D0089026

Engaging Students through Social Media

Engaging Students through Social Media

Evidence-Based Practices for Use in Student Affairs

Reynol Junco

Foreword by Mary Madden

JB JOSSEY-BASS™
A Wiley Brand

Consulting editor: John Schuh

Published by Jossey-Bass
A Wiley Brand
One Montgomery Street, Suite 1200, San Francisco, CA 94104-4594—www.josseybass.com/
highereducation

Jossey-Bass books and products are available through most bookstores. To contact Jossey-Bass
directly call our Customer Care Department within the U.S. at 800-956-7739, outside the U.S.
at 317-572-3986, or fax 317-572-4002.

Wiley publishes in a variety of print and electronic formats and by print-on-demand. Some
material included with standard print versions of this book may not be included in e-books or
in print-on-demand. If this book refers to media such as a CD or DVD that is not included in
the version you purchased, you may download this material at http://booksupport.wiley.com.
For more information about Wiley products, visit www.wiley.com.

**Library of Congress Cataloging-in-Publication Data has been applied for and is on file
with the Library of Congress**

ISBN 9781118647455 (cloth); ISBN 9781118903711 (ebk.); ISBN 9781118903308 (ebk.)

Printed in the United States of America
FIRST EDITION

HB Printing   10   9   8   7   6   5   4   3   2   1

CONTENTS

For Liam and Anja

FOREWORD

In 1994, a young psychology student at the University of Florida stood outside the library with a fellow classmate he had met through the campus psychology club. It was a pristine spring day, saturated with the kind of sunshine that shakes off any remaining chill from the winter and makes everything seem possible. The two friends, computer geeks who shared an interest in hacking and programming, stood chatting about some of the new technology services the university had started to offer to students.

The exchange went something like this:

Psych Student #1: "Did you know that you can have your *own* e-mail account now? I heard the school is giving out e-mail accounts for students who want to try it out. You should get one."

Psych Student #2: "Cool. But why would I want that? I don't know anyone else with e-mail."

A few weeks later, despite his reservations, Student #2 signed up for his first e-mail account. In the months that followed, its utility to him was indeed limited. He sent and received a few messages but was generally unimpressed. While other early adopters were wowed by the speed and efficiency of e-mail, the tool lacked the kinds of features that supported online community building, something Student #2 had grown accustomed to while hosting an early BBS (bulletin board system) as a teenager. More important, Student #2 was already invested in a network of friends who didn't use e-mail, so the social value of the tool wasn't readily apparent to him.

However, over time, and like most of his peers, Student #2 would become an avid user of e-mail. During his graduate studies at Pennsylvania State University, e-mail became an indispensable way for him to keep in touch with faculty, fellow students, and family back in Florida. By the time he graduated with a D.Ed. in counselor education in 2002, e-mail had become the primary means through which he and his far-flung advisors exchanged feedback and negotiated the final edits of his dissertation.

At the same time that e-mail was becoming a mainstream communications tool across the United States, Student #2 also embraced a range of new technologies that offered social features: instant messaging, blogging, and early social networking tools like Friendster and MySpace. In 2005, when Facebook started gaining popularity among young adults, Student #2 (who had since become Professor #2) began to think about how these growing platforms might help to inform and support the work of student affairs professionals.

In his first position as an instructor at Lock Haven University, before Facebook was available beyond the Ivy Leagues, he was asked by an eager student to contact Facebook to "see if they would come to Lock Haven next." (The student thought Lock Haven would have a better chance of getting access if a professor asked.) Professor #2, realizing that Facebook could be used to support student-to-student connections, reached out to the company with this request, and Lock Haven ultimately became one of the first among the state system schools to get accounts. The ensuing uptake across campus was stunning, and Professor

#2 had a front-row seat to witness and ultimately study the way this social media platform became integrated into the various dynamics of student life. Three books and more than thirty articles later, he has become one of the world's leading experts on educational outcomes associated with college students' social media use.

He also happens to be the author of this book.

Remembering his initial reaction to the idea of e-mail, Reynol Junco realized that the value of using social media in educationally relevant ways might not be readily apparent to those who weren't using the platforms and who might not have a connection to anyone else using them. Without firsthand experience of social media use in or out of the classroom, and with a host of negative news headlines to fuel concern, the perceived risks associated with these tools might easily appear to outweigh the potential benefits.

This book, in many ways, is the answer to the question that Rey asked in 1994: "Why would I want that?" In this case, the tool is social media, but the analytical and evaluative approach applied throughout the book could easily transfer to any new digital communications platform.

Yet what truly makes this volume stand apart is the extent to which the author addresses an equally important corollary for those whose careers are devoted to meeting students where they are: "Why would *they* want that?"

Much of my career has been devoted to understanding how and why teenagers and young adults have embraced social technologies. In 2002, during my first year of working for the Pew Internet and American Life Project, this meant studying music file sharing networks and instant messaging platforms. In later years, the analytical focus for youth research at Pew Internet moved to blogs, texting, and gaming environments. By 2007, after MySpace and Facebook had skyrocketed in popularity among teens, much of our research energy had shifted to understanding the emergent social networking sites (at the time, 55 percent of online teens ages 12–17 maintained a profile on a social networking site). Yet the use of social networking sites was still a niche activity for most adults over the age of 30—only 15 percent of online adults ages 30–49 had created a profile on a social networking site, and just 8 percent of adults ages 50–64 had done so.

Because social networking sites were so foreign to adults at the time, as researchers we were often asked to explain the appeal of these platforms. Why were teens spending so much time on MySpace and Facebook? What would possess them to share so much personal information about themselves—*on the Internet*? In our first major report on teens and social networking sites, we attempted to shed some light on this phenomenon:

> *Psychologists have long noted that the teenage years are host to a tumultuous period of identity formation and role development. Adolescents are intensely focused on social life during this time, and consequently have been eager and early adopters of Internet applications that help them engage with their peers ... Social networking sites appeal to teens, in part, because they encompass so many of the online tools and entertainment activities that teens know and love. They provide a centralized control center to access real-time and asynchronous communication features, blogging tools, photo, music and video sharing features, and the ability to post original creative work—all linked to a*

unique profile that can be customized and
updated on a regular basis.
(Amanda Lenhart and Mary Madden, "Teens, Privacy
and Online Social Networks," 2007)

In 2014, one hardly needs to explain what a social networking site is, or why people—teens or adults—would want to use it.
According to the latest Pew Internet surveys, 73 percent of online
adults and 81 percent of teens use social networking sites. And
many of these users are sharing a great deal of information about
themselves. Still, despite these high levels of adoption, many institutions are still struggling to figure out what—if anything—they
can gain through the professional use of social media.

To be sure, Facebook and Twitter were not designed with
student affairs professionals in mind. As such, their use may
require a certain amount of retrofitting. Today, there are countless
examples of these "off- label" uses of social media. Police
departments use Twitter to solicit tips to help solve crimes.
Patient groups who suffer from rare diseases use Facebook to
compare symptoms and share information about new treatments.
Even the tightly controlled Vatican communications office has
embraced the use of social media for evangelization and engagement with the world's faithful.

These uses, of course, are not without their side effects. If
social media are used in public or even semi-public ways, they
require frequent curation and moderation to maintain a sense of
presence and control over the messaging. Privacy choices need to
be made and often revised when applications are updated or use
patterns change. And like any online communications platform,
profiles can play host to various exchanges of misinformation or
inappropriate comments. While issues like these may be a deal
breaker for some institutions, many students will still hack out

their own educational uses of social media—whether that's creating Facebook groups associated with their courses or engaging directly with scholars like Reynol Junco who are active on Twitter.

One of the groundbreaking contributions this book makes is to help the reader understand how social media are *already* being used in effective ways across disciplines and, specifically, how they can best be used to meet the goals of student affairs professionals. As with any technology, these tools are not perfect. But they are ubiquitous, and their influence on campus life is undeniable. Through discussions of both the historical and cultural contexts that shaped the dominant platforms, the reader will gain a deeper understanding of the assumptions inherent in the early versions of the applications (such as exclusivity, simple privacy controls, and ad-free interfaces) and how these have changed quite dramatically over time.

The author is also a disciple of data. Every major insight in this book is backed by either his own research or that of established scholars in his field. As someone who works for a data-driven research institution, I am deeply appreciative of this perspective, which helps to ground every one of his recommendations in research. (For those who are already eager to explore the integration of social media into formal learning environments, the evidence-based practices list in chapter 5 is a plug-and-play road map that could be applied to any instructor's curricular development process.)

Yet, ultimately, while the author champions the uses of social media that he has found to have positive outcomes for student identity development, integration, and success, his enthusiasm is paired with a steady back channel of critical caveats. If your answer to the question "Why would I want that?" after you've read this book is, "Actually, I don't," he's okay with that. What you won't walk away with—contrary to popular news reports—is a sense that social media is inherently harmful to students. Instead, you'll be left with a mountain of thoughtful evidence and a host of innovative possibilities to engage with students and model the increasingly essential skills of how to survive and thrive in our networked world.

Mary Madden
Senior Researcher
Pew Research Center's
Internet & American Life Project
Washington, DC

PREFACE

This book examines how college students use social media, with a focus on connecting the available research to recommendations for student affairs practice. The intent is to provide balanced data and interpretations that allow the reader to more fully understand the benefits and the pitfalls of social media use in our profession. The book represents much of what I've discovered in the past five years of my ongoing research on the psychosocial and educational effects of social media on youth. As such, the book includes much of what I'm currently thinking about—issues such as how young people pass through stages of identity development and how their development is influenced by how they engage online; how a student affairs professional can most efficiently engage students and help them reach the desired outcomes of a college education; how learning can encompass facets that we often don't consider; and how living in a technology-based society changes us, for the better and worse.

The penetration of college campuses by social media makes it essential for student affairs professionals to understand how our students interact with these technologies and how they relate to educational outcomes. Student affairs graduate preparation programs are preserving a core curriculum focusing on basic competencies; however, as a national group, the programs are falling short of expanding these competencies to match the progress of technological change. While it is unreasonable to expect graduate preparation programs to chase a moving target, social media have been part of the student experience for more than a decade now. Most important, student affairs professionals need technology competencies not just to work effectively with students but also to develop their own online professional identity that will help them in their job search and career development. This book fills the gap in professional preparation by offering a comprehensive review of these issues.

THE GOALS OF THIS BOOK

This book is meant to help student affairs practitioners as well as other higher education professionals see the value of social media use with students. The book offers guidance and strategies for using social media effectively to enhance student learning. Specifically, the book is designed to do the following:

· Provide a research-based understanding of how students use social media.
· Dispel popular myths about how social media use affects students. For instance, there is no evidence to show that using social media detracts from face-to-face interactions, while there is evidence to show social media use supports such interactions.
· Describe how social media can harm and benefit student development and academic outcomes.
· Discuss the connection between educationally relevant uses of social media and student success.
· Promote the use of social media to engage students, to teach online civil discourse, and to support student development.

Throughout the book I discuss the adult normative and youth normative perspectives. The *adult normative* perspective takes a prescriptive and authoritarian approach to understanding youth social media use. Values related to the adult normative perspective include beliefs that social media use "ruins" young people's ability to have "normal" relationships. It is often propagated through media accounts of how terrible social media are for young people. The *youth normative* perspective, on the other hand, attempts to understand young people's experiences through their viewpoint. When student affairs professionals adopt the adult normative perspective, we've already lost—we go from being potential allies with our students to parental figures. While our students sometimes need parenting, we must remember that we are not their parents and should never try to be. Instead, we are educators who must challenge and support our students through their educational and psychosocial growth. The most effective way to do that is to understand students' viewpoints, for if you don't understand that viewpoint and where they are coming from, they are less likely to trust you to help them. If they don't trust you, then there is no way that you can engage in the important developmental work students need us to do.

So how do we understand the youth normative perspective? The growing body of literature on how college students use social media serves as an excellent resource to understand both the positives and the negatives of how youth are currently using technology and how it affects them psychosocially. Unfortunately, there is not a great deal of research focusing on social media in the field of student affairs. However, research from other disciplines sometimes examines constructs important to student affairs or constructs that are closely related to what we care about in student affairs. We can apply this research to understand constructs important to student affairs professionals. For example, Ellison and her colleagues (2007, 2011) examined how Facebook use influences the construct of social capital, which is closely related to Tinto's (1993) construct of social integration. I wrote this book to encourage an understanding of the youth normative perspective by reviewing relevant research and putting it in context for student affairs professionals. In doing so, I promote the idea that there is much to learn about how our students are using social media both in helpful and detrimental ways.

I consider myself an optimistic skeptic in terms of the adoption of new technologies. I focus on collecting and using data in order to make evaluations about how new technologies influence our students. As an undergraduate, I was in a psychology department that was heavily influenced by quantitative methodologies: in fact, we had to take more statistics and methodology courses than psychology students at other universities. Then in graduate school, quantitative methods were very important in both assessing clinical functioning and evaluating the outcomes of psychological therapies. The outcomes evaluation movement was in its prime in the field of clinical psychology while I was in graduate school. These two experiences have greatly influenced my theoretical and research framework. Ultimately, I am a quantitative methodologist who is interesting in using evidence-based approaches to practice. In this sense, the overarching question that guides my research is "What do the data show about the outcomes of college student social media use?" This question is addressed in the pages before you, but I also encourage you to keep a watchful eye out for emerging research that can inform your work with students. No doubt, some of the conclusions reached here will be refuted by additional research, while others will be strengthened, and some research will emerge to answer questions that have not yet been asked.

WHERE I'M COMING FROM

I've had perhaps three major formative experiences that inform my work with students generally but also more specifically when examining how they use social media:

First, I was a first-generation minority college student from a low socioeconomic background on a predominantly white and affluent campus. I was lucky to have been very successful in college, in no small part due to the fact that I had a network of friends whom I could rely on for support. In the parlance of this book, I had just enough social capital (the benefits accrued through interpersonal connections) to be successful. However, not all students with my background characteristics were as lucky; often, disenfranchisement because of minority status is promulgated and reproduced throughout the US educational system. Youth from low socioeconomic backgrounds generally attend schools in impoverished areas; these schools are not well funded and do not provide the appropriate support to lift youth from educational and economic insufficiencies. Therefore, I have a soft spot in my heart for supporting the success of all students, but specifically those who have been disenfranchised by cultural and social systems they cannot influence. The way I view the sociocultural norms of academia is a driving force in my work. I have found that we often only pay lip service to students who need extra help, and I have seen too many colleagues openly mocking students who weren't as smart, prepared, or motivated as my colleagues thought they themselves were as students. While openly mocking students, thankfully, is not the norm, not understanding our students can lead to widening the gulf between us and them—eroding our ability to effectively intervene to help them succeed.

Second, I have been a technology geek since my early years and was an early hacker and phreaker in the 1980s. Hacking is typically defined as exploiting weaknesses in technological systems, while phreaking was hacking's precursor, relating to exploiting telecommunication systems. One of my strongest skills was the ability to dial a phone number by just depressing the cradle switch repeatedly, called *switch-hooking*. This may sound like a useless task today: what the heck is a phone cradle? Back then, most payphones worked on the principle that putting money in the phone would "unlock" the dialing pad and allow you to dial a number; however, the cradle was always left "unlocked" so that a person could hang up before making the call or if they dialed the wrong series of numbers, get their money back, and redial. If one dialed a phone number by rapidly depressing the cradle switch (thereby emulating a rotary dial phone), then you could make the call for free. Hacking as a social movement has evolved a great deal since. For instance, *hacktivism*, or the hacking of systems to promote political ends, has emerged as a method and movement for social change. The interested reader is directed to Gabriella Coleman's (2012) work on the ethics of hacking and Molly Sauter's (2014) work on hacktivism. Say what you will about the actions of hackers and phreakers (and I might agree with some of your characterizations), but one important thread of hacker culture is the view that we do not have to follow along just because a powerful entity demands that we behave in ways that are not equitable, and that are perhaps even illegal or immoral. Another important value within hacker culture is the notion that just because we've done things a certain way in the past, we don't need to continue doing them in that same way. The most interesting psychological, sociological, educational, and technical discoveries come when we play at and with the boundaries of what has been prescribed and delimited by social norms.

Third, I was a DJ for many of my formative years, spinning, scratching, and mixing my way through college. A measure of DJ success in my community was how well one could mix songs—connect their beats to match but also creatively remix music by putting together disparate styles and beats, a precursor to what we now call *mashups*. For instance, a fellow DJ was highly praised for mashing together a specific dance track called 122 (which was basically electronic and bass drumbeats at the speed of 122 beats per minute) with incongruent styles like the song "Stand by Me" by Ben E. King. Since 122 was an electronic beat and "Stand by Me" used live percussion, he would have to monitor and "ride" the mix by making minor adjustments in the speed of the two records. The result was a fabulous juxtaposition of old and new, creating just enough dissonance between the two styles to please (and often impress) the listener. The game was always afoot—we'd test out methods of mixing disparate styles of music, often using speed, pitch, and even backmasking to achieve interesting results. This early experience left with me an appreciation for connecting disparate constructs into something that makes sense. In other words, I learned the value of the process of interdisciplinary collaboration before I ever entered academia—there was beauty, utility, and consonance in connecting different genres.

My ethnic and socioeconomic identity, my transplantation of the hacker ethos to issues of social and educational inequalities, and my interest in combining views of different disciplines into my own underlie the motivations for my research. My earliest work on student technology use focused on the field of student affairs; however, I quickly discovered that the scholarship in the growing field of Internet studies was being carried out by individuals from a broad range of backgrounds, such as sociology, communications, and computer science. I realized that in order to grow and expand my work I needed to pay attention to and incorporate the work happening in other fields into the work that I was doing; I also realized that I needed to collaborate with scholars in other fields in order to further this work. I have been greatly influenced by the Berkman Center for Internet and Society community. The Berkman Center is an interdisciplinary center that has as a core value an interest in bringing together individuals from a broad range of disciplinary backgrounds to collaborate and expand each other's work. Being part of this community and the processes it encourages has pushed the boundaries of how I understand college student development. It often seems that the further away I get from the restraints put in place by disciplinary thought, the more creative (and fun) my work becomes.

WHO SHOULD READ THIS BOOK

This book is for student affairs educators at all points along their career path. Established student affairs professionals will benefit from the knowledge contained about how social media can be and are being used in practice to support student development, while graduate students and new professionals will appreciate the connections between established student development theories and social media use. Furthermore, this book serves as a research base for understanding effective uses of social media, based on the currently available literature in the field. The combination of the research and the theoretical underpinnings can serve to help frame and guide effective uses of social media to improve student psychosocial development and learning outcomes.

HOW THIS BOOK IS ORGANIZED

Chapter 1 discusses why it's important for student affairs professionals to understand how social media influence students. Additionally, chapter 1 introduces the most popular social media sites for US college students, along with data about the popularity of each of the sites. Next, chapter 2 reviews what the research literature says about outcomes of interest to student affairs professionals—namely, student engagement, academic and social integration, and academic performance. The chapter reviews both the positive and negative outcomes of social media use and gives recommendations for evaluating research. Chapter 3 reviews major theories of identity development and discusses how the constructs of online identification, self-presentation, and disinhibition influence the development of identity through the use of social media.

Chapters 4 and 5 focus on how students use social media for informal and formal learning. These chapters also provide guidance to student affairs professionals about how they can best leverage these tools to support learning outcomes. Planning, implementing, and assessing interventions that use social media are discussed in chapter 6. Chapter 7 provides information on how social media can be used to promote professional development and gives recommendations for how to engage other colleagues effectively with social media. Furthermore, the chapter provides guidance to student affairs professionals about what to share in online social spaces. Lastly, chapter 8 describes the future of social media with an emphasis on the sociocultural processes that influence adoption and resistance.

A WORD ABOUT AGE

This book is not necessarily about traditional-aged or nontraditional-aged college students. I recognize that student affairs professionals are working with students of all ages, and while there are certainly differences between nontraditional-aged and traditional-aged students, there's not a lot of research on these differences in social media use. For the most part, I'll be talking about traditional-aged students, but that doesn't mean that the same principles don't apply to nontraditional-aged students. In fact, a lot of the variance in how social media are used has little to do with age and much more to do with exposure, use, and practice. For example, research on Internet skills shows that the more a person uses the Internet, the more types of social media that person will use and the better he or she will understand the cultural norms promoted by the communities on those sites.

At a few points in the book, I talk about the dichotomy between the adult normative and youth normative perspectives. While it's tempting to cast this as an adult versus youth dichotomy, it is in fact a cultural difference in how we view our students' experience: we are either mostly prescriptive and have little interest in their experience, or we are mostly descriptive and interested in learning from students what it's like to be a student. In this sense, the perspectives can hold for any age or for any type of relationship in which one person either imposes his or her view of reality on the other or else attempts to understand the other's view of reality without judgment.

ON BEST PRACTICES

I chose this book's title specifically to reflect how I feel about the term *best practices*, which educators like to throw around. Some may recognize the binary nature of such a term and instead use a phrase such as *better practices* or *more effective practices*. To me, the terms *best practices* and *better practices* imply that through extensive research we have distilled the best processes to use with students. However, the reality is very different—in student affairs in particular but also more broadly in all areas of human behavior. First, there is little outcomes-based research in student affairs. A literature search will show that even though the profession of student affairs has a long history, very little evidence has been collected to support interventions. Theoretical models are great as guiding principles for student affairs work; however, little is known about how using these models to guide practice affects student outcomes. Even the related fields of clinical and counseling psychology have, for decades, evaluated the effectiveness of psychotherapies (Butler, Chapman, Forman & Beck, 2005; Kazdin, 1990). Social media can offer student affairs professionals new forms of data collection, and it is imperative to collect information on the effectiveness of using these technologies with students, a matter discussed in further detail in chapter 6. Second, using a term such as *best practices* suggests that there are "one size fits all" practices and interventions, which of course is not the case. Some social media interventions may leave students from lower socioeconomic status backgrounds or from minority racial or ethnic backgrounds at a disadvantage. Therefore, this book uses the title and notion of *evidence-based practices*, which are those for which we have enough data to make recommendations. This term does not mean that these practices are necessarily better than others—just that there is research evidence to show that these practices are related to or have an impact on desired student outcomes.

Rey Junco
West Lafayette, Indiana

REFERENCES

Butler, A. C., Chapman, J. E., Forman, E. M., & Beck, A. T. (2005). The empirical status of cognitive-behavioral therapy: A review of meta-analyses. *Clinical Psychology Review, 26* (2006), 17–31.

Coleman, G. (2012). *Coding Freedom: The Ethics and Aesthetics of Hacking.* Princeton, NJ: Princeton University Press.

Ellison, N. B., Steinfield, C., & Lampe, C. (2007). The benefits of Facebook "friends": Social capital and college students' use of online social network sites. *Journal of Computer-Mediated Communication, 12*(4). 1143–1168. DOI:10.1111/j.1083–6101.2007.00367.x.

Ellison, N. B., Steinfield, C., & Lampe, C. (2011). Connection strategies: Social capital implications of Facebook-enabled communication practices. *New Media & Society.* DOI:10.1177/1461444810385389.

Kazdin, A. E. (1990). Psychotherapy for children and adolescents. *Annual Review of Psychology, 41*(1), 21–54.

Sauter, M. (2014). *Odd Letters.* Retrieved February 2, 2014, from http://oddletters.com/articlesmedia/.

Tinto, V. (1993). *Leaving College: Rethinking the Causes and Cures of Student Attrition* (2nd ed.). Chicago: University of Chicago Press.

ACKNOWLEDGMENTS

This book would not have been written without the support of my wonderful and generous partner, Rebecca Laster. Thank you for your unwavering encouragement, dedication, and help throughout my writing process. Your use of humor, bribery, and—most important—Excel spreadsheets helped keep me focused and on track. Thank you for the hours of driving, for the hours of Skype buffalo coworking sessions, for knowing what works, for helping me feel OK about not hitting my goals on a given day, for keeping me motivated, and for the constant feeling that we were in this together. When I was languishing on a section, you'd know exactly what I needed—whether that was a brisk walk or reassuring words—or even giving myself permission not to write and to just watch *Project Runway* instead. When I was overly critical about my work, you helped me see that my writing was good and that I could keep going, embodying the idea of not letting the perfect be the enemy of the good. When I was freaking out about getting the manuscript completed by the deadline, you asked me what I needed to do so—to which I responded, "I need you to help get everything out of my way so that I can focus on writing and nothing else." You didn't even think twice about it—you told me to write a to-do list of the things I needed you to get done. Two days later, you drove ten hours to Indiana, arriving late on a Sunday night. You spent all of Monday and Tuesday taking care of quite literally *everything* so that I could focus on writing; going so far as to cook enough of my favorite foods to last me weeks so that I would have healthy things to eat because I was too focused to cook for myself. Then, you left on Wednesday at four in the morning to drive another ten hours back because you needed to pick up Anja from school. You even left me a flower on the bathroom counter to help bring beauty into my space while you were gone. My words will never capture the depth of my gratitude for your love and support—I will leave that to my actions over a lifetime.

I am indebted to Urs Gasser, Executive Director of the Berkman Center for Internet and Society, who has been an ardent supporter of my work and who so graciously welcomed me into my academic home. Your friendship and colleagueship have helped me grow expansively as a researcher and as a public academic. I am also thankful to Sandra Cortesi, for being a strong supporter of my work and for always telling exactly what she thinks. I've spent many hours writing in the Youth and Media Lab bouncing ideas off of Urs and Sandra—it is through this process that my hypotheses about youth and media have expanded almost infinitely. Your research has been inspirational and has factored significantly in how I conceptualize youth and their interactions with technology. There's nothing more pleasing than finding a place where people are interested in the same research topic and who happen to be some of the kindest people I've ever met: thank you.

I'm extremely grateful to the members of the Berkman Book Club for their helpful feedback on a draft of the manuscript and their support throughout the writing process: Ethan Zuckerman for his help contextualizing the book around bringing research to bear to combat media misinformation; David Weinberger and Ethan for helping me find my nonacademic voice; Doc Searls for encouraging me to think about the consumer-customer dichotomy in social media use; and Judith Donath for highlighting my ability to clarify research for nonresearchers and for her encouragement throughout the writing process, especially her suggestion to "not be dutiful" and to "write only about what you find interesting."

I had planned to write this book at some point, but it was John Schuh's invitation that took the idea off of my back burner and put it at the top of a long list of projects. John's feedback on the first draft gave me great insight into how helpful the manuscript would be for student affairs professionals. My editor, Erin Null, at Jossey-Bass was instrumental in reviewing (and re-reviewing) the first and subsequent drafts all within my crazy timeline. I am grateful to Ed Cabellon, who provided a considerable amount of feedback on the first draft of the manuscript and provided helpful suggestions to reorder and rework the chapters to better suit a student affairs audience. Furthermore, Ed provided assistance with the contextualization of the training portion of chapter 6 as well as providing the hashtag archive for the ACPA 2012 national conference.

I am grateful for the feedback provided by Mary Madden on multiple drafts of the original manuscript, which especially helped solidify my thoughts about online identity development. I am thankful for master's student Candi Clem's help in formatting references and for her feedback on chapter 1. I am appreciative of Sharon Weiner's feedback on chapter 5, especially about information literacy, as well as Matt Pitstilli's feedback on chapter 6, which helped me shift from research to assessment mode. I am also grateful for TJ Logan's help in brainstorming additional ideas for professional development for chapter 7. A special thanks to James Baumann for sending me articles from the Talking Stick as well as the names of those using social media effectively in housing and residence life.

Kevin Valliere, Lisa Endersby, and Matt Brinton from the NASPA Technology Knowledge Community provided unpublished data and the preliminary results of their survey of social media use in student affairs, which were instrumental in framing chapter 4. A number of student affairs professionals provided examples of how they were using social media effectively with their students. I am grateful for the information provided by Sienna Abdulahad, Katie Bean, Cheryl Boncuore, Chris Butler, Justin Chase Brown, Jessica Fantini, Eric Heilmeier, Jennifer Keegin, Josh Kohnert, TJ Logan, Amma Marfo, James McHaley, Jeffrey Pelletier, Donna Talarico-Beerman, Kevin P. Thomas, and TJ Willis. Although I went in a different direction with the book, I appreciate Liz Gross's work in writing a draft chapter on social media marketing that I hope to see published elsewhere.

ABOUT THE AUTHOR

Rey Junco is an associate professor of education in the School of Education at Iowa State University and a fellow at the Berkman Center for Internet and Society at Harvard University. Rey's primary research interest is using quantitative methods to analyze the effects of social media on youth psychosocial development, engagement, and learning. His research has focused on informing best practices in using social technologies to enhance learning outcomes. Rey has found that technology, specifically social media like Facebook and Twitter, can be used in ways that improve engagement and academic performance. Rey is also interested in examining how social media affect interpersonal relationships, identity development, online discourse, and digital inequalities, and how the use of digital media promotes formal and informal learning. As part of his ongoing research program, Rey has explored the ability to use trace data (seemingly irrelevant data collected through natural uses of technology) to provide real-time and unobtrusive prediction of student outcomes. He tweets at @reyjunco, can be found at http://www.facebook.com/reyjunco, and blogs at http://blog.reyjunco.com.

Rey conducted the first large, multi-institution survey of student technology use and reported the results in a book he coauthored with Jeanna Mastrodicasa, *Connecting to the Net.Generation: What Higher Education Professionals Need to Know About Today's*

Students. In his second book, *Using Emerging Technologies to Enhance Student Engagement,* he and his colleagues provided a comprehensive analysis of social media's role in student engagement, technology's potential to improve retention, and blogs' potential to improve students' writing and marketing skills. His empirical work has been published in high-impact journals such as *Computers & Education, Computers in Human Behavior,* and the *Journal of Computer Assisted Learning.*

Rey's work has been cited in major news outlets such as the *New York Times, NPR, PBS, NBC, Time, US News & World Report, USA Today, The Guardian, The Atlantic, Huffington Post,* and *Mashable.* Rey is a regular guest on the *NPR* show *Tell Me More,* where he discusses how research informs the societal impact of social media use. Rey has given talks, workshops, and lectures at more than fifty national and international conferences, universities, and organizations. He enjoys talking about how technology affects college students, using social media in educationally relevant ways, teaching students about privacy, marketing university programs and services through social media, and developing effective first-year seminars.

Engaging Students through Social Media

CHAPTER 1

Introduction

Student affairs professionals aim to reach students where they are. Many college students are on Facebook and are highly engaged with the site. As a result, a growing number of student affairs professionals are interested in developing interventions that involve reaching students on Facebook and other social media. Facebook began to be popular among students between 2004 and 2005 and now is nearly ubiquitous on college campuses, but relatively little research is available on how Facebook use relates to student outcomes. The slow advancement of research on Facebook outcomes is mimicked by a slow progression of interest in and adoption of the platform by student affairs professionals. I have been researching social media sites since the early 2000s and have spoken to many student affairs professionals since, and I have consistently been surprised at administrators' xenophobia regarding the site. In most cases, student affairs administrators have preferred to stay away from Facebook, relegating it to students. Of course, that attitude has slowly changed; however, many upper-level student affairs administrators have only a cursory understanding of how Facebook is used and its effect on student development, learning, and interpersonal relationships. Indeed, in the absence of curiosity and knowledge about the platform, administrators are left with media accounts of why Facebook is "bad."

A quick search of news archives reveals traditional media outlets' sensationalism regarding Facebook. These headlines illustrate:

- Is Facebook leading to narcissist outlook? (Chowdhury, 2013)
- Facebook causes one-third of divorces (Allen, 2012)
- Study finds Facebook causes depression and isolation (Jimenez, 2013)
- Anxiety and alcohol use linked to Facebook (Moore, 2013)
- Facebook use can lower grades by 20 percent (Choney, 2010)
- Facebook is the worst social network for bullying (Gayle, 2013)

Many people who read these stories conclude that social media are the driving force behind negative outcomes. This result makes sense from an information-processing perspective: humans use unconscious, simple shortcuts to reduce the vast amounts of information we receive from the world into manageable data. The *availability heuristic* (Tversky & Kahneman, 1973) is one such unconscious shortcut, whereby we overestimate the probability of an event because of easy-to-remember examples. For instance, someone might overestimate the probability of being in a plane crash because media reports of plane crashes are easy to recall. The same holds true for social media: because the headlines typically report negative relationships and are widely broadcast, many people believe, for example, that today's youth are more

2

narcissistic than other generations because they use social media or that there is a high probability that children will get bullied if they use Facebook. These conclusions, however, are unwarranted based on available evidence concerning outcomes of social media use.

This book provides evidence to show that Facebook and other social media are a reflection of the offline world. Social media are no more than tools by which we communicate in a novel way (although the term *novel* is used with tongue in cheek here, as Facebook has been a part of our social milieu for so long). Social media are no more causative of an outcome than any other tool. Go back and reread the example headlines and substitute the phrase "using a shovel" for Facebook. It's silly to think that a shovel could cause your grades to decrease by 20 percent. Now you have a sense of how irresponsible it is to say that Facebook causes certain outcomes. That's not to say that there isn't a relationship between Facebook use and certain variables—just that there isn't a causative relationship.

Unfortunately, the vast majority of news reporters are not trained in differentiating between correlation and causation. So when they hear that a study found a negative correlation between time spent on Facebook and grades, reporters understand that to mean that Facebook caused lower grades. It is not possible to say that Facebook use caused lower grades because, as of this writing, no controlled experiments have examined a causal link between the two variables. Indeed, it would be extremely difficult to craft such a study, given the penetration of Facebook on college campuses. Later in this chapter, I'll highlight the research on digital inequalities, which shows that students who don't use Facebook tend to have sociodemographic characteristics in common; therefore, it would be nearly impossible to find a suitable group of Facebook nonusers to use as a sample for appropriate comparisons to the general population.

Take, for example, the headline "Facebook use can lower grades by 20 percent." The study in question was correlational and found a relationship between Facebook use and grades. Issues with sampling, methodology, and analyses aside, there are many reasons why there might be a correlation between Facebook use and grades. The most important reason is typically called the *third variable problem*—which I refer to as the *third, fourth, fifth, etc. variable problem*, as an infinite number of variables may actually cause the relationship between the original two variables to appear. In the case of Facebook use and grades, *self-regulation* (voluntary control of impulses in order to achieve goals) may be a reasonable culprit (see figure 1.1). Students who have poorer abilities to self-regulate typically get lower grades; because such students are less academically motivated, they may use Facebook in ways that keep them away from their studies. Another important point to remember in considering the relationship between Facebook use and grades is that it is impossible to tell directionality with a correlation. Students with lower grades tend to use Facebook more, but it could be that being a bad student drives increased Facebook use rather than that Facebook causes lower grades.

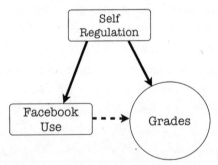

Figure 1.1. Depiction of hypothesized relationship showing that self-regulation may be the variable that causes the relationship observed between Facebook use and grades. Solid arrows suggest causal links, while the dotted arrow denotes a correlation.

These methodological issues are helpful to keep in mind when evaluating the literature on social media use. It's also helpful to understand the difference between *access* and *use* when thinking about outcomes of social media utilization. Just because any group of students uses Facebook doesn't mean that they will all use it in the same ways. And the ways in which those students use Facebook are much more important in predicting what they will get out of it. In other words, whether or not students use Facebook is less decisive in predicting outcomes than what they do on the site. Recall the example of the shovel as a tool: a shovel can be very effective for digging a hole in which to plant a tree; however, that same shovel is very ineffective when you try to use it to eat cereal.

A contributing, very problematic issue is that of disingenuous or ill-informed interpretation and communication of research findings by the researchers themselves. An original study of the relationship between Facebook use and academic performance was misrepresented by both the media and the person who conducted the research. Calls for accountability from other researchers were met with resistance and further misrepresentations of the limitations of the study. In the past year, I have read two research papers in high-impact, prestigious journals in which the researchers interpreted a nonsignificant result as significant. Sometimes it's hard for researchers to move beyond their biases and preexisting notions. These examples teach us the necessity of critically examining even peer-reviewed research.

Using evidence to guide thinking and practice is essential in student affairs. Up to now, however, higher education has been dominated by fearful myths about youth social media use based on inadequate or miscontextualized research. Myths about social media use don't sync with the reality of how youth use these technologies. The actual evidence paints a different picture, which is much more optimistic than popular assumptions. I'm not being naively optimistic about this; there are certainly both positive and negative outcomes associated with students' use of social media. However, it's imperative to understand how students' use of social technologies can be normative and beneficial. This book is an attempt to help the reader move beyond the limits that our culture has placed on our understanding of the phenomenon of youth social media use. Only then can we move forward and learn to leverage these technologies innovatively to support student engagement and learning.

WHAT ARE SOCIAL MEDIA?

For the purposes of this book, *social media* are defined as applications, services, and systems that allow users to create, remix, and share content. Social media typically have *social networking* features. That is, they allow interaction among users who may "friend," "follow," or "circle" one another. Although today's social media sites like Facebook and Twitter are easily recognizable containers for social interactions, using the Internet for social connection is not a new phenomenon (an issue explored in further detail in chapter 8). Most of the current social media sites and services have a specific function inherent in their design. For instance, Facebook is designed to allow users to readily connect with others and to share content, while Twitter is designed to allow users to broadcast short messages and to follow the short messages of others. Facebook is used to maintain social connections with family, friends, and people with whom users want to keep in touch, while Twitter is used to follow conversations, topics, and people of interest. Twitter updates are ephemeral, in that if a user who follows many people who tweet regularly isn't logged in to Twitter at the time someone the user follows posts an update, the user is likely to miss seeing the update. On Facebook, however, one is unlikely to miss an update from a significant friend because Facebook's algorithms ensure that important people's posts are seen, no matter when they were posted.

The design-specific and design-driven affordances of social media allow the user experience and resultant culture to develop in prescribed ways. For instance, when Facebook allowed users to subscribe to the public posts of others without being their friends, a new method was created for sharing and receiving memes posted on sites such as Tumblr and Instagram (in this context, *memes* are concepts that are spread rapidly on the Internet, usually in the form of a graphic and intended to be humorous; see figure 1.2 for an example). Facebook changed by allowing users to subscribe to the public posts of users they couldn't friend (for example, celebrities like George Takei), which changed the culture of Facebook by increasing the number of memes shared on the site. Additionally, Facebook added the pages feature, which allows any user to "like" and subscribe to a page and its updates. Pages can be used by public figures to connect with other Facebook users without having to use a personal account to "friend" them.

Figure 1.2. An example of a popular meme from 2012: Mckayla is not impressed.
Source: http://mckaylaisnotimpressed.tumblr.com/

Social media strategists in the business sector will extol the virtues of engagement with the audience when discussing good practices. In the social media marketing world, such engagement (in this context defined as interactive communication with your "audience") is directly related to an outcome (the promotion of a product—with *product* loosely defined here to mean a person, item, experience, or philosophy). These good practices for social media marketing stem directly from the user culture of social media sites, specifically Twitter and Facebook. On Twitter, the user culture is very interested in online engagement. Most Twitter users harbor the expectation that they will be able to interact with those they follow. The level of expectation that someone a user follows will respond to a tweet directed to that person (an "@ reply") is inversely proportional to the social status of that person. So, for instance, a user will be less likely to expect a response from the Barack Obama account than from my Twitter account. Early in 2011, I collected data from Twitter that showed that tweeting senior student affairs officers (SSAOs) were less likely to @ reply than a sample of tweeting student affairs professionals (Junco, 2011). Because of the correlational nature of the investigation, many variables could have played a role in the finding; however, it was curious to note the differences in culture between SSAOs and other student affairs professionals. An important question was whether SSAOs were treating Twitter as a method of broadcasting information, while the junior student affairs professionals were treating Twitter as a method to engage with others. This differential alone could lead to differences in student outcomes because of the ways that the interactions are perceived, with students perceiving more social distance between them and upper-level administrators. While that might be an intentional strategy for the administrator, it might work against facilitating students' academic integration.

While the affordances of social media often flow from the original intent of the site designers, as is clear from the previous examples, some affordances are realized when users engage with the site in novel ways. This dynamic provides opportunities for student affairs professionals. Understanding the affordances of a social media service can allow us to develop novel ways of communicating with and engaging with our students. As is explained in chapter 5, the affordances of Twitter make the service a more efficient tool for ongoing classroom discussions, while the affordances of Facebook make it more efficient for threaded class discussions and a more powerful tool than a learning management system (LMS). However, Facebook may be a more appropriate tool to advertise campus activities and programs through its pages feature.

Although an exhaustive review of all social media sites and services is well beyond the scope of this book, the following section reviews the most popular social media for college students in the United States as of this writing. Furthermore, the nature of social media and technological change is such that sites that are popular when this book was being written may decrease in popularity significantly by the time the book is published; conversely, sites that haven't even been launched yet may garner a huge following. Chapter 8 discusses the future of social media and how student affairs professionals can stay current (and perhaps ahead of the curve) with emerging sites and technologies. Although the most popular social media sites and services will be described, it is valuable for readers unfamiliar with these platforms to investigate them, not just by signing up for accounts and actively engaging on them, but also by asking students how they use these platforms.

Why Focus on Social Media?

Social media sites and services are incredibly popular among college students. College students use the Internet and social media at higher rates than the general population, perhaps because college students typically have greater and relatively unfettered access to hardware and broadband (Jones, Johnson-Yale, Millermaier & Pérez, 2009; Smith, Rainie & Zickuhr, 2011). In addition, college students engage through social media to help in their transition from high school. Their social media use acts as a bridge between the uncertain feelings of transition and the solidification of social and academic integration at their college or university. Because such a large percentage of students use social media and because social media use is related to academic and psychosocial outcomes, it behooves student affairs professionals to understand how they can use these technologies in beneficial ways.

Using social media in educationally relevant ways has been shown to be related to student engagement, campus involvement, adjustment to college, and academic outcomes such as grades and persistence (DeAndrea, Ellison, LaRose, Steinfield & Fiore, 2011; Heiberger & Harper, 2008; Junco, 2012a; Junco 2012b; Junco, Elavsky & Heiberger, 2012; Junco, Heiberger & Loken, 2011; Karpinski, Kirschner, Ozer, Mellott & Ochwo, 2012; Valenzuela, Park & Kee, 2009; Yang & Brown, 2013). Therefore, student affairs professionals can leverage social media in ways to help students attain the desired outcomes of a college education. Social media can also be leveraged as powerful tools to predict student behaviors and characteristics with the goal of early identification of students at risk for academic failure. For instance, Kosinski, Stillwell, and Graepel (2013) were able to predict with a high degree of accuracy traits such as gender, sexual orientation, race, religious preference, and political affiliation using only Facebook likes. While research in this area has not yet included the higher education context, these researchers' methods show promise for the field of education. Such methods along with the related field of learning analytics are examined in chapter 8.

At the very least, student affairs professionals should understand how social media are used by students in order to have a better understanding of how these media interact with the developmental processes most important to our profession. Indeed, 96 percent of respondents to the NASPA Technology Knowledge Community social media survey believed that new student affairs professionals should have social media skills (compared with 99 percent who said they should have Microsoft Word skills; Valliere, Endersby & Brinton, 2013). While some research has already been conducted showing connections between social media use and student development, student affairs professionals are encouraged to document the learning and psychosocial outcomes obtainable through social media interventions. Later chapters will focus specifically on how students develop identity using social media; how social media use is related to student engagement; how social media can improve student academic and social integration; how to plan, get support for, and implement social media interventions; and how student affairs professionals can evaluate the outcomes of social media interventions.

A Word of Caution

"If you are not paying for it, you're not the customer; you're the product being sold." Blue_beetle (2010) wrote that now-famous quote about the changes to the social news aggregation site Digg in 2010. While perhaps an oversimplification, the general idea is true. On Google and Facebook, advertisers are the customers, and users are the product being sold to those customers. Ultimately, these companies are responsible to their advertisers. As social media users, we tend to conflate *consumers* and *customers*. Let's take Google and Facebook as examples. We are *users* and *consumers* of Google products such as Gmail and Facebook; however, we are *not* Google's customers. What does this distinction mean in practice? Facebook has had a long history of disregarding user privacy. A chronological list of Facebook's privacy faux pas can be found on the "Criticism of Facebook" page of Wikipedia ("Criticism of Facebook," 2014). Standard practice at Facebook seems to be to update or add features, change privacy settings, and change the user interface in ways that compel users to share more information, often without users knowing they are doing so. Perhaps this is related to the history of Facebook and to how Facebook's creator and CEO sees the world (an issue discussed in more detail in chapter 3), but it is also likely related to Facebook's business model. If Facebook can get users to share more information about themselves, Facebook can then mine this information for its advertisers more effectively. Also, if users share more, they and their friends are likely to be more engaged on the site. This issue is not just confined to Facebook. Google relies on advertising for a large proportion of its revenue, as do Twitter, Yahoo, and many of the other social media sites and services. Making this structure even more problematic, most Internet users have little idea how their online browsing data are being mined to predict their purchasing behaviors.

To add to these concerns, in the summer of 2013, technology companies, including Google, Facebook, Microsoft, and Apple, came under scrutiny for their participation in the National Security Agency's PRISM program, which covertly mines massive amounts of user data (Greenwald & MacAskill, 2013). Twitter was the only one of eight major technology companies to refuse to make it easier for the National Security Agency (NSA) to have access to user data (Miller, 2013). Although Facebook, Google, Yahoo, and others have asked for greater transparency about domestic spying from the US government in an effort to alleviate the bad publicity they have received from the PRISM revelation, questions remain about how much was shared, how much access was given, and how willing the companies have been to turn over information (Auerbach, Mayer & Eckersley, 2013). Participation in the PRISM program is especially disquieting in light of research showing that NSA domestic surveillance programs have produced little actionable information (Schneier, 2013; 2014). The PRISM imbroglio crystallizes concerns about large Internet companies that possess a great deal of information about their users. Even when expressing a desire to "not be evil" (an unofficial Google company philosophy), these companies can easily cite market forces and other outside pressures to throw users under the bus.

Students are not particularly bothered by the fact that sites like Facebook mine users' personal data to obtain advertising revenue (Madden, Lenhart, Cortesi, Gasser, Duggan, Smith & Beaton, 2013). I believe one reason is that youth are not fully aware of how advertisers are using this information. This concern is not limited to youth. Many adults don't seem to completely understand how their online activities are tracked for advertising and marketing purposes. This lack of clarity is no doubt due in part to the reality that companies like Google don't want to divulge trade secrets; however, such practices keep users uninformed about how their information is being used. Furthermore, sites and services like Facebook and Google are so ingrained into our online experience that it would seem difficult if not impossible for users to leave or switch to a competitor. Indeed, a number of sites and services (like Diaspora) have been developed with the idea to give users more control over their privacy and to provide more transparency. Unfortunately, these sites dwindle with a tiny user base and haven't yet been popular with those outside of the tech geek set.

Changes to these marketing and privacy dynamics are unlikely in the near future. Therefore, it is critical for student affairs professionals and other educators to familiarize themselves with these issues and dynamics, not just to make appropriate choices about tools to use with students but also to teach students about the trade-offs of using these "free" services. There is no federal oversight of companies like Facebook and Google, and that's likely a good thing, because those who should be exercising oversight are actually worse actors than the technology companies themselves (PRISM being an excellent case in point). Luckily, youth report high levels of confidence in their ability to manage their privacy settings and take steps to shape their reputations, and the majority of teen users keep their Facebook profiles private (Madden, Lenhart, Cortesi, Gasser, Duggan, Smith & Beaton, 2013). We can use this preexisting knowledge to help students develop even stronger privacy knowledge and skills. As we learn more about these processes and help educate our students, we can become greater advocates for our Internet rights and perhaps even develop effective methods for oversight, to the benefit of society at large.

Student affairs professionals can help students by becoming familiar with both the technical and the psychological aspects of privacy and communicating these distinctions to students. *Technical* aspects of privacy include such matters as privacy controls on sites like Facebook as well as the provisions of the Family Educational Rights and Privacy Act (FERPA). *Psychological* aspects of privacy involve how both educators and students perceive online privacy. Research by Wang and colleagues (2011) found that Facebook users regretted posts they made containing sensitive topics (such as alcohol and drug use, sex, religion and politics, and profanity), content with strong sentiment (offensive comments and arguments), and lies and secrets. The researchers discovered the following reasons people made posts they later regretted: (1) they wanted to be perceived favorably, (2) they didn't consider their reasons for posting or the possible consequences, (3) they misjudged cultural norms in their friend circle or circles, (4) they posted when in an emotionally charged state such as anger, (5) they didn't think about the audience that would see the post, (6) they did not foresee how their post would be interpreted by their intended audience, and (7) they did not understand how the Facebook platform works (Wang et al., 2011). These causes suggest areas for discussion and education with students; however, adopting an adult normative perspective in these conversations would likely backfire. Educators are encouraged to learn about these processes and to open up a broader discussion with students about their understanding of privacy. Begin by learning where students are coming from, then lead them through learning the necessary information.

Students may be unaware of how some of their posts could be deleterious to their future employment or educational plans. For instance, they may not be aware that 26 percent of admissions officers and 37 percent of company hiring managers use social media to screen applicants (CareerBuilder.com, 2012; Kaplan, 2012). The fact that online content can be permanent (that is, impossible to delete) can also cause long-term problems for students. In late 2012, the online news site Jezebel engaged in the public shaming of teens who posted racist tweets after Obama's reelection. The original post identified only the teens' Twitter accounts, but a commenter on that post uncovered and shared some of their personal information, like their high schools. Responding to this comment, the author of the original Jezebel post wrote a new story posting the teens' real names, their high schools, and the phone numbers to their high schools and encouraged readers to call and complain to administrators about the teens' online behavior. In this case, Jezebel used its considerable power and influence to attempt to ruin these teenagers' future job and educational opportunities. In fact, the editor of Jezebel was quoted as saying, "And I think there's something larger at play here, and we're going to see this kind of story over and over again until it's innately understood that the line between 'online' and 'in real life' is basically nonexistent" (Hill, 2012). Not only does this statement show a lack of journalistic ethics, but it also highlights the worldview that Jezebel has chosen to espouse: that young people have no right to make mistakes nor the right to have their online mistakes forgotten. Just after the article was published, top hits from a Google search of the names of some of the teens showed the article labeling them as racist. Unfortunately, potential employers and college representatives may view the racist tweets not as a mistake of youth but from an adult framework of well-developed moral and ethnic identity development.

A growing legislative movement aims to protect youth from their own developmentally normative mistakes. "Right to be forgotten" legislation allows youth to erase online content they have posted. In 2012, the European Commission included a right to be forgotten in the draft updates to the Data Protection Directive, and in 2011, Representative Edward Markey proposed amending the Children's Online Privacy Protection Act with the Do Not Track Kids Act, a bill that would have required sites and services to provide an "eraser button" for online content. While the 2011 Do Not Track Kids Act bill was unsuccessful, Markey and other sponsors reintroduced it in late 2013 (Govtrack.us, 2014). Signed just before the Do Not Track Kids Act was introduced, California bill SB568 gives minors the right to remove information they've posted online. While there are certainly limits to these legislative efforts—for instance, they don't grant youth the ability to delete information posted *about* them, only information posted *by* them—such efforts are a good first step to helping support development by allowing youth the freedom to remove content they might not post later in life. In the meantime, however, it will be up to educators to help students learn about online privacy from a youth-normative perspective.

The issues raised by university and employer monitoring of social media, the permanence of online content, and others' willingness to engage in a mob mentality and ruin a student's reputation show the need for teaching not just about privacy, but about civil discourse and ethical and moral online decision making. While it may be difficult to cover these topics comprehensively, educators have the responsibility to at least touch on and model

16

these constructs. Chances are that most students will not be receiving much information about privacy, civil discourse, or ethical and moral online decision making in their courses, and when they do, instruction will almost always be from an adult normative perspective. Therefore, student affairs professionals have an opportunity to instruct students in ways that are both youth normative and helpful for their lives after college. At the very least, issues that arise on social media, such as what happened with the teens in the Jezebel story, can be used as teachable moments. Perhaps with time, higher education institutions will agree upon and adopt learning outcomes that include the effective use of social media in students' post-college lives.

SOCIAL NETWORKING

Social networking sites (SNSs) and services are the most popular category of social media. SNSs typically allow users to create profiles and to add and interact with a group of friends (boyd, 2007; Junco & Mastrodicasa, 2007). The Pew Internet and American Life Project found that between 67 percent and 75 percent of college-aged young adults (who may not necessarily be enrolled in college) use social networking websites (Jones & Fox, 2009; Lenhart, 2009; Lenhart, Purcell, Smith & Zickuhr, 2010). The most popular social networking website among US college students is Facebook. Research shows that anywhere between 79 and 99 percent of college students use Facebook (Hargittai, 2008; Junco, 2012b; Junco, 2013b; Matney & Borland, 2009; Smith, Rainie & Zickuhr, 2011). Data collected by the EDUCAUSE Center for Applied Research (ECAR) found that 90 percent of college students used Facebook, with 58 percent using it several times a day (Dahlstrom, de Boor, Grunwald & Vockley, 2011). A study of a large sample of college students published in 2012 showed that 92 percent of students used Facebook and reported spending an average of more than one hour and forty minutes a day on the site (Junco, 2012b); however, data collected using computer monitoring software measuring actual Facebook use showed that students really spent only twenty-six minutes per day on the site (Junco, 2013a; 2013b).

Because of its popularity with college students, its dominance among SNSs, and the amount of research available on the site as compared to other SNSs, much of the research and examples in this book will focus on Facebook. It is worth noting that the SNS land-scape can and does change quite rapidly. The case of Myspace is a perfect example: an early competitor to Facebook, the site is now used by only 7 percent of teen social media users (Madden, Lenhart, Cortesi, Gasser, Duggan, Smith & Beaton, 2013). In May 2013, the national news media propagated the myth that youth were aban-doning Facebook for other platforms, in a misrepresentation of Pew Internet and American Life Project data showing that teens were actually diversifying their social media portfolio while main-taining Facebook as the site they use most often (Madden, 2013; Madden, Lenhart, Cortesi, Gasser, Duggan, Smith & Beaton, 2013). Although some teens are becoming dissatisfied with Facebook because of "increasing adult presence, the high stakes of managing self-presentation on the site, the burden of negative social interac-tions ('drama'), or feeling overwhelmed by friends who share too much," it is still too early to tell whether this dissatisfaction will fuel a desire to abandon the site in favor of others (Madden, 2013). As explained in chapter 8, whatever replacement for Facebook eventually emerges, it will have to include affordances similar to Facebook's (allowing youth to connect and share with each other) as well as address users' dissatisfactions with Facebook.

Facebook

Throughout history, processes repeat in societies, institutions, and other social ecosystems. Processes involved in the develop-ment of any given phenomenon tend to be replicated in further applications of the system. In the case of Facebook, for instance, understanding its history as an exclusive network for Ivy League students helps us understand how students use Facebook today and how Facebook has developed features that allow for specific affordances. Facebook's initial exclusivity to Ivy League schools helped drive its adoption when it became available to students at non–Ivy League colleges and universities. Furthermore, its exclusivity to college students was a driving force in building a large user base before being opened to the general public.

Mark Zuckerberg conceived Facebook when he was an undergraduate at Harvard University. Zuckerberg created Facemash, the predecessor to Facebook, in 2003. Facemash culled the online pictures of Harvard College students and made them readily accessible online. The interface was much like the then-popular website Hot or Not and, like that site, asked users to rate which of two Harvard College students pictured was "hotter." The site was very popular and received more than 22,000 photo views in the first few hours after it went live. Harvard administrators quickly shut down the site, and Zuckerberg was called before the Administrative Board on charges of breaching security, violating copyright, and violating individual privacy, charges that were later dropped (Kaplan, 2003).

After the Facemash incident, Zuckerberg created the first iteration of Facebook, which launched to Harvard College students in early 2004. As with Facemash, thefacebook.com was very popular with Harvard undergraduate students, with more than half of them signing up within the first month. Clearly, Zuckerberg had stumbled onto something that students were craving—a unified and online facebook, which had not yet existed at Harvard (Harvard houses had issued their own paper "facebooks," directories with student pictures, since the 1980s), and a way for students to have an exclusive and seemingly private off-campus network to connect with their peers. Later, Facebook was launched at other Ivy League schools and was slowly rolled out to all colleges and universities, to student fanfare similar to that at Harvard. The site expanded to high school students in 2005 and then to the general population in late 2006. Since then, it has become one of the most popular online destinations in the English-speaking world.

An example of how Facebook's history has influenced its current state is the use of real names on the site. Facemash was created by uploading the pictures of Harvard College students, and then the first iteration of Facebook focused on actual offline identities. Because of Mark Zuckerberg's insistence that users engage online with their real names, as well as his focus on making users share as much as possible, the culture of Facebook is one where users typically use their real names. Even though it is open to everyone today, Facebook has less of a problem with fake and "creepy" accounts than its early rival Myspace, which was also open to all. Interestingly, Facebook's current business model is predicated on encouraging people to share as much as possible and mining data to push advertisements tailored specifically to each user. Facebook does this through advanced predictive modeling that presumably takes into account a large number of variables, including a person's interests, the interests of their friends, the interests of the friends they interact with the most, the topics of the posts they comment on or like the most, and so on.

Google+

Google+ is Google's social networking service and was developed as a direct competitor to Facebook. Google+ launched as invitation-only in June 2011. At the time, the reaction from the technology sector was that Google+ would be a "Facebook killer" because of both its focus on user privacy and the rate at which users were signing up for the service (DeRosa, 2011; Vaughan-

Nichols, 2011). Google+ offered compelling features, such as the ability to easily place those you follow in "circles" and to share selectively with those groups. Another unique feature of Google+ is the "hangout," which allows as many as ten users to simultaneously engage in video chats (and also simultaneously watch YouTube videos). The hangout feature has been used effectively for educational communication for research meetings, distance education cohort meetings, and professional development opportunities like the live video chats hosted by Ed Cabellon (2014). However, Google+ has not lived up to the "Facebook killer" label; while users originally registered at high rates, user engagement on the site is low, with many users visiting the site only three times a month (Ingraham, 2013).

MICROBLOGGING

Microblogging sites are similar to longer-form blogs; however, their content is typically much shorter, such as short sentences, individual pictures, or links (Twitter, 2014). The most popular microblogging service in the United States is Twitter, with more than 200 million active users (Wickre, 2013).

Twitter

Twitter was the brainchild of Jack Dorsey and was conceived during a brainstorming session held by the board members of Odeo (a podcasting company). At the time, Dorsey proposed a service by which users could use text messaging to communicate with a group of friends (Twitter, 2014). Twitter was first used as an internal service by Odeo employees and then was launched publicly in July of 2006. Twitter's popularity exploded during the 2007 South by Southwest Interactive (SxSWi) conference, when daily tweets tripled from 20,000 to 60,000 (Twitter, 2014). The

SxSWi conference focuses on emerging technologies and is known as a place where technorati congregate to share new ideas and technologies and have an all-around good time. If a technology is able to capture the attention of conference goers, it has a great chance of being successful. Indeed, a number of start-ups have been catapulted to success thanks, in no small part, to their adoption and adoration at SxSWi. Twitter is probably the most famous of these start-ups, but some other notable services launched at SxSWi include Foursquare, Storify, GroupMe, Ushahidi, Foodspotting, and Flavors.me. Of particular interest in the development of Twitter is the fact that like Facebook, Twitter's popularity boost came from use by an "exclusive" group—in this case, well-to-do technology industry members.

Twitter allows users to share short (140 characters or less) messages (*tweets*) with their *followers*—people who have chosen to receive these messages in their Twitter *feed*. Users subscribe to the posts of others, and the timeline is a real-time running archive of what is being posted by those you follow. Like Facebook, Twitter allows users to share images. Because of the restricted number of characters, *url shorteners* are often used when sharing links. In contrast with Facebook, these links are inserted into the text of the message, and no preview is provided. Therefore, Twitter users must ensure that they provide enough context when posting urls. The differences relative to Facebook can often be described as shorthand versus long-form writing. Indeed, to the uninitiated, the "language" of Twitter often seems confusing and the stream overwhelming because of its constantly running nature. If a user follows many other users who post frequently, the user's stream may move rather quickly (and while the stream doesn't move automatically, requiring a user to click or refresh a page to see new tweets, the Twitter feed can still be overwhelming).

Twitter also allows for the use of *hashtags*: keywords that are preceded by a # sign and are clickable based on the interface used to access the site. Hashtags have been such a popular feature of Twitter that Facebook, Google+, Instagram, and Vine have also adopted them. Figure 1.3 shows an example tweet that uses a hashtag. In academic settings, hashtags have been used to aggregate tweets around conferences, workshops, and other events. Following a conference hashtag allows those in attendance to communicate about conference content but also about social events; it also allows those not in attendance to follow along and

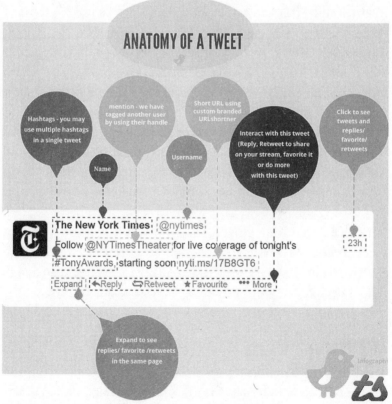

Figure 1.3. Anatomy of a tweet showing a hashtag.
Source: Ann Smarty, Teksocial, and the *New York Times*

learn about what is being discussed. In other words, nonattendees can have some experience of what being at the conference is like and therefore are afforded a low- to no-cost method of professional development. Another noteworthy affordance of Twitter is the large number and wide variety of applications that can be used to access the service. Mayo (2012) found that only around 24 percent of users access Twitter through Twitter.com, the rest accessing the site through mobile and other third-party applications and services. TweetDeck, one such application, was so popular that Twitter ended up buying it in 2011.

Like Facebook, Twitter is more likely used by youth. Pew Internet and American Life Project data show that 31 percent of those 18–29 and 24 percent of 12- to 17-year-olds use Twitter, compared with 19 percent of 30- to 49-year-olds (Duggan & Smith, 2013; Madden, Lenhart, Cortesi, Gasser, Duggan, Smith & Beaton, 2013). Of particular interest, multiple sources show that African American youth are more likely to use Twitter than white youth. In 2011, 31 percent of African American teens used Twitter, compared to 12 percent of white teens (Pew Internet and American Life Project, 2011). In 2013, 39 percent of African American teens used Twitter, compared to 23 percent of white teens (Madden, Lenhart, Cortesi, Gasser, Duggan, Smith & Beaton, 2013). Hargittai and Litt (2011) found that African American students and those with greater Internet skills were more likely to use Twitter, while students with parents who had less than a high school degree were less likely to be Twitter users.

Tumblr

Tumblr is the second most popular microblogging platform in the United States in terms of traffic (Alexa, 2013a). While Tumblr is a very popular website in the United States and the second most popular microblogging site, very little research has been conducted on the Tumblr user experience. The Pew Internet and American Life Project found that while 16 percent of all online adults used Twitter, only 6 percent use Tumblr (Duggan & Brenner, 2013). Tumblr is most popular among 18- to 29-year-olds, with 13 percent saying they use the site (Duggan & Brenner, 2013). A study using computer monitoring data found that of the thirty-one minutes students spent on social networking websites daily, only four minutes were spent using Tumblr (Junco, 2013b). Some have speculated that there is a geographic or cultural leaning in Tumblr use toward those in northeastern cities such as New York; however, this speculation may be fueled by the fact that Tumblr user demographics skew toward the urban and educated (Duggan & Brenner, 2013).

In terms of affordances, Tumblr has features very similar to Twitter. Users can post short blogs, follow the microblogs of other users, and post multimedia content. Unlike Twitter, Tumblr does not limit posts to 140 characters. Although Tumblr's use by college students is currently limited, it is helpful for student affairs professionals to be aware of the patterns of Tumblr use at their institutions; if Tumblr use skews toward those in urban settings, we may miss a significant part of the minority student experience if we do not consider the site in connection with our social media intervention strategies (Junco, 2013c).

IMAGE AND VIDEO SHARING

Instagram

Instagram is an online photo-sharing service that enables users to take pictures with their mobile devices, add a variety of filters, and post those pictures to a stream. Perhaps one of the early draws of Instagram was the ability to easily apply photo filters (see figure

Figure 1.4. An example of an Instagram photo with filter. Creative Commons License: catepol—http://i-am-cc.org/instagram/catepol/237350.

1.4), which made poorer-quality mobile phone pictures more interesting and artistic. As with Twitter, one can follow the Instagram stream of other users and see the photos they post in real time. Also as with Twitter, one can use hashtags to aggregate pictures under a common theme. Unlike Twitter, Instagram allows users to "like" and comment on pictures. The Pew Internet and American Life Project found that 13 percent of Internet users overall used Instagram (Duggan & Brenner, 2013). In another study, the Pew Internet and American Life Project and Berkman Center for Internet and Society found that 3 percent of teens used Instagram. Teen Instagram users expressed excitement about the platform, noting the absence of "drama" such as is found on Facebook as well as the opportunities for creative expression (Madden, Lenhart, Cortesi, Gasser, Duggan, Smith & Beaton, 2013). As is true for Tumblr, little research has been conducted on users' experience of Instagram—so there's also little research on Instragram that has been conducted in education settings.

Vine

Vine can be best thought of as "Instagram for video clips"—although in order to compete with Vine, Instagram added the ability to share videos. Vine was founded in June 2012 and was quickly acquired by Twitter in October of the same year (Vine, 2014). Vine is accessed through a mobile application that allows users to post short videos of up to six seconds. The app interface easily allows users to start and stop recording and instantly publish the video to their feed. Given the emergent nature of Vine at the time of this writing, it is unclear as to its penetration among college students. Vine is so new to the social media scene that even the latest (as of this writing) Pew Internet and American Life Project and Berkman Center for Internet and Society report did not include Vine as a social media site in their questions (Madden, Lenhart, Cortesi, Gasser, Duggan, Smith & Beaton, 2013). Vine is certainly an app to watch in the near future, as its ability to easily share short videos allows for creative educational opportunities.

Pinterest

Pinterest is an image- and video-sharing service that allows users to aggregate content in theme-based pinboards. Like Twitter and Instagram, Pinterest allows users to follow other users. Pinterest users can also like content as well as "repin" it to their own boards. Users can upload pictures to their pinboards via their computers or mobile devices or through web links. In February 2014, Pinterest was the twelfth most visited site in the United States (Alexa, 2013b). As such, it is a more popular web destination than Instagram. However, while Instagram was used by 11 percent of respondents in the Pew Internet and American Life Project and Berkman Center for Internet and Society study, only 1 percent reported having a Pinterest account (Madden, Lenhart, Cortesi, Gasser, Duggan, Smith & Beaton, 2013). Pinterest is more popular among college students. Unpublished data collected on more than four hundred college students using computer monitoring software showed that 26 percent used Pinterest at least once during the monthlong data collection period (Junco, 2014). As is true for Tumblr, Instagram, and Vine, little research has been conducted on the Pinterest user experience or on the use of Pinterest in educational settings. However, the penetration rate of Pinterest among college students might lead to more research interest in examining the service as a learning tool compared to other image platforms.

SnapChat

SnapChat is a mobile photo- and video-messaging application that allows users to set a limit on how long a recipient can view a photo or video before it is "deleted" from the mobile device. A unique feature of SnapChat is the ability to doodle and to add text to picture and video, which gives users the ability to easily create memes. While SnapChat gives the illusion of increased privacy because pictures are automatically deleted, there are a number of ways to bypass this feature. Recipients can take a screen capture of the message (as easy as pressing the home and the power buttons simultaneously on an iPhone or the volume down and power buttons simultaneously on newer Android devices). While SnapChat will inform the sender if a screencap is taken, the privacy breach has already occurred. Further, there are other technical (running SnapChat in an emulator) and nontechnical (taking a picture of the phone screen with another camera) ways to thwart the perceived privacy of the app.

SnapChat was developed by Stanford student Evan Spiegel as part of one of his design courses. Spiegel said that he created the app to help bring fun back into online communications, because people had been hyperfocused on presenting spotless online identities. He theorized that SnapChat would allow people to get back to their truer selves without the pressure of possible career and educational ruin (Colao, 2012). The app launched in September 2011, and by May 2012 it was processing about 25 images every second (Gallagher, 2012). SnapChat's popularity continues to increase, and data collected by the Pew Internet and American Life Project and the Berman Center for Internet and Society showed that teens who used SnapChat were very excited about it (Madden, Lenhart, Cortesi, Gasser, Duggan, Smith & Beaton, 2013). As is true for Tumblr, Instagram, and Vine, at the time of this writing no research has yet been published on the user experience or outcomes of SnapChat use. The provocative nature of SnapChat—many media mentions note the affordances of SnapChat as a safer alternative to sexting—is likely to spur more research on the platform in the near term as compared to Tumblr, Instagram, and Vine.

DEVICES

While social media sites started as web-based platforms, the increased availability and affordability of smartphones and the availability of tablets has led to a concomitant increase in the use of mobile platforms to access these sites. Smartphone ownership has increased dramatically in a few short years: in 2013, 37 percent of teens in the United States owned a smartphone, compared to 23 percent in 2011 (Madden, Lenhart, Duggan, Cortesi

& Gasser, 2013). Additionally, 23 percent of teens owned a tablet computer. Almost three quarters (74 percent) of all teens 12–17 reported at least occasionally accessing the Internet on cell phones, tablets, or other mobile devices (Madden, Lenhart, Duggan, Cortesi & Gasser, 2013). Interestingly, especially for issues related to digital inequalities, 25 percent of teens reported that their cell phones are the primary way that they access the Internet, a percentage that rises to 50 percent for teen smartphone users (Madden, Lenhart, Duggan, Cortesi & Gasser, 2013). Some of my earlier research found that African American students were less likely to own a cell phone than white students; however, African American cell phone owners sent more texts and spent more time talking on the phone than white cell phone owners (Junco, Merson & Salter, 2010).

There are at least two principal ways that accessing social media on mobile devices can alter the user experience and by extension how students use these sites: (1) While mobile applications for social media have overlapping functionality with their web-based components, mobile applications also have additional functions providing supplementary affordances. The Facebook application allows users to post pictures directly from the mobile applications (and from the devices that youth typically use to take pictures). Instagram, on the other hand, is primarily a mobile service with very limited web-based functionality. (2) Access patterns are different on mobile devices. Students tend not to spend as much time logged in and interacting with social media when they are on mobile devices as when they are using computer-based applications. Often, students will check social media on their phones briefly throughout the day. Research has found that accessing Facebook in different ways (logging in fewer times for longer amounts of time versus logging in frequently for shorter amounts of time) is differentially related to student outcomes with students who log in frequently for shorter amounts of time having more positive outcomes (Junco, 2012a; 2012b). As more research is conducted, it will be important to learn how data from mobile use of social media can enhance our understanding of how students interact with these sites.

DIGITAL INEQUALITIES

Many educators make the mistake of assuming that "all of today's students are technologically savvy," to the detriment of educators' work with students. While it is indeed the case that many college students use social media, we must pay special attention to those who don't for various reasons. In one analysis, boyd (2007) distinguished between two types of youth who don't use social media: those who are disenfranchised and those who are "conscientious objectors." *Conscientious objectors* are youth who choose to refrain from social media use for personal or political reasons. Student affairs professionals should be particularly concerned about those students who don't use social media because they are disenfranchised as a result of their socioeconomic or racial or ethnic backgrounds. Furthermore, the mere fact that students use social media does not mean that they use social media in ways that are beneficial for their academic and developmental outcomes. The distinction between *access* and *use* is extremely important when considering digital inequalities. These inequalities persist over time and can have far-reaching effects for students.

Digital inequalities can impact the college admissions process. Take for example, Kaplan's (2012) survey of college admissions officers. In this survey, 26 percent of admissions officers admitted visiting an applicant's social networking profile, and 27 percent reported Googling an applicant to learn more about them. What is most disturbing is that 35 percent said that they found something online that negatively impacted a student's application; however, there was no follow-up conducted to examine what kind of things the admissions officers found online that would negatively impact the application. Admissions processes are typically standardized at each institution in order to remove as much bias from admissions decisions as possible. For example, admissions officers at public institutions can't base an admissions decision on an applicant's religion. Therefore, such "off the books" evaluations using social media are incredibly problematic. An admissions officer reviewing a student's Facebook profile might find out the student is Muslim, and while the officer might not make a decision based on this fact, the reality is that information not shared by the student on the application is being considered as part of the admissions decision.

Even if reviewing social media profiles and Googling students were to be made a standard part of the admissions process, there is no way that admissions officers could evaluate student social media profiles fairly. First, there is a lack of resources. Admissions offices barely have enough staff to keep the machinery of recruitment and the traditional evaluation process going, let alone to review the Facebook profiles of all entering students. Even if admissions offices had the necessary resources to evaluate every applicant's Facebook profile, the process would still be inherently unfair. Some students have the requisite skills (and forethought) to hide their profiles from admissions officers or to create ideal-self profiles that highlight their most positive attributes. Unfortunately, having these skills is related to sociodemographics such as parental education, household income, and race and ethnicity. For instance, Hargittai (2010) found that women, African Americans, Latinos, and those whose parents had lower educational attainment had lower levels of Internet skills even when controlling for Internet access and experience. Furthermore, those with higher levels of Internet skills engaged in more types of activities online.

Research has also revealed differences in how students from minority racial and ethnic backgrounds and from lower socioeconomic statuses access social media. In an early study, Hargittai (2008) found that Latino students were less likely to use Facebook than Caucasians and Asian Americans and were more likely to use Myspace. Women were also more likely to use Myspace than men were, and Asian American students were more likely to use Facebook but less likely to use Myspace (Hargittai, 2008). Furthermore, Hargittai (2008) found that students whose parents had a college degree were more likely to use Facebook than students whose parents did not have a college degree. However, the social media ecosystem has changed dramatically since that study was published, with participation on Myspace dropping to an all-time low of 7 percent of teen social media users, while Facebook adoption has reached 94 percent (Madden, Lenhart, Cortesi, Gasser, Duggan, Smith & Beaton, 2013). More recently, Hargittai and Litt (2011) found that African American students and students with greater Internet skills were more likely to use Twitter, while students from lower socioeconomic levels were less likely to be Twitter users. The Pew Internet and American Life Project also found that African Americans were more likely to use Twitter; however, the researchers did not find differences in use based on socioeconomic status (Duggan & Brenner, 2013).

There are gender and race/ethnicity differences in the use of image-sharing social media sites. An analysis of user profiles by Chrzan (2012) found that globally, 83 percent of Pinterest users were female. Pinterest is more popular among female Internet users in the United States as well, with 25 percent of women using Pinterest compared to 5 percent of men (Duggan & Brenner, 2013). Pinterest is more popular among wealthier individuals and those with greater educational attainment (Duggan & Brenner, 2013). Female college students in the United States use Pinterest more than male students: unpublished computer usage data show that 35 percent of the female students in the sample used Pinterest during the monthlong study period, while only 12 percent of the men did so (Junco, 2014). There is a similar pattern with Instagram: women were significantly more likely to use the service than men (Duggan & Brenner, 2013). Additionally, African Americans and Latinos were significantly more likely to use Instagram than whites (Duggan & Brenner, 2013).

Studies have shown that while access has begun to equalize across groups for some social media sites and services, *how* students use the sites varies by sociodemographic characteristics. Muscanell and Guadagno (2011) found that men were more likely to report using social networking websites to make new friends while women were more likely to report using the sites to maintain current relationships. Furthermore, they found that men were more likely to play games on social networking websites while women were more likely to post public messages, send private messages, send friend requests, and post photographs (Muscanell and Guadagno, 2011). My own research shows that even though time spent on the site was the same across groups, women were more likely to use Facebook for communication, African Americans were less likely to use Facebook to check up on friends, and students from lower socioeconomic levels were less likely to use Facebook for communication and sharing (Junco, 2013c).

These sociodemographic differences highlight some of the ways that youth who may already be at a disadvantage are disadvantaged further by their lack of social media skills. In my research, the differences in how Facebook was used by members of minority groups was related to their understanding of the cultural norms and mores of the site as well as to their level of skill. Students with higher levels of skill are more able to do things like enable privacy settings so that their profiles are not searchable. And because not all students are sophisticated enough to hide their profiles from admissions officers (or to create ideal-self profiles), they are at the mercy of admissions officers looking for an easy way to make their applicant pool smaller. Facebook-stalking and Googling applicants thus can be seen as discriminatory admissions practices similar to other banned forms of discriminatory practices.

Affluent students have more parental input into what they post online and have a more thorough understanding of how their online self-presentation might affect their college, career, and interpersonal prospects. Indeed, research has shown that the interpersonal benefits accrued from technology use vary by socioeconomic status. Zhao (2009) found that seventh and tenth graders from schools in middle- and high-income suburbs were more likely to use instant messaging (IM) than those from schools in lower-income urban areas. At the time of the study, IM was used for communication and connection with a peer group, helping youth build and strengthen friendships. Zhao's (2009) research then suggests that youth from areas of lower socioeconomic status are at a disadvantage when using IM for building social capital (an issue that will be discussed in further detail in later chapters).

Knowing that Facebook's and Twitter's early development and popularity were sustained by members of exclusive communities (Harvard students and SxSWi attendees) helps us to understand the cultural environment of these sites. Additionally, understanding that there is variability in how sites are accessed and used based on background characteristics allows educators to have a more complete understanding of how all students use technology. Even if there were equal access and use by all members of society, sites like Facebook and Twitter have a history of being analogous to exclusive country clubs that extend membership only to societal and cultural elites. It is no surprise that when we examine differences in how these sites are used, we find that

35

students from minority racial, ethnic, and socioeconomic backgrounds are at a disadvantage. The following section builds on this framework of digital inequalities and examines how these inequalities affect education and how they are perpetuated through educational systems.

Digital Inequalities in Education

Some studies of elementary or high school students or of both have found academic benefits from using educational technology (Shapley, Sheehan, Maloney & Caranikas-Walker, 2010; Suhr, Hernandez, Grimes & Warschauer, 2010; Tienken & Wilson, 2007). On the contrary, other studies find technology use and academic outcomes to be negatively related in primary and secondary schools (Aypay, Erdogan & Sozer, 2007; Waight & Abd-El-Khalick, 2007). Research on technology use in higher education helps to resolve these conflicting findings: Bliuc, Ellis, Goodyear, and Piggott (2010) found that students who used discussion boards as tools to seek answers—instead of improving their understanding of a topic—were using them in ways that encouraged reproduction and task completion rather than deep learning; those students also had lower final course grades. Rizzuto, LeDoux, and Hatala (2009) discovered a positive relationship between the use of a course management system for required actions such as posting comments and course test scores. Related research has found that students who were provided lecture slides via a course management system had lower exam scores than a control section, possibly due to decreased attendance (Weatherly, Grabe & Arthur, 2003). In other words, it's not whether technologies were used as part of the educational process, but how students used those technologies, that made a difference in outcomes.

Although research on college students has focused on institutionally supported technologies like learning and course management systems, a small number of studies have found substantial benefits in incorporating social media (Junco, 2012a; 2012b; Junco, Elavsky & Heiberger, 2012; Junco, Heiberger & Loken, 2011). For example, my research has found that specific uses of Facebook, such as checking to see what friends were up to and sharing links, were positively related to overall grade point average (Junco, 2012a). In a related study, certain Facebook activities predicted more of the variance in student engagement than time spent on the site (Junco, 2012b). Specific Facebook activities such as creating or RSVP'ing to events, commenting, and viewing photos were positively predictive of engagement, whereas playing games, posting photos, using Facebook chat, and checking up on friends were negatively predictive. In controlled classroom experiments, using Twitter for educational purposes both increased student engagement and improved overall student first-semester grade point averages (Junco, Elavsky & Heiberger, 2012; Junco, Heiberger & Loken, 2011).

Unfortunately, research on digital inequalities in education has shown that the benefits obtained by using educational technology are distributed unequally across gender, race, and socioeconomic status. However, a majority of this research has examined high school students. Brown, Higgins, and Hartley (2001), Milone and Salpeter (1996), Pisapia (1994), and Warschauer, Knobel, and Stone (2004) found that public school students in areas of lower socioeconomic status were more likely to use computers for academic practice and quizzing, while students in areas of higher socioeconomic status were more than three times as likely to be learning how to program computers. In their review, Warschauer and Matuchniak (2010) found that students from lower socioeconomic levels as well as those from minority ethnic and racial backgrounds were at a disadvantage because of how they used

37

technology in school and because they were less likely to own a computer. These disadvantages translated into negative impacts on academic achievement (Warschauer & Matuchniak, 2010).

In summary, digital inequalities work in two ways: they may begin at an early age and be perpetuated throughout a student's schooling so as to put some students at an educational and, by extension, a socioeconomic disadvantage; or socioeconomically and educationally disadvantaged youth may be more likely to suffer from these inequalities. For students, the chances of being successful in today's workforce increase with the ability to use computers and other information and communications technologies. This is especially true for social media, as they are increasingly used as platforms to find employment and for career development. In the case of Facebook, research has found the use of the platform to be related to behavior supporting future employment potential, such as the building and maintenance of social capital, student engagement in academic and cocurricular activities, and possibilities for peer-to-peer learning (Ellison, Steinfield & Lampe, 2011; Ellison, Steinfield & Lampe, 2007; Ellison, Vitak, Gray, & Lampe, 2014; Jenkins, Clinton, Purushotma, Robison & Weigel, 2009; Junco, 2012b). Therefore, inequalities in Facebook usage may put students at an "engagement disadvantage," which would affect their social integration, and by extension their persistence towards graduation (Tinto, 1993).

Unfortunately, relatively little work has been conducted on digital inequalities, presumably because most researchers, like society at large, conclude that all youth are born with these digital skills. Prensky (2001) is credited with coining the term "digital native." From his perspective, all youth, because they spend time around technology, have equivalent access and skills. As has been reported in this section, nothing can be further from the truth. In fact, adopting the "digital native" myth is dangerous for student affairs professionals, as it misses the goal of ensuring success for all students, especially those who have been traditionally underserved or underrepresented in higher education. Not only is the "digital native" myth contradicted by the reality of digital inequalities, the word *native* can be (and has been) used in derogatory ways, increasing social distance and emphasizing inequalities. It is imperative that student affairs professionals actively and consistently consider the assumptions they are making about student technology use and take steps to ensure that digital resources are inclusive. Student affairs professionals can do so not only by communicating information through multiple online venues, but also by developing programming that serves to level the digital "playing field."

CONCLUSION

Social media sites and services are incredibly popular among college students. Even with the high adoption rates of sites and services such as Facebook, it is helpful to keep in mind that not all students are on these sites and that there are differences based on sociodemographic characteristics in the ways these sites are used. These differences in access and use are of great import when thinking about how to meet students where they are on social media and when developing effective social media programs and interventions. It is essential to understand the research that has been conducted on these sites that relates to issues of importance for student affairs professionals—namely student development, student engagement, and student success (covered in chapters 2, 3, 4, and 5). Chapter 4 reviews how social media can be and have been used in student affairs to improve student engagement, implement programming, and improve communication between students and student affairs professionals. While most of these interventions are focused on the most popular social media sites as of this writing, it will be crucial to consider how the principles of online engagement can be applied to emerging technologies, an issue that will be covered in chapter 8. Furthermore, chapter 5 will outline the ways that social media can be used effectively to promote formal learning, processes relevant to all educators. Other chapters will explore how to assess social media interventions to see whether they are effective (chapter 6) and how social media can be used for professional development (chapter 7).

Practical Tips

1. Question media reports of social media use by critically evaluating the research on which they are based.
2. Be aware of the differences in outcomes between social media access and use.
3. Understand and communicate the costs of using "free" sites and services like Facebook and Twitter.
4. Recognize that while social media are popular among many students, there are those who are at a disadvantage because of digital inequalities.
5. Take steps to ensure that you do not propagate digital inequalities in your work with students.

REFERENCES

Alexa. (2013a). Tumblr.com. Retrieved August 22, 2013, from http://www.alexa.com/siteinfo/tumblr.com.

Alexa. (2013b). Top sites in the United States. Retrieved February 2, 2014, from http://www.alexa.com/topsites/countries/US.

Allen, M. (2012). Study: Facebook causes one third of divorces. *Opposing Views*. Retrieved from http://www.opposingviews.com/i/technology/internet/study-facebook-causes-one-third-divorces.

Auerbach, D., Mayer, J., & Eckersley, P. (2013). What we need to know about PRISM. *The Electronic Frontier Foundation*. Retrieved August 22, 2013, from https://www.eff.org/deeplinks/2013/06/what-we-need-to-know-about-prism.

Aypay, A., Erdogan, M., & Sozer, M. A. (2007). Variation among schools on classroom practices in science based on TIMSS-1999 in Turkey. *Journal of Research in Science Teaching, 44*(10), 1417–1435.

Bliuc, A. M., Ellis, R., Goodyear, P., & Piggott, L. (2010). Learning through face-to-face and online discussions: Associations between students' conceptions, approaches and academic performance in political science. *British Journal of Educational Technology, 41*(3), 512–524. doi:10.1111/j.1467–8535.2009.00966.x.

Blue_beetle, (2010). Metafilter discussion thread. Retrieved August 22, 2013, from http://www.metafilter.com/95152/Userdriven-discontent#3256046.

boyd, d. (2007). *Why Youth (Heart) Social Network Sites: The Role of Networked Publics in Teenage Social Life*. MacArthur Foundation Series on Digital Learning: Youth, Identity, and Digital Media (ed. David Buckingham). Cambridge, MA: MIT Press.

Brown, M. R., Higgins, K., & Hartley, K. (2001). Teachers and technology equity. *Teaching Exceptional Children, 33*(4), 32–39.

Cabellon, E. (2014). Student Affairs Live. Retrieved January 31, 2014, from http://higheredlive.com/tag/student-affairs-live/.

CareerBuilder.com. (2012). Thirty-seven percent of companies use social networks to research potential job candidates, according to new CareerBuilder Survey. Retrieved January 31, 2014, from http://www.careerbuilder.com/share/aboutus/pressreleasesdetail.aspx?id=pr691&sd=4%2F18%2F2012&ed=4%2F18%2F2099.

Choney, S. (2010). Facebook use can lower grades by 20 percent, study says. *NBC Bay Area*. Retrieved February 2, 2014, from http://www.nbcbayarea.com/news/tech/Facebook_use_can_lower_grades_by_20_percent__study_says-102372359.html.

Chowdhury, A. (2013). Is Facebook leading to narcissist outlook? *CoolAge*. Retrieved January 31, 2014, from http://www.coolage.in/2013/05/13/is-facebook-leading-to-narcissist-outlook-top-3/.

Chrzan, Q. (2012). Pinterest: A review of social media's newest sweetheart. *Engauge Insight Report*. Retrieved January 31, 2014, from http://www.engauge.com/assets/pdf/Engauge-Pinterest.pdf.

Colao, J. J. (2012). Snapchat: The biggest no-revenue mobile app since Instagram. Retrieved January 31, 2014, from http://www.forbes.com/sites/jjcolao/2012/11/27/snapchat-the-biggest-no-revenue-mobile-app-since-instagram/.

Criticism of Facebook. (2014). In Wikipedia. Retrieved January 31, 2014, from http://en.wikipedia.org/wiki/Criticism_of_Facebook#Privacy_concerns.

Dahlstrom, E., de Boor, T., Grunwald, P., & Vockley, M. (2011). *The ECAR National Study of Undergraduate Students and Information Technology, 2011*. Boulder, CO: EDUCAUSE Center for Applied Research.

DeAndrea, D. C., Ellison, N. B., LaRose, R., Steinfield, C., & Fiore, A. (2011). Serious social media: On the use of social media for improving students' adjustment to college. *The Internet and Higher Education*, 1–9. doi:10.1016/j.iheduc.2011.05.009.

DeRosa, A. (2011). Is Google+ a Facebook killer or another Google Wave? Retrieved January 31, 2014, from http://blogs.reuters.com/anthony-derosa/2011/06/30/is-google-a-facebook-killer-or-another-google-wave/.

Duggan, M., & Brenner, J. (2013). *The Demographics of Social Media Users—2012*. Pew Internet and American Life Report. Retrieved January 31, 2014, from http://www.pewinternet.org/Reports/2013/Social-media-users.aspx.

Duggan, M., & Smith, A. (2013). *Social Media Update 2013*. Pew Internet and American Life Project Report. Retrieved February 2, 2014, from http://www.pewinternet.org/Reports/2013/Social-Media-Update.aspx.

Ellison, N. B., Steinfield, C., & Lampe, C. (2007). The benefits of Facebook "friends": Exploring the relationship between college students' use of online social networks and social capital. *Journal of Computer Mediated Communication, 12,* 1143–1168.

Ellison, N. B., Steinfield, C., & Lampe C. (2011). Connection strategies: Social capital implications of Facebook-enabled communication practices. *New Media and Society, 13*(6), 873–892.

Ellison, N. B., Vitak, J., Gray, R., & Lampe, C. (2014). Cultivating social resources on social network sites: Facebook relationship maintenance behaviors and their role in social capital processes. *Journal of Computer-Mediated Communication,* DOI: 10.1111/jcc4.12078.

Gallagher, B. (2012). No, Snapchat isn't about sexting, says co-founder Evan Spiegel. Retrieved January 31, 2014, from http://techcrunch.com/2012/05/12/snapchat-not-sexting/.

Gayle, D. (2013). Facebook is the worst social network for bullying with 19-year-old BOYS the most common victims. *Daily Mail.* Retrieved January 31, 2014, from http://www.dailymail.co.uk/sciencetech/article-2294023/Facebook-worst-social-network-bullying-New-survey-shows-youngsters-targeted-online-else.html.

Govtrack.us. (2014). H.R. 1895 (112th): Do Not Track Kids Act of 2011. Retrieved February 2, 2014, from https://www.govtrack.us/congress/bills/112/hr1895.

Greenwald, G., & MacAskill, E. (2013). NSA Prism program taps in to user data of Apple, Google and others. *The Guardian,* Thursday, June 6, 2013. Retrieved August 22, 2013, from http://www.theguardian.com/world/2013/jun/06/us-tech-giants-nsa-data.

Hargittai, E. (2008). Whose space? Differences among users and non-users of social network sites. *Journal of Computer-Mediated Communication, 13*(1), 276–297.

Hargittai, E. (2010). Digital na(t)ives? Variation in Internet skills and uses among members of the "Net Generation." *Sociological Inquiry, 80*(1), 92–113.

Hargittai, E., & Litt, E. (2011). The tweet smell of celebrity success: Explaining variation in Twitter adoption among a diverse group of young adults. *New Media & Society, 13*(5), 824–842.

Heiberger, G., & Harper, R. (2008). Have you Facebooked Astin lately? Using technology to increase student involvement. *New Directions for Student Services, 124*, 19–35. doi:10.1002/ss.293

Hill, K. (2012). Should teenagers have racist election tweets in their Google results for life? Jezebel votes yes. Retrieved January 31, 2014, from http://www.forbes.com/sites/kashmirhill/2012/11/09/should-teenagers-have-racist-election-tweets-in-their-google-results-for-life-jezebel-votes-yes/.

Ingraham, N. (2013). Google+ trending down? Data suggests users only visit the site three times a month. Retrieved January 31, 2014, from http://www.theverge.com/web/2012/2/28/2832136/google-plus-engagement-user-data.

Jenkins, H., Clinton, K., Purushotma, R., Robison, A. J., & Weigel, M. (2009). *Confronting the Challenges of Participatory Culture: Media Education for the 21 Century.* The John D. and Catherine T. MacArthur Foundation Reports on Digital Media and Learning. Retrieved January 31, 2014, from http://mitpress.mit.edu/sites/default/files/titles/free_download/9780262513623_Confronting_the_Challenges.pdf.

Jimenez, F. (2013). Social envy—Study finds Facebook causes depression and isolation. *World Crunch.* Retrieved January 31, 2014, from http://www.worldcrunch.com/culture-society/social-envy-study-finds-facebook-causes-depression-and-isolation/zuckerberg-social-network-health-depression-fb/c3s10718/.

Jones, S., & Fox, S. (2009). *Generations Online in 2009.* Data memo. Washington, DC: Pew Internet and American Life Project. Retrieved February 2, 2014, from http://www.pewinternet.org/~/media//Files/Reports/2009/PIP_Generations_2009.pdf.

Jones, S., Johnson-Yale, C., Millermaier, S., & Pérez, F. S. (2009). Everyday life, online: U.S. college students' use of the Internet. *First Monday, 14*(10). Retrieved April 4, 2014, from http://firstmonday.org/ojs/index.php/fm/article/view/2649/2301.

Junco, R. (2011, April 28). Tweeting SSAO's less interested in engaging in conversations. *Social Media in Higher Education* (blog). Retrieved April 4, 2014, from: http://blog.reyjunco.com/tweeting-ssao%E2%80%99s-less-interested-in-engaging-in-conversations.

Junco, R. (2012a). Too much face and not enough books: The relationship between multiple indices of Facebook use and academic performance. *Computers in Human Behavior, 28*(1), 187–198.

Junco, R. (2012b). The relationship between frequency of Facebook use, participation in Facebook activities, and student engagement. *Computers & Education, 58*(1), 162–171.

Junco, R. (2013a). Comparing actual and self-reported measures of Facebook use. *Computers in Human Behavior, 29*(3), 626–631.

Junco, R. (2013b). iSpy: Seeing what students really do online. *Learning, Media and Technology, 39*(1), 75–89.

Junco, R. (2013c). Inequalities in Facebook use. *Computers in Human Behavior, 29*(6), 2328–2336.

Junco, R. (2014). Predicting student outcomes using data from computer monitoring software. Unpublished raw data.

Junco, R., Elavsky, C. M., & Heiberger, G. (2012). Putting Twitter to the test: Assessing outcomes for student collaboration, engagement, and success. *British Journal of Educational Technology, 44*(2), 273–287.

Junco, R., Heiberger, G., & Loken, E. (2011). The effect of Twitter on college student engagement and grades. *Journal of Computer Assisted Learning, 27*(2), 119–132.

Junco, R., & Mastrodicasa, J. (2007). *Connecting to the Net.Generation: What Higher Education Professionals Need to Know about Today's Students.* Washington, DC: NASPA.

Junco, R., Merson, D., & Salter, D. W. (2010). The effect of gender, ethnicity, and income on college students' use of communication technologies. *Cyberpsychology, Behavior, and Social Networking, 13*(6), 619–627.

Junco, R., & Timm, D. M. (2008). Editors' notes. In R. Junco & D. M. Timm (eds.), Using Emerging Technologies to Enhance Student Engagement. *New Directions for Student Services*, Issue 124, pp. 55–70. San Francisco: Jossey-Bass.

Kaplan, K. (2003). Facemash creator survives ad board. *The Harvard Crimson*, November 19, 2003. Retrieved January 31, 2014, from http://www.thecrimson.com/article/2003/11/19/facemash -creator-survives-ad-board-the/.

Kaplan. (2012). *Kaplan Test Prep's 2012 Survey of College Admissions Officers*. Retrieved January 31, 2014, from http://press.kaptest.com/httppress-kaptest-comresearch/kaplan-test-preps-2012-survey-of-college-admissions-officers.

Karpinski, A. C., Kirschner, P. A., Ozer, I., Mellott, J. A., & Ochwo, P. (2012). An exploration of social networking site use, multitasking, and academic performance among United States and European university students. *Computers in Human Behavior, 29*(3), 1182–1192.

Kosinski, M., Stillwell, D., & Graepel, T. (2013). Private traits and attributes are predictable from digital records of human behavior. *Proceedings of the National Academy of Sciences of the United States of America, 110*(15), 5802–5805.

Lenhart, A. (2009). *Adults and Social Network Websites*. Pew Internet and American Life Project Report. Retrieved January 31, 2014, from http://www.pewinternet.org/Reports/2009/Adults-and-Social-Network-Websites.aspx.

Lenhart, A., Purcell, K., Smith, A., & Zickuhr, K. (2010). *Social Media and Young Adults*. Pew Internet and American Life Report. Retrieved January 31, 2014, from http://www.pewinternet.org/Reports/2010/Social-Media-and-Young-Adults.aspx.

Madden, M. (2013). *Teens Haven't Abandoned Facebook (Yet)*. Pew Internet and American Life Project Commentary. Retrieved January 31, 2014, from http://pewinternet.org/Commentary/2013/August/Teens-Havent-Abandoned-Facebook-Yet.aspx.

Madden, A., Lenhart, A., Cortesi, S., Gasser, U., Duggan, M., Smith, A., & Beaton, M. (2013). *Teens, Social Media, and Privacy*. Pew Internet and American Life Project Report. Retrieved January 31, 2014, from http://www.pewinternet.org/Reports/2013/Teens-Social-Media-And-Privacy.aspx.

Madden, A., Lenhart, A., Duggan, M., Cortesi, S., & Gasser, U. (2013). *Teens and Technology 2013*. Pew Internet and American Life Project Report. Retrieved February 2, 2014, from http://www.pewinternet.org/Reports/2013/Teens-and-Tech.aspx.

Matney, M., & Borland, K. (2009). Facebook, blogs, tweets: How staff and units can use social networking to enhance student learning. Presentation at the annual meeting of the National Association for Student Personnel Administrators, Seattle, WA.

Mayo, B. (2012). How many people use Twitter's own apps? Retrieved January 31, 2014, from http://benjaminmayo.co.uk/how-many -people-use-twitter-s-own-apps.

Miller, C. C. (2013). Tech companies concede to surveillance program. *The New York Times,* June 7, 2013. Retrieved August 22, 2013, from http:// www.nytimes.com/2013/06/08/technology/tech-companies -bristling-concede-to-government-surveillance-efforts.html.

Milone, M. N., & Salpeter, J. (1996). Technology and equity issues. *Technology and Learning, 16*(4), 38–47.

Moore, E. A. (2013). Study: Anxiety and alcohol use linked to Facebook. *CNET.* Retrieved April 11, 2014, from http://www.cnet.com/news/ study-anxiety-and-alcohol-use-linked-to-facebook/.

Muscanell, N. L., & Guadagno, R. E. (2011). Make new friends or keep the old: Gender and personality differences in social networking use. *Computers in Human Behavior, 28*(1), 107–112.

Pew Internet and American Life Project. (2011). July 2011—Teens and Online Behavior [Dataset]. Retrieved from http://pewinternet.org/ Shared-Content/Data-Sets/2011/July-2011-Teens-and-Online -Behavior.aspx.

Pisapia, J. (1994). *Technology: The Equity Issue.* Richmond, VA: Metropolitan Educational Research Consortium.

Prensky, M. (2001). Digital natives, digital immigrants: Part 1. *On the Horizon, 9*(5), 1–6.

Rizzuto, T. E., LeDoux, J., & Hatala, J. P. (2009). It's not just what you know, it's who you know: Testing a model of the relative importance of social networks to academic performance. *Social Psychology of Education, 12*(2), 175–189. doi:10.1007/s11218-008 -9080-0.

Schneier, B. (2013). Could U.S. have stopped Syria's chemical attack? *CNN.* Retrieved February 14, 2014, from http://www .cnn.com/2013/09/11/opinion/schneier-intelligence-limitation.

Schneier, B. (2014). How the NSA threatens national security. *The Atlantic.* Retrieved February 14, 2014, from http://www.theatlantic.com/

technology/archive/2014/01/how-the-nsa-threatens-national
-security/282822/.

Shapley, K. S., Sheehan, D., Maloney, C., & Caranikas-Walker, F. (2010). Evaluating the implementation fidelity of technology immersion and its relationship with student achievement. *The Journal of Technology, Learning and Assessment, 9*(4). Retrieved April 11, 2014, from http://ejournals.bc.edu/ojs/index.php/jtla/article/view/1609/.

Smith, A., Rainie, L., & Zickuhr, K. (2011). College students and technology. Pew Internet and American Life Project Report. Retrieved April 4, 2014, from http://www.pewinternet.org/2011/07/19/college-students-and-technology/.

Suhr, K. A., Hernandez, D. A., Grimes, D., & Warschauer, M. (2010). Laptops and fourth grade literacy: Assisting the jump over the fourth-grade slump. *The Journal of Technology, Learning and Assessment, 9*(5). Retrieved April 11, 2014, from http://ejournals.bc.edu/ojs/index.php/jtla/article/view/1610.

Tienken, C., & Wilson, M. (2007). The impact of computer assisted instruction on seventh grade students' mathematics achievement. *Planning and Changing, 38*(3–4), 181–190.

Tinto, V. (1993). *Leaving College: Rethinking the Causes and Cures of Student Attrition* (2nd ed.). Chicago: The University of Chicago Press.

Tversky, A., & Kahneman, D. (1973). Availability: A heuristic for judging frequency and probability. *Cognitive Psychology, 5*(2), 207–233.

Twitter. (2014). In Wikipedia. Retrieved February 2, 2014, from http://en.wikipedia.org/wiki/Twitter#Creation_and_initial_reaction.

Valenzuela, S., Park, N., & Kee, K. F. (2009). Is there social capital in a social network site? Facebook use and college students' life satisfaction, trust, and participation. *Journal of Computer-Mediated Communication, 14*(4), 875–901.

Valliere, K., Endersby, L., & Brinton, M. (2013). *Student Affairs Technology Competencies Survey*. NASPA Technology Knowledge Community.

Vaughan-Nichols, S. (2011). Can Google+ be a Facebook killer? Retrieved February 2, 2014, from http://www.zdnet.com/blog/networking/can-google-be-a-facebook-killer/1250.

Vine. (2014). In Wikipedia. Retrieved February 2, 2014, from http://en.wikipedia.org/wiki/Vine_(app).

Waight, N., & Abd-El-Khalick, F. (2007). The impact of technology on the enactment of "inquiry" in a technology enthusiast's sixth grade science classroom. *Journal of Research in Science Teaching, 44*(1), 154–182.

Wang, Y., Komanduri, S., Leon, P., Norcie, G., Acquisti, A., & Cranor, L. (2011). "I regretted the minute I pressed share": A qualitative study of regrets on Facebook. *Symposium on Usable Privacy and Security (SOUPS) 2011*, Pittsburgh, PA, July 20–22, 2011.

Warschauer, M., Knobel, M., & Stone, L. (2004). Technology and equity in schooling: Deconstructing the digital divide. *Educational Policy, 18*(4), 562–588.

Warschauer, M., & Matuchniak, T. (2010). New technology and digital worlds: Analyzing evidence of equity in access, use, and outcomes. *Review of Research in Education, 34*(1), 179–255. doi:10.3102/0091732X09349791.

Weatherly, J. N., Grabe, M., & Arthur, E. I. L. (2003). Providing introductory psychology students access to lecture slides via Blackboard 5: A negative impact on performance. *Journal of Educational Technology Systems, 31*(4), 463–474.

Wickre, K. (2013). Celebrating #Twitter7. Retrieved February 2, 2014, from https://blog.twitter.com/2013/celebrating-twitter7.

Yang, C., & Brown, B. B. (2013). Motives for using Facebook, patterns of Facebook activities, and late adolescents' social adjustment to college. *Journal of Youth and Adolescence, 42*(3), 403–416.

Zhao, S. (2009). Teen adoption of MySpace and IM: Inner-city versus suburban differences. *Cyberpsychology & Behavior, 12*(1), 55–58.

CHAPTER 2

Research on Social Media

As with any other intervention, with social media use in education it's important to know what works and what doesn't. There is a lot of excitement about using social media from newer student affairs professionals and other educators, and less excitement from those who have been in the profession longer. As is also elucidated in chapter 6, the champions of social media use on campus have to convince their supervisors of the value of these technologies. Therefore, it is critical to have data to show *how* social media can be used to help support students. Understanding what works and what doesn't is essential in planning how to use these sites and services effectively with students. Furthermore, in conversations to garner support for using social media with students, you'll earn a lot more clout when you can reference research showing how social media can be used in productive ways as well as how social media can negatively impact student learning and engagement.

"Facebook use can lower grades by 20 percent" (Choney, 2010), Luckily, that headline is not true—or this book wouldn't have been written. But *why* is the headline false? First, the research study that prompted the story used a correlational design, and so causation cannot be inferred. To date, there have been no published studies of how Facebook use *causes* anything. While it might seem like methodological hair splitting, correlational designs can only suggest relationships between two or more variables. With correlational designs, there is no way of knowing whether additional variables may be causing the outcome in question. Second, additional research conducted on the connection between Facebook use and grades suggests that the relationship is complex and that other factors, such as how students use Facebook, are more important in determining academic outcomes. This chapter reviews the research conducted on social media in order to contextualize how students use these technologies as well as to show how such uses relate to three broad academic outcomes: student engagement, student academic and social integration, and student success.

OUTCOMES OF SOCIAL MEDIA USE

Enough time has passed in the "age of social media" to warrant an accumulation of research on how these sites are used and the outcomes of their use. For instance, researchers have examined how Facebook use is related to self-esteem (Gonzales & Hancock, 2011; Mehdizadeh, 2010; Tazghini & Siedlecki, 2013), shyness (Orr et al., 2009), the Big Five personality traits (Bachrach, Kosinski, Graepel, Kohli & Stillwell, 2012; Gosling, Augustine, Vazire, Holtzman & Gaddis, 2011; Moore & McElroy, 2012; Ong, Ang, Ho, Lim & Goh, 2011; Ross et al., 2009; Seidman, 2012), political participation (Kim & Khang, 2014; Vitak et al., 2011), life satisfaction, social trust, civic engagement, and political participation (Valenzuela, Park & Kee, 2009), development of identity and peer relationships (Pempek, Yermolayeva & Calvert, 2009), perceptions of social support (DeAndrea, Ellison, LaRose, Steinfield & Fiore, 2011; Manago, Taylor & Greenfield, 2012), and relationship building and maintenance (Ellison, Steinfield & Lampe, 2007; 2011; Ellison, Vitak, Gray, & Lampe, 2014; Manago, Taylor & Greenfield, 2012; Valenzuela, Park & Kee, 2009; Yang & Brown, 2013). Although interesting, an exhaustive review of the literature on these issues is, well, exhaustive and incongruent with the goals of the chapter and this book (see Tess (2013) for a review of empirical studies of social media use in higher education classes). This chapter will examine research on social media that is relevant for student affairs professionals. Major issues include the relationship of social media use to student engagement, student academic and social integration, and student success.

Student Engagement

What do we mean when we use the term *engagement*? There are many definitions in the educational literature. For instance, Finn (1989) and Finn and Rock's (1997) taxonomy of student engagement includes three progressive levels: acquiescence to school, initiative taking, and social involvement. Tison, Bateman, and Culver (2011) defined engagement as a composite of level of academic challenge, active and collaborative learning, and skill development, and Skinner, Kindermann, and Furrer (2008) defined engagement as "the quality of a student's connection or involvement with the endeavor of schooling" (p. 2). Fredricks and McColskey (2011) reviewed twenty-one instruments designed to measure student engagement through diverse methods, from classroom observations to teacher and student self-report, and with different definitions of engagement. Student affairs professionals, however, tend to focus on the construct of student engagement based on the work of Alexander Astin (1984).

According to Astin (1984), engagement is "the amount of physical and psychological energy that the student devotes to the academic experience" (p. 518). His theory of student engagement includes five tenets: (1) engagement involves investment of physical and psychological energy; (2) engagement occurs along a continuum (some students are more engaged than others, and individual students are engaged in different activities at differing levels); (3) engagement has both quantitative and qualitative features; (4) the amount of student learning and development associated with an educational program is directly related to the quality and quantity of student engagement in that program; and (5) the effectiveness of any educational practice is directly related to the ability of that practice to increase student engagement.

Today, engagement is conceptualized as the time and effort students devote to educational activities that are empirically linked to desired college outcomes (Kuh, 2009). Engagement encompasses various factors, including investment in the academic experience of college, involvement in cocurricular activities, and interactions with peers and faculty (Kuh, 2009; Pascarella & Terenzini, 2005). Kuh (2009) emphasizes two major aspects: academic (in-class) engagement and engagement in educationally related cocurricular (out-of-class) activities, both of which are important to student success. Since 1984, the construct of engagement has been researched extensively. As Kuh (2009) states: "student engagement and its historical antecedents...are supported by decades of research showing positive associations with a range of desired outcomes of college" (p. 698). In their review of the research on how college affects students, Pascarella and Terenzini (2005) highlight the relationship between student engagement, student development, and success:

- Close interactions between faculty and students on college campuses is related to improved critical thinking, knowledge acquisition, analytic competencies, and intellectual development.
- Persistence and educational attainment are maximized by close on-campus peer relationships and engagement in college-sponsored activities.
- Psychological adjustment and maturity are maximized in environments that emphasize engagement in class discussions and involvement with faculty in the academic community; students' perception of faculty as caring, helpful and accessible promotes persistence and degree completion.
- Extracurricular involvement has a positive effect on persistence and educational attainment, development of a positive social self-concept, and women's choice of nontraditional careers.
- Students' levels of knowledge acquisition and cognitive growth increase with a higher level of student engagement in academic work and in the academic experience of college.
- Interaction with peers is an influential force in student persistence and degree completion.

To summarize, academic and cocurricular engagement play major roles in both student psychosocial development and academic success. With increased engagement, added improvements in grades and persistence are found among minority students, first-generation students, and students who are not adequately prepared for college academic work (Kuh, Cruce, Shoup, Kinzie & Gonyea, 2008; Pascarella & Terenzini, 2005). Instead of students who are already engaged, we need to reach the students who are less engaged so that we can help them achieve the desired outcomes of a college education. Even though student engagement has been researched extensively in offline environments (Pascarella & Terenzini, 2005), little research has been done on the relationship between student engagement and social media use.

55

Student Academic and Social Integration

Vincent Tinto (1993) developed a model of student departure that accounted for multiple variables related to a student's decision to persist at an institution. Unlike previous theories of why students persisted or dropped out, this model took into account pre-entry student attributes like family background, skills and ability, and prior schooling as well as student intentions, commitments, institutional experiences, and, most important, integration into the institution. According to Tinto (1993), student integration is one of the few factors that is readily changeable by the institution. Tinto's (1993) model therefore highlights the influence of both the academic system (academic performance and faculty-staff interactions) as well as the social system (extracurricular activities and peer group interactions) in student integration. Tinto (1993) notes that a student's level of integration refers to the extent to which the student connects with and accepts the values and goals of peers and faculty at the college or university. A higher level of integration leads to stronger commitment to the student's personal goals as well as to the academic institution (Tinto, 1993). Therefore, academic and social integration become important motivators in decisions to persist at or to leave a college or university (Tinto, 1993).

Research shows that students who are more interactive with faculty, staff, and their peer group at their institution are more likely to persist (Pascarella & Terenzini, 2005). Specifically, students who believe that the norms of their peers and faculty support persistence are more likely to persist themselves (Bank & Slavings, 1990). In addition, student engagement, which involves interactions with faculty and peers, is positively related to educational attainment and persistence (Pascarella & Terenzini, 2005). Research has also shown the academic benefits of social integration. For example, a social network analysis by Thomas (2000) showed that students with strong ties outside of their peer group (broad ties) persisted at a higher rate. Additionally, relationships that were reciprocated had a positive and direct impact on social integration and persistence (Thomas, 2000). More recently, social network analysis was used to analyze the impact on retention of a cohort of first-year full-time students at a small, private institution (Eckles & Stradley, 2012). Eckles and Stradley (2012) found that "attrition and retention behaviors among students' friends had a significant impact on whether students returned for their sophomore year" (p. 13).

Facebook and Student Engagement

It makes sense to examine the relationship between Facebook use and student engagement for two general reasons: (1) many of today's college students use Facebook at high rates, as illustrated by the statistics presented in chapter 1, and (2) Facebook was developed as and intended to be an engaging platform and measures its own success in terms of user engagement (Heiberger & Harper, 2008; Morrin, 2007). Therefore, it is possible that students may be using Facebook in ways that influence or are influenced by real-world engagement. More specifically, we can conceptualize student use and involvement on Facebook along Astin's (1984) five tenets of engagement:

1. *Engagement refers to the investment of physical and psychological energy:* Students invest a great deal of psychological energy in using Facebook, as evidenced by usage statistics and emotional connections to the site.
2. *Engagement occurs along a continuum:* Some students are more engaged on Facebook than others, while some don't use social media at all.
3. *Engagement has both quantitative and qualitative features:* Students can spend a great deal of time using Facebook (a

quantitative feature) and may engage in a wide variety of activities on the platform (qualitative features).

4. *The amount of student learning and development associated with an educational program is directly related to the quality and quantity of student engagement in that program:* It is possible that Facebook use is related to real-world student engagement in tangible ways. As suggested in the next chapter, the quality of student online interactions can influence identity development.

5. *The effectiveness of any educational practice is directly related to the ability of that practice to increase student engagement:* If Facebook indeed increases engagement, then it is possible that it could be used in educationally relevant ways to improve student academic outcomes.

Early research on Facebook use and student engagement found a relationship between time spent on the site and offline engagement. The Higher Education Research Institute (2007) used the Your First College Year (YFCY) survey to collect data from more than 31,000 students at 114 colleges and universities about their general social networking website use. Heiberger and Harper (2008) conducted a smaller study of 377 undergraduate students at one institution and focused solely on Facebook. Both studies found positive correlations between Facebook (and social networking website) use and student engagement. For instance, a greater percentage of heavy users of social networking websites participated in and spent more time in campus organizations than low users (Heiberger & Harper, 2008; HERI, 2007). Additionally, heavy users were more likely to report that they interacted daily offline with close friends (HERI, 2007) and felt stronger connections to them (Heiberger & Harper, 2008).

Previous research measured engagement through single questions (such as perceived connection with friends) and used survey items truncating time spent on Facebook into categories such as less than 1 hour, 1–2 hours, 2–3 hours, and so on. Recent research has expanded earlier work by (1) expanding the quantification of engagement beyond single-item measures and (2) using continuous measures of time spent on Facebook. Engagement is a construct that encompasses at least two factors (in-class and cocurricular engagement) and therefore may be best measured with multiple items. Relying on questions about Facebook frequency of use with categorical choices is problematic because doing so may reflect the researcher's a priori, biased estimate of the distribution of time spent on the site. Furthermore, categorical choices artificially truncate variance in ways that reduce measurement precision.

Since activity on Facebook had yet to be measured in relation to any outcome, I developed a study where I asked students to rate the frequency with which they engaged in a list of fourteen broad categories of Facebook activities (Junco, 2012a):

Playing games (FarmVille, MafiaWars, and so on)
Posting status updates
Sharing links
Sending private messages
Commenting (on statuses, wall posts, pictures, and so on)
Chatting on Facebook chat
Checking in to see what someone is up to
Creating or RSVP'ing to events
Posting photos
Tagging photos
Viewing photos
Posting videos
Tagging videos
Viewing videos

For this study, data were collected from 2,368 students on their time spent on Facebook, how frequently they checked

Facebook each day, and how frequently they engaged in the fourteen Facebook activities. Also measured were student engagement via a nineteen-item scale developed based on the National Survey of Student Engagement (NSSE) (Junco, Heiberger & Loken, 2012), how much time students spent preparing for class, and how much time they spent engaging in cocurricular activities (Junco, 2012a).

Surprisingly, there was a negative relationship between time spent on Facebook and student engagement as measured by the nineteen-item scale; of particular interest, however, was the fact that frequency of engaging in certain Facebook activities was more strongly predictive of engagement than time spent on the site (Junco, 2012a). For instance, frequency of creating or RSVP'ing to events on Facebook was a much stronger positive predictor of engagement than time spent on the site. Furthermore, chatting on Facebook chat was a strong negative predictor of engagement. This emphasizes that what students do on Facebook is of greater importance when examining engagement outcomes than whether or not students use the site. Put another way, it's not using Facebook that is related to engagement; it's how students use the site that more strongly predicts benefits or drawbacks. It's worthwhile to highlight that some uses of Facebook predict positive engagement outcomes, while others predict negative outcomes. Other results from that study are also noteworthy: time spent on Facebook was not predictive of time spent preparing for class; however, time spent chatting on Facebook chat was negatively predictive. As was suggested by earlier studies, time spent on Facebook was positively related to time spent in cocurricular activities (Junco, 2012a).

Facebook and Student Social and Academic Integration

There is some research showing the advantages of using social technologies to improve student engagement and in turn to improve social and academic integration (Junco, 2012a; Junco,

Elavsky & Heiberger, 2012; Junco, Heiberger & Loken, 2011). The findings of my study on Facebook use and student engagement (and as described in the next section, the study on Twitter use and student engagement) suggest that using social technologies like Twitter and Facebook in ways that improve student interactions with peers and faculty members will also increase social and academic integration and lead to improved student persistence (Junco, 2012a). In my study, time spent on Facebook was positively related to time spent in offline extracurricular activities (Junco, 2012a). Additionally, time spent on the site was not as strong of a predictor of involvement in offline campus activities as the types of activities students engaged in on Facebook (Junco, 2012a). Furthermore, Ward (2010) found that students who used social networking sites to learn about on-campus activities were retained at higher rates and participated in face-to-face activities at higher levels.

New students typically maintain a connection with high school friends on Facebook as they transition to college (Ellison, Steinfield & Lampe, 2007; 2011; Junco & Mastrodicasa, 2007). Ellison and colleagues (2007) found that students used Facebook to form and maintain friendships, and those friendships on Facebook flow from offline to online. In other words, students are using Facebook to maintain and strengthen offline relationships; they are not meeting new friends on Facebook and then building offline connections. This affordance of Facebook leads to stronger bonds on campus and increased social integration. In a newer study, Ellison and colleagues (2011) found that it's not common for students to initiate contact with strangers on Facebook; instead, students use it for maintaining ties with close friends and for *social information seeking*—discovering information about someone with whom they have an offline connection. Adding to this, Stutzman (2011) found that the use of Facebook for social information seeking and to receive support positively influences adaptation to college for students in transition.

Research by Selwyn (2009) provides data about how students are using Facebook to improve their social and academic integration. He studied the wall posts of 612 social science students and found that 4 percent of the 68,169 posts made during the study period were related to students' academic experiences. The following were the five main themes found in Selwyn's (2009) analyses:

1. *Recounting and reflecting on the college experience.* Students used their Facebook walls to describe and deliberate on recent experiences. For instance, students commented on a class lecture they just attended. Some of these posts were students seeking justifications from their peers for missing a class or not understanding the material. Selwyn (2009) reports that, often, students were posting negative comments about the learning experience.

2. *Exchange of practical information.* Selwyn (2009) described these exchanges as focusing on the "job" of being a student. They were focused on information seeking about assignment deadlines, course scheduling, assignment requirements (such as word counts for papers), and exam format. Students also relayed information they received from faculty and other college or university staff.

3. *Exchange of academic information.* These posts were peer guidance: students exchanging more academically focused information like the content of examinations and course readings. Some students, however, were using Facebook in novel ways to exchange academic information, such as sharing references or recruiting participants for a research project.

4. *Displays of supplication and disengagement.* These were posts in which students attempted to attract sympathy for their academic situation, often portraying themselves as helpless. Other students not only presented themselves as helpless but also as "defiantly disengaged" from academics.

5. *Banter.* These more playful statements were humorous and often sarcastic: students criticized those who were better students, provided joke responses to exam answers, and shared funny and disparaging stories about faculty members and lectures.

Selwyn's (2009) findings point to the powerful role played by student Facebook use in academic integration: students use the site to develop their identity as college students. In this way, students become more academically integrated by learning the cultural mores and norms of academia or at the very least what it's like to be a student in an institution of higher education. Through these interactions, students learn how to navigate the college environment and seek information and support from their peers, thus also enhancing their social integration. Students therefore use Facebook to make and strengthen connections with friends at their college or university, for important cultural and normative information seeking, and to maintain their "safety net" of friends from high school in the transition to college. Using Facebook for these types of connection strategies helps students strengthen their social bonds, which leads to a greater sense of commitment to the institution and to increased motivation to perform better academically (Tinto, 1993).

Other research has found similar results. Yu, Tian, Vogel, and Kwok (2010) conducted a study evaluating how Facebook use was related to proxies for social and academic integration (social acceptance and acculturation to the university culture) and how these constructs predicted cognitive, affective, and skills-based learning outcomes. The researchers found that Facebook use had a direct impact on the three learning outcomes they measured: self-esteem, satisfaction with university life, and students' perceived ability to solve problems and perform tasks (performance proficiency). Furthermore, the researchers discovered that

63

the mediating effects of social and academic integration could transform Facebook engagement into learning outcomes. Specifically, Yu and colleagues found that engagement on Facebook was directly related both to increased social acceptance by peers and to acculturation to university culture and that through this path, Facebook use was more strongly related to learning outcomes. Lastly, the researchers found that social integration was more strongly related to cognitive learning outcomes, while academic integration was more strongly related to satisfaction with university life (Yu, Tian, Vogel & Kwok, 2010).

These findings demonstrate that what might before have been considered purely social interactions on Facebook can greatly influence academic and social integration and by extension have an effect on student persistence, as suggested by Tinto's (1993) model. Students, then, use Facebook for social information seeking that leads to improved social capital and better integration with their peer group. Students post cues on Facebook that allow their peers to engage in learning the culture and norms of the university environment. These behaviors on Facebook lead students to have stronger connections with and feel more accepted by peers at their institution (social integration) and to feel more comfortable with their cognitive skills (academic integration). It is important to note that these studies all describe how students use Facebook naturally, without guidance from educators, and presumably using these sites as part of the educational process would improve these processes even more so.

Although these findings are specific to Facebook, they support Tinto's (1993) model and demonstrate that peer influences are strong predictors of student persistence. Furthermore, the Facebook findings show that social networking sites can assist students in forming and maintaining relationships that lead to increased social and academic integration. With an increased use of Twitter among the college student age demographic, an examination of the ability of Twitter to influence such peer interaction yielding social and academic benefits should follow (Smith & Brenner, 2012).

Twitter and Student Engagement

Even though my findings regarding Facebook use and student engagement are intriguing, the fact remains that the research was correlational. It is impossible to discern the directionality of the relationship between Facebook use and engagement, or whether third, fourth, fifth, or more variables were causing the relationship between the two (Junco, 2012a). It could be that more engaged students spend less time on Facebook, or that students who are more engaged spend more time creating or RSVP'ing to events because they are already engaged. In such cases, the research is certainly suggestive of a link, but because the design is correlational, more investigation is warranted. In order to make causal inferences, studies using an experimental design must be conducted. To date, there are no such studies that focus on Facebook use (perhaps because of the difficulty obtaining a representative sample of Facebook nonusers); however, there is research examining the causal link between Twitter use and student engagement.

In 2010, we set out to evaluate whether integrating social media into a course could indeed affect student engagement (Junco, Heiberger & Loken, 2011). At the time of the study, Twitter was an ideal platform to study for two reasons:

1. Facebook penetration on college campuses was very high (hovering around 90 percent in most studies), making it difficult to find a sample of students who were not users of the

platform so they could be randomly assigned into a group that would use Facebook and another that wouldn't. In other words, there was no way to control for preexisting familiarity with the platform. Even if a group of Facebook nonusers were identified, their nonuse would be related to a host of other variables related to Internet skills and academic performance (see the discussion of digital inequalities in chapter 1).

2. In contrast to faculty attitudes toward Facebook, faculty were much more willing to explore integrating Twitter in their courses. Of course, the "much more willing" faculty in this case were still a small minority of faculty, who were interested in examining new, technology-enhanced curricular interventions. Even still, that minority was much larger than those interested in using Facebook in their courses. Faculty saw (and continue to see) Twitter as a more useful academic tool for a few reasons. First, Twitter saw an adoption spike at academic conferences because of its use as a back channel. A *back channel* is a running conversation that happens "behind the scenes" of an event (usually a talk—in this case, an academic talk) and allows participants to engage with each other and sometimes with the presenter. Faculty who recognized the affordances of Twitter in facilitating back channels saw an opportunity for a similar process in their courses. Second, while many faculty considered Facebook to be a more private (and protected) space for students with its very personal and social pictures and comments, Twitter was seen as more simply a conversation tool.

To conduct the study, we randomly assigned all students taking a first-year seminar in a pre-health professional program to one of two conditions: the experimental group, which would use Twitter in educationally relevant ways, and the control group, which would receive the same information and attention from faculty, but would do so using Ning, a service that allowed users to create their own social networking site. Ning was used in previous semesters as the seminar's course management system. We developed twelve educationally relevant ways to use Twitter in the classroom based on Chickering and Gamson's (1987) seven principles for good practice in undergraduate education. To measure student engagement, we developed a nineteen-item scale based on the NSSE, which was given to students at the beginning and end of the fourteen-week research period (Junco, Heiberger & Loken, 2011). Validity data collected as part of our study supported the notion that the nineteen-item scale was an overall measure of both academic and cocurricular student engagement. Results from the pretest administration showed that students in both the experimental and control groups had equal levels of engagement. This finding also lends support to the effectiveness of the random assignment, for if students were not randomly assigned, there might be differences in preexisting levels of engagement.

At the time, I didn't think that the Twitter intervention would impact student engagement for two reasons: (1) the effect of using Twitter might not be large enough to influence engagement in a significant way; and (2) the nineteen-item instrument might not capture short-term changes in engagement. I was so skeptical of finding a positive impact on student engagement that I even said as much in a presentation of the preliminary results at the Berkman Center (see Junco, 2009). However, the results at the end of the fourteen-week research period were surprising: students who were in the Twitter group had significantly increased engagement over those in the control group. The average engagement score increase over the entire semester for the Twitter group was more than double that of the control group. Controlling for preexisting engagement levels and increases in engagement allowed us to account for the fact that student engagement will increase naturally over the first semester. The control group engagement increase could then be interpreted as the natural increase in student engagement without any additional intervention, while the increase in engagement for the Twitter group could almost surely be due only to the Twitter intervention.

What does this finding mean? As stated previously, the Twitter intervention seemed to have been the driving force for the significant increase in student engagement. Let's remember, however, that research had already suggested that *how* students use social media is as important or perhaps more important than *whether* students use social media. This dichotomy makes it difficult to say something like "Twitter increases student engagement." A more apt summary would be that "Twitter used in specific ways increases student engagement." Our original study did not measure differences in Twitter implementation (Junco, Heiberger & Loken, 2011). However, in a follow-up study, we compared *how* Twitter was used and the resultant effect (Junco, Elavsky & Heiberger, 2012). Two sets of classrooms were used in the follow-up study: the original set of classrooms that used Twitter for the educationally relevant purposes mentioned earlier and another large-lecture classroom that used Twitter as part of the class. In the large-lecture classroom, (1) students were not required to use Twitter for any assignments; (2) while there were no active Twitter users at the onset of the original Twitter study (Junco, Heiberger & Loken, 2011), 43 percent of students reported using or exploring Twitter; (3) Twitter was projected on a screen and used as a back channel during class discussion time (it was not used in the times between class sessions as in the original study) (Junco, Heiberger & Loken, 2011); and (4) instructors did not engage with students on Twitter and made few explicit references to the Twitter back channel during discussions.

The results of the follow-up study helped clarify the essential elements of integrating Twitter into a course (Junco, Elavsky &

Heiberger, 2012). We found that the students who used Twitter in the large-lecture course, while certainly engaging with the class content at levels similar to those in the first course, did not exhibit the increases in engagement seen with students in the first course.

These are some key elements of obtaining improved engagement when using Twitter as part of a course (Junco, Elavsky & Heiberger, 2012):

- *Students must be required to use Twitter.* Allowing students to choose whether or not they used Twitter may have created a dynamic by which only those students who were more engaged to begin with used Twitter, while those who needed help being more engaged stayed away from the Twitter conversations.
- *Twitter must be integrated into a course in educationally relevant ways.* The first set of classrooms used a theoretical framework (Chickering and Gamson's (1987) seven principles for good practice in undergraduate education) to guide Twitter implementation in the course; however, the second classroom allowed students to use Twitter in emergent ways. In other words, students who received benefit from using Twitter were guided by faculty to use Twitter in ways that would produce positive outcomes.
- *Faculty must engage with students on the platform.* Even though the instructors in the second classroom were interested in using Twitter in educationally relevant ways, they did not engage on the platform as the faculty in the first set of classrooms did.

Twitter and Student Social and Academic Integration

The increased engagement seen with the students in our original Twitter study reached beyond their first semester. Follow-up work showed that these students were significantly more likely to persist into their second year than the students who did not use Twitter (Junco, Heiberger & Alonso-Garcia, in preparation; Junco, Heiberger & Loken, 2011). In fact, 88 percent of students in the Twitter group persisted into the second year, as compared with only 70 percent of students in the control group. The 18 percentage point difference between the group that received the intervention and the control was substantially larger than the 5 percentage point average difference found by Fidler (1991) in his meta-analysis of the effects of first-year seminars. First-year seminars have been the most adopted of the many interventions aimed at improving first-year student outcomes.

One-year follow-up interviews with students in both the Twitter and control groups discovered that students who used Twitter were more socially and academically integrated into the institution than those who didn't. They were more connected to their peer group, more involved in campus activities, and built stronger bonds with faculty and staff (Junco, Heiberger & Alonso-Garcia, in preparation). Indeed, without our encouragement, students already use social media in ways that strengthen these bonds. Ward (2010) found that students who used social networking sites to learn about on-campus activities participated in face-to-face activities at higher levels and were retained at higher rates. Additionally, time spent on Facebook was positively related to time spent in offline extracurricular activities (Junco, 2012a). Furthermore, the types of activities students engaged in on Facebook were stronger predictors of involvement in offline campus activities than time spent on the site (Junco, 2012a). The payoff from such interventions is enormous in terms of the desired outcomes of a college education. With little added effort, meeting students where they are on social media, we can efficiently improve their academic and social integration and, by extension, their persistence. Student affairs professionals can use the results of the aforementioned studies to inform their work. Engaging with students on social media in educationally relevant ways is the most important factor in supporting student growth using these technologies.

Before moving to issues of academic performance, it's important to discuss the sources of variance in the aforementioned positive engagement results. Of particular importance is how we (the researchers) interacted with the students and how this affected outcomes. The *observer effect* is a threat to the internal validity of a research study. This effect occurs when the outcome of interest changes because of unconscious biases held by the researcher that influence participant behavior. In the case of Twitter and student engagement, we might have expected that the students who used Twitter would be more engaged, and then we might have behaved in subtle and unconscious ways that improved student engagement but that had nothing to do with the social media intervention. This process is not restricted to social science research. Indeed, the observer effect also occurs in the natural sciences. In physics, for instance, the act of observing a phenomenon alters the state of what is being measured. Crook (2008) described a specific type of observer effect in educational uses of technology, which he termed the *Web 2.0 mentality*. Crook (2008) suggested that educators who are more likely to integrate social media in their courses share other important engaging characteristics that are related to improved student outcomes. For instance, an educator who is willing to try new educational interventions may be someone who is (1) keeping up on the research focusing on teaching and learning, (2) more willing to take "educational risks" by being open to engage in new teaching methods and learning strategies, (3) more interested in engaging students, and (4) more willing to remove traditional barriers between students and professors (in other words, more interested in being a "guide on the side" than a "sage on the stage" in the classroom, allowing students to construct their own knowledge). Such an educator might have other characteristics that make them more effective at reaching students—and it is these characteristics that perhaps are the most important predictors of student outcomes.

Consider this question: who are the most effective student affairs practitioners on your campus? Think about a hall director who makes it a point to know what is going on with all of her or his residents and gets to know them on an individual basis. The hall director may build strong connections with residents by making sure to interact with them every day, or just by showing care and concern during regular interactions. This hall director might also be someone who implements more innovative programs in the residence hall. So does the fact that their students are more engaged come from the innovative programming, the director's engaging style, or both? Both can be true, because there is often an interaction effect in these processes. Therefore, it is helpful to recognize that social media interventions function the same way: there will be an interaction between a professor or student affairs professional's style and how that person is using a technology for educational purposes. This is certainly an area for further research to examine how we can parse out the variance in personality styles, interventions, and the interactions between them.

Facebook and Academic Performance

"Facebook use can lower grades by 20 percent" (Choney, 2010). If you were to read that popular news headline, you might reach a conclusion that looks a little something like this: Maria Luisa, a great student with a 3.85 in pre-med biology, signs up for Facebook in her third semester, and just like that her GPA drops to 3.08. That just sounds silly; in addition, it's important to consider the problem of third, fourth, fifth, etc. variables, mentioned earlier in this chapter. So many variables can contribute to student fluctuations in GPA. What if Maria Luisa had a close relative die in the previous semester (and perhaps her signing up for Facebook was driven by a desire to connect with family members)? What if all of her courses last semester were "weed-out" courses? What if the format of her courses went from interactive small group work and assessments in the previous semester to large lecture courses with multiple-choice tests? The point is that we don't know how many other variables could have contributed to her GPA drop. Also, we can't assume such direct prediction from the study discussed in the news article.

So that leaves us with the question of what effect, if any, Facebook use has on academic performance. If we know that students spend a lot of time on Facebook, might it not be one of the corollaries to their academic performance? Indeed, an early study in this area was extremely provocative and received a great deal of media attention. Unfortunately, the study had not been published or peer-reviewed, and it suffered from methodological issues such that making generalizations about the results was nearly impossible. Since then, four published, peer-reviewed studies have examined the relationship between Facebook use and grades (Junco, 2012b; Kirschner & Karpinski, 2010; Kolek & Saunders, 2008; Pasek, More & Hargittai, 2009). Pasek and colleagues (2009) examined the relationship between Facebook use and academic performance and found there was no relationship between Facebook use and grades. Kolek and Saunders (2008) found that there were no differences in overall GPA between users and nonusers of Facebook. Kirschner and Karpinski (2010), on the other hand, found that Facebook users reported a lower mean GPA than

73

nonusers; additionally, Facebook users reported studying fewer hours per week than nonusers (Kirschner & Karpinski, 2010).

There were clear discrepancies in the aforementioned studies: two studies found no relationship between Facebook use and grades, and another found a negative relationship between the two. Weaknesses of previous research included how "Facebook use" had been operationalized (as dichotomous or interval-level variables), the sampling methods used, the generalizability of the samples, and reliance on self-reported grades. Furthermore, none of these earlier studies examined *what students did* on Facebook. As already reviewed in an earlier section on Facebook use and student engagement, what students do on Facebook predicts more of the variance in outcomes than the time students spend on the site. Finally, previous studies had not taken into account consequential control variables such as gender, ethnicity, socioeconomic status, and student preexisting ability (for instance, high school GPA) in their analyses.

One of my studies was designed to address these limitations of previous work (Junco, 2012b). In this study, multiple indices of Facebook use were evaluated, as well as actual grades from the university registrar (Junco, 2012b). Furthermore, the sample size for the study was 1,839 and representative of the institution where the data were collected. Lastly, gender, race and ethnicity, and socioeconomic status were included as control variables to account for issues of digital inequalities and the uneven influence of these variables on student technology use and academic success (Junco, 2012b). As with the study on the relationship between Facebook use and student engagement, data were collected on time spent on Facebook as well as activities students engaged in on the site (Junco, 2012a).

Time spent on Facebook was indeed negatively related to overall student GPA; however, the real-world significance of the effect was minimal (Junco, 2012b). Specifically, every 93 minutes that students spent on Facebook above the average time spent on the site per day (106 minutes) was related only to a 0.12-point drop in overall GPA. To put it in context, time spent on Facebook was only half as strong a predictor of overall college GPA as high school GPA was. As was found in the study on Facebook use and student engagement, however, certain Facebook activities were positively related to GPA, while others were negatively related. Checking to see what friends were up to and sharing links on Facebook were positive predictors of overall GPA, while posting status updates was negatively predictive of GPA. Additionally, being from a higher socioeconomic status (SES) was predictive of higher GPA, while being male or African American were negatively predictive. Time spent on Facebook was negatively predictive of time spent preparing for class, although, as with GPA, the relationship was not strong. However, the number of times students checked Facebook was not predictive of time spent preparing for class yet was negatively predictive of GPA (again, not a strong relationship).

As was found with student engagement, the ways that students used Facebook were important in predicting academic outcomes. First, there was a difference in outcomes between time spent on Facebook and number of times students checked Facebook. Time spent on Facebook seemed to predict more negative outcomes than checking Facebook. Indeed, on average students spent little time on Facebook each time they checked. A possible interpretation is that checking Facebook for short periods of time does not strongly impact academic performance; however, spending a great deal of time on Facebook does. Second, outcomes differed by what students did on Facebook: large amounts of time spent posting status updates predicted lower GPAs, whereas checking to see what friends were up to and sharing links predicted higher GPAs. This finding led to the following conclusion: "It seems that using Facebook for activities that involve collecting

75

and sharing information (checking to see what friends are up to and sharing links, respectively) is more positively predictive of outcomes than using Facebook for socializing (status updates and chatting)" (Junco, 2012b, p. 11).

Twitter and Academic Performance

Taken as a whole, the findings of research on Facebook use and student engagement (Junco, 2012a) and academic performance (Junco, 2012b) showed a similar pattern in the results: student behaviors on the site mattered more when predicting outcomes than whether or not students used the site. It is for this reason that we decided to also examine whether using Twitter in educationally relevant ways could influence academic performance (Junco, Heiberger & Loken, 2011). As was the case with Twitter and student engagement, I didn't think Twitter use would have an impact on academic performance. In the same talk at the Berkman Center that I mentioned earlier (Junco, 2009), I reported that it would be surprising if the effect size of the intervention would be large enough to influence grades and that I believed there would be a truncation of variance (limited range of student grades) because all students were pre-health professionals and would earn good grades. This time the results were astonishing. We found that the Twitter group had significantly higher overall first semester GPAs than the control group by more than 0.5 of a grade point (Junco, Heiberger & Loken, 2011). It is noteworthy to underscore that the groups were randomly assigned and that analyses revealed no preexisting differences in student ability as measured by high school GPA. Therefore, we concluded that using Twitter in educationally relevant ways can improve student academic performance, not just in the course that is using Twitter but in other courses (Junco, Heiberger & Loken, 2011). Our follow-up work to this study suggests that this effect was due to increased academic integration—with students being more comfortable engaging in class discussions, talking with faculty members, and participating in study groups.

Additional data support the notion that how Twitter was used was important in the effect on grades. Our study examining the two different Twitter course interventions found that the classroom where faculty did not engage with students on Twitter, did not make Twitter a requirement, and did not integrate Twitter using an a priori theoretical model, did not see increases in student academic performance (Junco, Elavsky & Heiberger, 2012). Indeed, those students who used Twitter in the second classroom did not have end-of-semester grades that were higher or lower than those who didn't use Twitter.

DANGERS OF SOCIAL MEDIA USE

Up to this point, the (mostly) positive effects of certain types of social media use on student engagement and academic performance have been discussed. However, there is a growing body of research examining negative factors related to social media use. It seems that every week, new studies are released showing a relationship between social media use and undesirable constructs such as narcissistic personality traits (Mehdizadeh, 2010; Ong, Ang, Ho, Lim & Goh, 2011). A popular area of examination is the effect of media multitasking on student learning and academic performance. In this chapter, the popular term *multitasking* is understood as often being used to describe the phenomena of divided attention and task switching, concepts from the cognitive sciences literature that are more representative of how humans attend to and process information (Chun, Golomb & Turk-Browne, 2011). Therefore, *multitasking* is here defined as divided attention and nonsequential task switching for ill-defined tasks as they are performed in learning situations—for example, when a student is text messaging a friend while studying for an examination. The widespread use of laptops, availability of wifi on college campuses, use of cell phones, and use of social media have contributed to the fear that student learning may be affected because of students' serial switching between tasks.

There has been a great deal of research in the cognitive sciences examining the effects of multitasking on human information processing. This research supports the idea of what has been long termed a "cognitive bottleneck," a limitation in decision making that slows a second task (Welford, 1967). For instance, Koch and colleagues (2011) found significant performance costs in both accuracy and reaction time when switching between two auditory stimuli; these costs were not reduced by advance preparation of the participant's attention. Tombu and colleagues (2011) found that participants responded more slowly and had poorer accuracy on dual-task trials than on single-task trials for both auditory-vocal and visual-manual tasks. In summary, trying to attend to or process more than one task at a time "clogs up" the bottleneck and overloads the capacity of the human information processing system, which results in real-world consequences due to the costs of task switching (Koch, Lawo, Fels & Vorländer, 2011; Marois & Ivanoff, 2005; Strayer & Drews, 2004; Tombu et al., 2011; Wood & Cowan, 1995).

Because of the work conducted in the cognitive sciences, researchers have wondered how the costs of multitasking affect educational outcomes (Fried, 2008; Junco & Cotten, 2011; 2012; Mayer & Moreno, 2003; Rosen, Lim, Carrier & Cheever, 2011; and Wood et al., 2012). Mayer and Moreno (2003) proposed a framework by which we can understand how multitasking might affect the learning process, which is based on four assumptions about the human information processing system:

1. The human information processing system has two channels by which it can take in information: visual and auditory.

2. Each channel has a limited capacity for cognitive processing.
3. This capacity is used when selecting and processing stimuli.
4. Meaningful learning can happen only by using a substantial amount of capacity (cognitive processing) in either the visual or auditory channels.

Cognitive overload occurs when processing demands evoked by a learning task exceed the processing capacity of the cognitive system (Mayer & Moreno, 2003). Given the widespread use of technologies and the now-ubiquitous laptop initiatives that encourage or even require students to own a laptop computer, researchers have wondered how much capacity is being taken up by the mere act of using technology (Weaver & Nilson, 2005). For example, might just having a laptop available increase a student's cognitive load so that meaningful learning cannot occur? Indeed, research has shown that unstructured use of laptops (that is, use of laptops without incorporating them into the learning process) is related to performing more off-task activities such as checking e-mail and playing games during class (Kay & Lauricella, 2011). Research by Fried (2008) has shown that student use of laptops for non-class-related ("off-task") activities is negatively related to their course performance. However, laptop initiatives have been touted for helping to support facets of student learning. Therefore, it is critical to evaluate how student technology use can both help and hinder the learning process.

A number of studies have examined how social media (as well as other technologies) affect learning. One of our early surveys of students at four universities discovered that students who reported studying while sending and receiving instant messages (IMs) were more likely to report that instant messaging interfered with their ability to complete their homework (Junco & Cotten, 2011). However, the study was correlational and collected only self-reported data. In a more recent study, we collected GPA data

79

from the university registrar as well as surveys on a large sample of students (n = 1839) (Junco & Cotten, 2012). Controlling for background variables and high school GPA, we found that using Facebook and texting while studying were negatively related to overall college GPA; however, we found that e-mailing, searching for content not related to courses, talking on the phone, and instant messaging while preparing for class were not related to GPA (Junco & Cotten, 2012). In yet another study, students frequently sent and received text messages during class, and there was a negative relationship between text messaging and Facebook use during class and GPA even after controlling for gender, race and ethnicity, high school GPA, and Internet skill; however, as we found in our earlier study, e-mailing and searching for content not related to the class were not related to GPA (Junco, 2012c; Junco & Cotten, 2012).

Some studies have found a negative relationship between Facebook use and academic performance (Junco, 2012b; Kirschner & Karpinski, 2010), whereas others have found no relationship between the two (Kolek & Saunders, 2008; Pasek, More & Hargittai, 2009). As reported in my Facebook and academic performance paper, the ways that students use Facebook are perhaps the most important factors in influencing academic outcomes (Junco, 2012b). Additional research has discovered that the negative relationship seen between Facebook use and academic performance is likely predicted by multitasking. In a manuscript currently under review, the time students spent doing schoolwork while using Facebook was split from other time spent on Facebook (Junco, under review). Time spent on Facebook was negatively related to student overall GPA for first-year students, but not for sophomores, juniors, and seniors. Furthermore, time spent multitasking while on Facebook was negatively related to GPA for students at all levels except seniors. Not only does multitasking predict the negative relationship between Facebook use and academic performance, then, but also perhaps first-year students have not developed the appropriate self-regulation skills to keep their Facebook use from impacting their academic performance.

The aforementioned studies were based on self-report measures of multitasking (Junco & Cotten, 2011; 2012; Junco, under review). As has been discovered with technology use (Junco, 2013) and in other areas ranging from health-related behaviors (Celis-Morales et al., 2012; Hald, Overgaard & Grau, 2003) to TV viewing (Otten, Littenberg & Harvey-Berino, 2010), self-reported measures of behavior are notoriously inaccurate in capturing actual behaviors. In methodological terms, self-reported measures lack evidence of criterion validity. Furthermore, the aforementioned studies were correlational in nature—perhaps students with poorer academic skills are more likely to multitask. In order to extend these findings, Rosen and colleagues (2013) observed students during fifteen-minute study periods in their natural environments. The researchers found that students who accessed Facebook during the study period had lower GPAs than those who didn't and concluded that the drive to check Facebook is related to the emotional gratification derived from reading posts, commenting on content, or posting status updates (Rosen, Carrier & Cheever, 2013).

Other studies have examined social media, multitasking, and academic outcomes using experimental designs. For instance, a study by Wood and colleagues (2012) used an experimental design to examine the effects of Facebook, text messaging, IM, and e-mail during a simulated lecture. The researchers found that students who used Facebook while attending to a lecture scored significantly lower on tests of lecture material than those who were only allowed to take notes using paper and pencil; however, the scores of students who texted, e-mailed, or sent IMs did not differ significantly from students in control groups. In a related study, Rosen and colleagues (2011) had students watch a thirty-minute lecture video. The researchers asked students to respond to text messages sent out at even intervals throughout the lecture by researchers. Students were split into a low text messaging group (which received 0–7 messages), a moderate text messaging group (8–15 messages), and a high text messaging group (16 or more messages). The researchers found that the high text messaging group performed worse (by one letter grade) on an information post-test than the low text messaging group; however, the moderate text messaging group showed no difference on the post-test compared with the other two groups. These studies leave open questions about the interaction of technologies with multitasking behaviors to produce differential outcomes. Future research may elucidate the process by which some activities lead to negative outcomes and others to positive outcomes.

ON EVALUATING RESEARCH

As educators, it is our duty to be critical about the research we read. Whenever you see an intriguing news story about a new research study, don't just read the story and accept it at face value—read the original study and evaluate it critically. As a matter of fact, it's good practice *not* to trust a reporter's interpretation of a scientific study. Remember that reporters are trained to do just that—report on stories. They are, quite often, not subject area experts. Of course, many of them are very good at talking about the fields they cover, but again they are not researchers and don't have the requisite research evaluation skills. Additionally, provocative stories sell more papers and get more clicks—so the more intriguing a reporter can make a story sound, the better. Therefore, it's up to you to evaluate the research yourself. Make it a point not to share, retweet, or forward a story that you haven't read or that cites research that you don't understand. One well-publicized study had (generally) great methodology and found interesting results; however, the authors overreached when discussing their findings—they interpreted a nonsignificant effect as significant because it "showed a trend towards significance," a statistical no-no. In statistics the standard convention is that a p-value that isn't below .05 is simply not interpretable.

Questions to Ask When Evaluating Research

1. Why did the researchers conduct the study?
2. Did they include research supporting their theoretical underpinnings and, by extension, their research questions?
3. How rigorous were the methods?
   a. How was the sample selected for the study?
      i. Was the sample representative of the population being studied?
      ii. Did the sample match the population in terms of gender, race, ethnicity, socioeconomic status, level of computer and Internet skill, diversity of majors, academic ability, and so on?
      iii. If there were assignments into groups, were the participants randomly assigned?
   b. How were data collected?
      i. How were the variables operationalized? For instance, if the researchers were studying engagement, how did they measure engagement?
      ii. Did the researchers use established measures of the variables being examined? If not, why not? Using new or untested measures does not automatically send up a red flag but it should make the reader curious as to why these measures were chosen.
      iii. It is essential that researchers provide data on how well their questions, surveys, or tests provided similar results under similar testing conditions and

whether these instruments measured what they were intended to measure. In other words, the researchers should provide data about the reliability and validity of their instruments.

iv. How were the data collected? Were surveys conducted online? Paper and pencil? How were observational data collected? How were data from the institution obtained? How were data coded and interpreted?

c. Were the appropriate statistical methods used?

i. Thinking critically about statistical methods requires that student affairs professionals understand and be able to interpret statistics. As also explored in chapter 6, student affairs professionals don't go into the field to be researchers. Knowing this, many student affairs graduate preparation programs have *lightened* the research requirements. The cycle continues with new faculty who have graduated from these programs entering their teaching positions with little in the way of quantitative research skills. Therefore, it is incumbent on student affairs professionals to engage in the appropriate levels of professional development in order to build their ability to critically evaluate statistical methods.

ii. Do the statistical procedures match the data? For instance, are the data normally distributed? Are the data on an ordinal, interval, or ratio scale? Do the data meet the assumptions of the statistical procedures being used? Are the procedures warranted? For instance, does a control variable need to be included in a correlation (using a partial correlation) or a regression? Are there any variables that should have been included that would have influenced the results? For instance, if semester GPA is being used as an outcome variable, has preexisting ability (that is, high school GPA) been included as a control?

d. Were the results explained in a way that can be understood, and were the results appropriately evaluated?

   i.   Did the researchers follow standard reporting techniques for statistical tests (such as providing degrees of freedom)?

   ii. Do the results reach significance (that is, $p < .05$)?

   iii. If the results are significant, are the real-world implications of the results substantial? Are effect size estimates included? For instance, if there is a significant difference in semester GPA for a group that uses Twitter, is the difference between the GPA of the two groups substantial enough to warrant focus?

e. Do the conclusions fit with what was done?

   i.   How did the researchers tie in the theoretical model used, research questions, and results?

   ii. Were any inferential leaps not corroborated with evidence?

   iii. Do the conclusions make sense based on the statistical evidence?

   iv. How would you have interpreted what was found?

f. Were limitations appropriately explored?

   i.   Did the researchers discuss key limitations of the study such as sampling problems, methodological problems, and problems with making inferences to other populations?

   ii. What other limitations would you have included?

CONCLUSION

Student affairs professionals are at their best when they use evidence-based strategies to support students. The following chapters review how we can translate the research on social media into effective practices, and chapter 6 explains the importance of evaluating social media interventions. In times of increased scrutiny of higher education and calls for improved accountability, it is essential that we properly evaluate our programs and services, social media or otherwise, to provide evidence of positive outcomes. Therefore, the benefits are twofold—we can best support our students by ensuring that what we do *actually matters* as well as supporting the continued growth of the profession. As part of that goal, we need to change the culture of academia as a whole—a concept not foreign to student affairs professionals. For our students, we must model critical thinking in all aspects of what we do—and that includes the evaluation of research.

Practical Tips

1. Appreciate the impact of student engagement, academic, and social integration on the desired outcomes of a college education.
2. Remember that social media can be used in helpful and harmful ways with respect to student learning outcomes.
3. Remember that how students use social media is more predictive of outcomes than whether or not they use these technologies.
4. Integrate research on how social media influence student development into your practice.
5. Critically evaluate research studies by asking the questions discussed in this chapter.

REFERENCES

Astin, A. W. (1984). Student involvement: A developmental theory for higher education. *Journal of College Student Personnel, 25*(4), 297–308.

Bachrach, Y., Kosinski, M., Graepel, T., Kohli, P., & Stillwell, D. (2012). Personality and patterns of Facebook usage. *Proceedings of the 3rd Annual ACM Web Science Conference,* 24–32.

Bank, B., & Slavings, R. (1990). Effects of peer, faculty, and parental influences on students' persistence. *Sociology of Education, 63*(2), 208–225.

Celis-Morales, C. A., Perez-Bravo, F., Ibañez, L., Salas, C., Bailey, M. E. S., & Gill, J. M. R. (2012). Objective vs. self-reported physical activity and sedentary time: Effects of measurement method on relationships with risk biomarkers. *PLOS ONE, 7*(5).

Chickering, A., & Gamson, Z. (1987). Seven principles of good practice in undergraduate education. *AAHE Bulletin, 39,* 3–7.

Choney, S. (2010). Facebook use can lower grades by 20 percent, study says. *NBC News.* Retrieved February 2, 2014, from http://www.nbcnews.com/id/39038581/ns/technology_and_science-back_to_school/t/facebook-use-can-lower-grades-percent-study-says/.

Chun, M. M., Golomb, J. D., & Turk-Browne, N. B. (2011). A taxonomy of external and internal attention. *Annual Review of Psychology, 62,* 73–101.

Crook, C. (2008). *Web 2.0 Technologies for Learning: The Current Landscape— Opportunities, Challenges and Tensions.* British Educational Communications and Technology Agency (BECTA) Report: Web 2.0 Technologies for Learning at Key Stages 3 and 4. Retrieved February 3, 2014, from http://dera.ioe.ac.uk/1474/1/becta_2008_web2_currentlandscape_litrev.pdf.

DeAndrea, D. C., Ellison, N. B., LaRose, R., Steinfield, C., & Fiore, A. (2011). Serious social media: On the use of social media for improving students' adjustment to college. *The Internet and Higher Education, 15*(1), 15–23.

Eckles, J. E., & Stradley, E. G. (2012). A social network analysis of student retention using archival data. *Social Psychology of Education, 15*(2), 165–180.

Ellison, N. B., Steinfield, C., & Lampe, C. (2007). The benefits of Facebook "friends:" Social capital and college students' use of online social network sites. *Journal of Computer-Mediated Communication, 12*(4), 1143–1168.

Ellison, N. B., Steinfield, C., & Lampe, C. (2011). Connection strategies: Social capital implications of Facebook-enabled communication practices. *New Media & Society, 13*(6), 873–892.

Ellison, N. B., Vitak, J., Gray, R., & Lampe, C. (2014). Cultivating social resources on social network sites: Facebook relationship maintenance behaviors and their role in social capital processes. *Journal of Computer-Mediated Communication,* DOI: 10.1111/jcc4.12078.

Fidler, P. P. (1991). Relationship of freshman orientation seminars to sophomore return rates. *Journal of the Freshman Year Experience, 3*(1), 7–39.

Finn, J. (1989). Withdrawing from school. *Review of Educational Research, 59,* 117–142.

Finn, J. D., & Rock, D. A. (1997). Academic success among students at risk for school failure. *Journal of Applied Psychology, 82*(2), 221–34.

Fredricks, J., & McColskey, W. (2011). *Measuring Student Engagement in Upper Elementary Through High School: A Description of 21 Instruments.* U.S. Department of Education, Institute of Education Sciences Report. Retrieved February 3, 2014, from http://ies.ed.gov/ncee/edlabs/projects/project.asp?ProjectID=268.

Fried, C. (2008). In-class laptop use and its effects on student learning. *Computers & Education, 50*(3), 906–914.

Gonzales, A. L., & Hancock, J. T. (2011). Mirror, mirror on my Facebook wall: Effects of exposure to Facebook on self-esteem. *Cyberpsychology, Behavior, and Social Networking, 14*(1–2), 79–83.

Gosling, S. D., Augustine, A. A., Vazire, S., Holtzman, N., & Gaddis, S. (2011). Manifestations of personality in online social networks: Self-reported Facebook-related behaviors and observable profile information. *Cyberpsychology, Behavior, and Social Networking, 14*(9), 483–488.

Hald, J., Overgaard J., & Grau, C. (2003). Evaluation of objective measures of smoking status—a prospective clinical study in a group of head and neck cancer patients treated with radiotherapy. *Acta Oncologica, 42*(2), 154–159.

Heiberger, G., & Harper, R. (2008). Have you Facebooked Astin lately? Using technology to increase student involvement. In R. Junco & D. M. Timm (eds.), Using emerging technologies to enhance student engagement. *New Directions for Student Services*, Issue 124, pp. 19–35. San Francisco: Jossey-Bass.

Higher Education Research Institute (HERI) (2007). College freshmen and online social networking sites. Retrieved April 7, 2013, from http://www.heri.ucla.edu/PDFs/pubs/briefs/brief-091107 -SocialNetworking.pdf.

Junco, R. (2009). Teaching teens to Twitter: Supporting engagement in the college classroom. Presentation at the Berkman Center for Internet & Society Luncheon Series. Retrieved September 15, 2013, from https://www.youtube.com/watch?v=qAD6Nd2Wx-I.

Junco, R. (2012a). The relationship between frequency of Facebook use, participation in Facebook activities, and student engagement. *Computers & Education, 58*(1), 162–171.

Junco, R. (2012b). Too much face and not enough books: The relationship between multiple indices of Facebook use and academic performance. *Computers in Human Behavior, 28*(1), 187–198.

Junco, R. (2012c). In-class multitasking and academic performance. *Computers in Human Behavior, 28*(6), 2236–2243.

Junco, R. (2013). Comparing actual and self-reported measures of Facebook use. *Computers in Human Behavior, 29*(3), 626–631.

Junco. R. (under review). Student class standing, Facebook use, and academic outcomes.

Junco, R., & Cotten, S. R. (2011). Perceived academic effects of instant messaging use. *Computers & Education, 56*(2), 370–378.

Junco, R., & Cotten, S. R. (2012). No A 4 U: The relationship between multitasking and academic performance. *Computers & Education, 59*, 505–514.

Junco, R., Elavsky, C. M., & Heiberger, G. (2012). Putting Twitter to the test: Assessing outcomes for student collaboration, engagement, and success. *British Journal of Educational Technology, 44*(2), 273–287.

Junco, R., Heiberger, G., & Alonso-Garcia, N. (in preparation). Tweeting to stay: Fostering academic and social integration through Twitter.

Junco, R., Heiberger, G., & Loken, E. (2011). The effect of Twitter on college student engagement and grades. *Journal of Computer Assisted Learning, 27*(2), 119–132.

Junco, R., & Mastrodicasa, J. (2007). *Connecting to the Net.Generation: What Higher Education Professionals Need to Know about Today's Students.* Washington, DC: NASPA.

Kay, R. H., & Lauricella, S. (2011). Unstructured vs. structured use of laptops in higher education. *Journal of Information Technology Education, 10*, 33–40.

Kim, Y., & Khang, H. (2014). Revisiting civic voluntarism predictors of college students' political participation in the context of social media. *Computers in Human Behavior, 36*, 114–121.

Kirschner, P. A., & Karpinski, A. C. (2010). Facebook and academic performance. *Computers in Human Behavior, 26*, 1237–1245.

Koch, I., Lawo, V., Fels, J., & Vorländer, M. (2011). Switching in the cocktail party: Exploring intentional control of auditory selective attention. *Journal of Experimental Psychology: Human Perception and Performance, 37*(4), 1140–1147.

Kolek, E. A., & Saunders, D. (2008). Online disclosure: An empirical examination of undergraduate Facebook profiles. *National Association of Student Personnel Administrators Journal, 45*(1), 1–25.

Kuh, G. D. (2009). What student affairs professionals need to know about student engagement. *Journal of College Student Development, 50*(6), 683–706.

Kuh, G. D., Cruce, T. M., Shoup, R., Kinzie, J., & Gonyea, R. M. (2008). Unmasking the effects of student engagement on first-year college grades and persistence. *Journal of Higher Education, 79*(5), 540–563.

Manago, A. M., Taylor, T., & Greenfield, P. M. (2012). Me and my 400 friends: The anatomy of college students' Facebook networks, their communication patterns, and well-being. *Developmental Psychology, 48*(2), 369–380.

Marois, R., & Ivanoff, J. (2005). Capacity limits of information processing in the brain. *Trends in Cognitive Sciences, 9*(6), 296–305.

Mayer, R., & Moreno, R. (2003). Nine ways to reduce cognitive load in multimedia learning. *Educational Psychologist, 38*(1), 43–52.

Mehdizadeh, S. (2010). Self-presentation 2.0: Narcissism and self-esteem on Facebook. *Cyberpsychology, Behavior, and Social Networking, 13*(4), 357–64.

Moore, K., & McElroy, J. C. (2012). The influence of personality on Facebook usage, wall postings, and regret. *Computers in Human Behavior, 28*(1), 267–274.

Morrin, D. (2007, August 29). A shift to engagement. *Facebook Developers* (blog). Retrieved February 2, 2014, from https://developers.facebook.com/blog/post/30.

Ong, E., Ang, R., Ho, J., Lim, J., & Goh, D. (2011). Narcissism, extraversion, and adolescents' self-presentation on Facebook. *Personality and Individual Differences, 50*, 180–185.

Orr, E. S., Sisic, M., Ross, C., Simmering, M. G., Arseneault, J. M., & Orr, R. R. (2009). The influence of shyness on the use of Facebook in an undergraduate sample. *CyberPsychology & Behavior, 12*(3), 337–40.

Otten, J. J., Littenberg, B., & Harvey-Berino, J. R. (2010). Relationship between self-report and an objective measure of television-viewing time in adults. *Obesity, 18*(6), 1273–1275.

Pascarella, E. T., & Terenzini, P. T. (2005). *How College Affects Students: A Third Decade of Research.* San Francisco: Jossey-Bass.

Pasek, J., More, E., & Hargittai, E. (2009). Facebook and academic performance: Reconciling a media sensation with data. *First Monday, 14*(5). Retrieved February 3, 2014, from http://journals.uic.edu/ojs/index.php/fm/article/viewArticle/2498/2181.

Pempek, T. A., Yermolayeva, Y. A., & Calvert, S. L. (2009). College students' social networking experiences on Facebook. *Journal of Applied Developmental Psychology, 30*(3), 227–238.

Rosen, L. D., Carrier, L. M., & Cheever, N. A. (2013). Facebook and texting made me do it: Media-induced task-switching while studying. *Computers in Human Behavior, 29*(3), 948–958.

Rosen, L. D., Lim, A. F., Carrier, L. M., & Cheever, N. A. (2011). An empirical examination of the educational impact of text message-induced task switching in the classroom: Educational implications and strategies to enhance learning. *Psicologia Educativa, 17*(2), 163–177.

Ross, C., Orr, E. S., Sisic, M., Arseneault, J. M., Simmering, M. G., & Orr, R. R. (2009). Personality and motivations associated with Facebook use. *Computers in Human Behavior, 25*(2), 578–586.

Seidman, G. (2012). Self-presentation and belonging on Facebook: How personality influences social media use and motivations. *Personality and Individual Differences, 54*(3), 402–407.

Selwyn, N. (2009). Faceworking: Exploring students' education-related use of Facebook. *Learning, Media and Technology, 34*(2), 157–174.

Skinner, E. A., Kindermann, T. A., & Furrer, C. J. (2008). A motivational perspective on engagement and disaffection: Conceptualization and assessment of children's behavioral and emotional participation in academic activities in the classroom. *Educational and Psychological Measurement, 69*(3), 493–525.

Smith, A., & Brenner, J. (2012). *Twitter Use 2012*. Pew Internet and American Life Project Report. Retrieved April 11, 2014, from http://www.pewinternet.org/2012/05/31/twitter-use-2012/.

Strayer, D. L., & Drews, F. A. (2004). Profiles in driver distraction: Effects of cell phone conversations on younger and older drivers. *Human Factors, 46*(4), 640–649.

Stutzman, F. D. (2011). *Networked Information Behavior in Life Transition*. Ph.D. diss., University of North Carolina at Chapel Hill.

Tazghini, S., & Siedlecki, K. L. (2013). A mixed method approach to examining Facebook use and its relationship to self-esteem. *Computers in Human Behavior 29*(3), 827–832.

Tess, P. A. (2013). The role of social media in higher education classes (real and virtual): A literature review. *Computers in Human Behavior, 29*(5), A60–A68.

Thomas, S. L. (2000). Ties that bind: A social network approach to understanding student integration and persistence. *Journal of Higher Education, 71*(5), 591–615.

Tinto, V. (1993). *Leaving College: Rethinking the Causes and Cures of Student Attrition* (2nd ed.). Chicago: The University of Chicago Press.

Tison, E. B., Bateman, T., & Culver, S. M. (2011). Examination of the gender-student engagement relationship at one university. *Assessment & Evaluation in Higher Education, 36*(1), 27–49.

Tombu, M. N., Asplund, C. L., Dux, P. E., Godwin, D., Martin, J. W., & Marois, R. (2011). A unified attentional bottleneck in the human brain. *Proceedings of the National Academy of Sciences, 108*(33), 13426–13431.

Valenzuela, S., Park, N., & Kee, K. F. (2009). Is there social capital in a social network site?: Facebook use and college students' life satisfaction, trust, and participation. *Journal of Computer-Mediated Communication, 14*(4), 875–901.

Vitak, J., Zube, P., Smock, A., Carr, C. T., Ellison, N., & Lampe, C. (2011). It's complicated: Facebook users' political participation in the 2008 election. *Cyberpsychology, Behavior and Social Networking, 14*(3), 107–114.

Ward, T. H. (2010). *Social network site use and student retention at a four-year private university.* Ph.D. diss., The Claremont Graduate University.

Weaver, B. E., & Nilson, L. B. (2005). Laptops in class: What are they good for? What can you do with them? *New Directions for Teaching and Learning, 2005*(101), 3–13.

Welford, A. (1967). Single-channel operation in the brain. *Acta Psychologica, 27*, 5–22.

Wood, N., & Cowan, N. (1995). The cocktail party phenomenon revisited. How frequent are attention shifts to one's name in an irrelevant auditory channel? *Journal of Experimental Psychology: Learning, Memory, and Cognition, 21*(1), 255–260.

Wood, E., Zivcakova, L., Gentile, P., Archer, K., De Pasquale, D., & Nosko, A. (2012). Examining the impact of off-task multi-tasking with technology on real-time classroom learning. *Computers & Education, 58*(1), 365–374.

Yang, C., & Brown, B. B. (2013). Motives for using Facebook, patterns of Facebook activities, and late adolescents' social adjustment to college. *Journal of Youth and Adolescence, 42*(3), 403–416.

Yu, A. Y., Tian, S. W., Vogel, D., & Kwok, R. C.-W. (2010). Can learning be virtually boosted? An investigation of online social networking impacts. *Computers & Education, 55*, 1495–1503.

CHAPTER 3

Social Media and Student Identity Development

Very little attention has been given to how social media influence student development, although these sites and services are central to the lives of our students. There is a stark disconnect between student use of social media websites and the use of and interest in these sites by student affairs professionals. Of course, some student affairs professionals are true champions of social media; however, these individuals are few and far between. There are also student affairs professionals and other educators with explicit animosity toward the sites and services; these individuals are also few and far between. Most student affairs professionals fall somewhere in the middle of the spectrum—anywhere between having a passing interest in social media, to more active use, to thinking that these technologies might be beneficial to students. What is missing in this ecosystem are student affairs professionals who understand how student behaviors on social media are connected to students' overall development and how to put into practice strategies that help students along their developmental paths.

Generally, educators take a prescriptive approach in the rare instances when they do teach students about social media. A typical strategy is to discuss why "oversharing" is bad and how it could hurt a student's future career prospects. While the pitfalls of sharing personal information online *should* be discussed, they need to be placed within a broader context of supporting student learning and development. When student affairs professionals take such a cynical approach, they are viewing student technology use from an *adult normative perspective*, by which they define what is appropriate based on their own expectations and norms; these expectations are no doubt influenced by popular media portrayals of social media as detrimental to youth development (see table 3.1). Perhaps an adult normative perspective is warranted at times and in certain situations; however, like other forms of education, there must be a balance. If we tell students how to behave on *their* social media sites without considering their psychological, emotional, and sociological relationship to the sites, then we've already lost them.

Unfortunately and surprisingly, by the time youth get to college, they have been the recipients of many adult normative messages about social media. For instance, social media sites are banned in almost all K–12 schools. The implicit message is that

Table 3.1. Differences between the adult normative and youth normative perspectives

	Adult normative	Youth normative
Viewpoint	Adult experience	Youth experience
Approach	Prescriptive	Inquisitive
Beliefs about social media	Negative	Balanced
Source of information	Self	Other

these sites are nonacademic in nature and can only serve to distract from the educational mission of the school. Additionally, policies in K–12 school districts ban educators from using social media with their students. Again, the implicit message is that the only reason that educators would use social media with students is to cross a boundary in the teacher-student relationship. These implicit messages, fueled by popular media stories about the evils of social media, get communicated to students.

A few years ago when I published a paper on the relationship between student use of Facebook and academic performance, I spoke to many campus newspaper reporters. These reporters were very interested in my finding that *how* students used Facebook was a stronger predictor of grades than time spent on the site (see chapter 2; Junco, 2012) and that Facebook use, in and of itself, was not related to poorer academic outcomes. Most of these reporters shared my results with their friends before contacting me, and every one of them said how they and their friends were all surprised. They said that they had heard many media reports about how Facebook *causes* students to have lower grades. In other words, these students had accepted the adult normative view that Facebook was harming them academically.

Student affairs professionals and other educators must ask themselves what harm they are doing by telling students that something they do daily, as an integral and normal part of their lives, is harming them. It's as if educators have subconsciously accepted the proposition that each and every one of our students is an addict, so in subtle ways we shame students for making social media such a significant part of their lives. Imagine how students feel being on the receiving end of such messages, especially from educators whom students trust yet who have no idea of what students' online world is like. Indeed, it is highly likely that one of your students is alive today because of a support system developed on Facebook that helped the student through a challenging time.

The time has come to move away from the adult normative perspective and see how social media use can, and does, support student psychosocial development. With this understanding, we can begin to reframe student social media use and understand its benefits and pitfalls. Only when we truly empathize with our students' experience can we educate them about how best to use social media to support their growth. Up to this point, I've been discussing taking an unempathic adult normative perspective in relation to social media; however, imagine if student affairs professionals behaved this way with students in other domains. For instance, imagine a residence hall director who tells residents to go to sleep at 8 pm because it's what the director does. Social media are no different. Indeed, one mistaken assumption adults make when engaging in the adult normative perspective is that what happens on social media bears no relationship to what happens in the real world. Not only is this a philosophical falsehood, but there is research to show that is not the case. For instance, students who are more extroverted in the offline world are also more extroverted on Facebook (Bachrach, Kosinski, Graepel, Kohli & Stillwell, 2012; Ong, Ang, Ho, Lim & Goh, 2011; Ross et al., 2009; Seidman, 2012).

By the time most students reach college, they have spent countless hours using social media. What youth are doing online is quite consonant with established models of human personality and identity development, such as those proposed by Erikson (1968) and Chickering and Reisser (1993). Unfortunately, most educators believe that youth are only using these sites for pointless activities. Many even state that youth use social media for "socializing," as if social interactions, in and of themselves, were pointless (Roblyer, McDaniel, Webb, Herman & Witty, 2010). This adult normative view of youth social media use is far from the reality of the benefits students get from these sites. Youth actually use social media to engage in and support a critical maturation task, *identity development*. Imagine a young person who is coming to terms with a gay sexual identity but, because of geographic location, has no offline space to explore this facet of identity without suffering serious social or physical consequences. It is only through online exploration of this identity that the young person can engage in healthy development. But how exactly does this happen? This chapter connects traditional models of youth identity development with the identity work that youth are engaging in on social media.

In order to understand just how social media use influences and is congruent with student identity development, it is first important to review the relevant theories. An exhaustive review of all models of student development is beyond the scope of this book in general and this chapter in particular; however, student social media use will be examined in relation to Erik Erikson's (1968) theory of psychosocial development; the Atkinson, Morten, and Sue (1998) and Sue and Sue (2003) Racial and Cultural Identity Development (RCID) model; D'Augelli's (1994) model of lesbian, gay, and bisexual identity development; and Chickering & Reisser's (1993) seven vectors of student identity development.

IDENTITY FORMATION

Identity is a "conscious sense of individual uniqueness" and an "unconscious striving for a continuity of experience" (Erikson, 1968, p. 208). Erikson's (1968) theory of psychosocial development includes eight stages through which healthy individuals pass during their lives. Each stage has a *virtue* (strength), the favorable outcome of the resolution of the tension between the internal self and external environment within each particular life stage challenge. The virtue for the fifth stage in this model is *fidelity* and is reached through successful navigation of the *identity versus role confusion* duality. Youth pass through the fidelity stage typically

99

between the ages of thirteen and nineteen, and Erikson viewed this stage as a crucial integration of previous stages and a preparation for future ones. The main developmental task in the fidelity stage is for adolescents to solidify a stable sense of identity. To put it in layperson's terms, youth at this stage are trying to figure out who they are while being confronted with many new roles and adult statuses. The traditional-aged first-year student, for instance, is faced with the transition from high school, where the student likely had a great deal of parental input, support, and direction, to college, where the student is now living on his or her own and must engage internal motivation to reach goals.

Identity formation involves the development of a stable sense of self. There is an "important need for trust in oneself and in others" (Erikson, 1968, p. 128). At this stage, youth have to develop an "inner sameness" that is matched to how their "sameness" is recognized by others. Perhaps this developmental stage accounts for youth's preoccupation with how others see them as compared to how they feel they are (Erikson, 1968). In this sense, youth are attempting to understand who they are within the context of their environment; once they have formed their identity, they know that who they are is consistent across situations and that others recognize this consistency. Youth who have not successfully traversed the fifth stage do not have strong relationships with others, have lower levels of self-esteem, are likely to be shy, and have more difficulty adapting to college environments (Kroger, 2008). Indeed, Erikson (1968) indicates that true intimacy is possible only once the task of identity formation is under way.

Racial and Cultural Identity Development

Erikson (1968) recognized the connections between his construct of identity and how the term was used in the literature on the African American experience of his day. Indeed, one can easily see how Erikson's model might account for the development of a racial identity—for the development of a sense of self with its resultant interactions between internal and external environments should include how the person is situated within the wider cultural milieu of the society in which the person lives. Numerous theories address the development of racial and ethnic identity. The interested reader is referred to the excellent summaries of these theories found in Evans, Forney, Guido, Patton, and Renn (2009). Because racial and ethnic identity development models share dynamics that are based in the Atkinson, Morten, and Sue (1998) and Sue and Sue (2003) Racial and Cultural Identity Development (RCID) model, only the RCID model will be reviewed here.

The Racial and Cultural Identity Development (RCID) model stages are as follows (Atkinson, Morten & Sue, 1998; Sue & Sue, 2003):

1. *Conformity:* Individuals have a preference for and identify with white culture, often harboring negative attitudes toward themselves and other members of their minority group.
2. *Dissonance:* While denial is used a great deal in the conformity stage, it begins to break down in the dissonance stage. It is usually a gradual process but an external event or challenges to the person's negative attitudes about their minority group may propel them to the next stage.
3. *Resistance and immersion:* Once the conflicts of the previous stage begin to be resolved, the person "flips" the views held in the conformity stage and now identifies with views held by the minority group and rejects those held by the dominant culture.
4. *Introspection:* The individual is disaffected from the rigid and polarized views held in the resistance and immersion stage and begins to move toward greater individual autonomy. The

101

individual starts to recognize that perhaps not everything in the dominant culture is "bad," adopting a more balanced view and able to hold both the positives and the negatives.

5. *Synergistic articulation and awareness:* The conflicts from the introspection stage have been resolved, and the individual feels a sense of fulfillment in relation to their cultural identity. The values of both the dominant culture and minority culture are examined objectively.

LGBT Identity Development

Like racial and ethnic identity models, there are a number of lesbian, gay, bisexual, and transgender (LGBT) identity development models (Evans, Forney, Guido, Patton & Renn, 2009). However, only one will be reviewed here—D'Augelli's (1994) model of LGB identity development. D'Augelli's original work focused only on LGB identity development, but Bilodeau (2005) found that the processes in D'Augelli's model also applied to the development of transgender identity. As such, D'Augelli's original model will be considered to encompass transgender identity development and will be labeled as LGBT throughout this chapter. D'Augelli (1994) argued that explaining the LGBT identity process without reference to historical, community, or social contexts in which such development occurs reduces homosexuality to a "dysfunctional individual identity detached from the common experience" (p. 317).

Three factors are involved in the D'Augelli (1994) model of LGBT identity development:

1. *Subjectivities and actions:* "How individuals feel about their sexual identities over their lives, how they engage in diverse sexual activities with different meanings, and how they construct their sexual lives and feel about them" (p. 318).

102

2. *Interactive intimacies:* "How sexuality is developed by parental and familial factors, how age-peer interactions shape and modify the impact of early parental and familial socialization, and how this learning affects and is affected by intimate partnerships of different kinds" (p. 318).

3. *Sociohistorical connections:* "Social norms and expectations of various geographic and subcultural communities; local and national social customs, policies, and laws; and major cultural and historical continuities and discontinuities" (p. 318).

D'Augelli's (1994) model is a life-span development model that emphasizes the fact that people grow and develop throughout their entire lives. The model notes the importance of plasticity (that human functioning is very responsive to environmental, physical, and biological factors) and interindividual differences— or that each person's developmental path is different and that there is a broad continuum of sexual feelings and experience.

D'Augelli (1994) identified the following six processes that play a role in LGBT identity development. He noted that they are not stages such as those found in traditional identity development models but are dynamic processes mediated by the sociopolitical and cultural contexts in which they occur (D'Augelli, 1994).

1. *Exiting heterosexual identity:* This involves understanding that one's attractions are not heterosexual. It also involves telling others about one's identity, a process often referred to as "coming out."

2. *Developing a personal lesbian/gay/bisexual identity status:* This involves developing, within the context of the lesbian /gay/bisexual community, one's own definition of what it means to be lesbian, gay, or bisexual. An essential facet of this process is working through internalized myths about nonheterosexuality.

3. *Developing a lesbian/gay/bisexual social identity:* This is a lifelong process of building a network of friends who know and accept the individual's sexual identity and who can offer support.

4. *Becoming a lesbian/gay/bisexual offspring:* The major task of this process is coming out to one's parents. Often, the relationship with parents is disrupted after disclosure of sexual orientation. Luckily, this is often a temporary state that reverts with input from the lesbian, gay, or bisexual person.

5. *Developing a lesbian/gay/bisexual intimacy status:* The relative invisibility of lesbian and gay couples in our society as compared with heterosexual couples leads to uncertainty and ambiguity in the development of meaningful homosexual relationships.

6. *Entering a lesbian/gay/bisexual community:* This involves becoming politically and socially active. Some never do so because of the dangers inherent in being "out" in our society or because they view their sexuality as a purely private matter.

Student Identity Development

In 1969, Arthur Chickering published *Education and Identity*, introducing his theory of student identity development. He later collaborated with Linda Reisser in 1993 to refine the theory. Chickering and Reisser's (1993) theory consists of seven vectors and is an incremental developmental model whereby a student progresses through discrete stages. The theory allows for the fact that entering a new vector may bring up issues from previous vectors that need to be resolved along with the new developmental tasks. Chickering and Reisser's (1993) seven vectors can be seen as breaking down Erikson's (1968) fifth stage into granular components, as follows:

1. *Developing competence:* There are three types of competences that develop in college—intellectual, physical, and interpersonal.

2. *Managing emotions:* College students begin to recognize their emotions and develop intrapsychic strategies for coping with them.

3. *Moving through autonomy toward interdependence:* Students first learn to become self-sufficient and to function without the input and direction of others (like parents); then students realize that they cannot function independently of others and move toward interdependence.

4. *Developing mature interpersonal relationships:* This involves the capacity to tolerate and appreciate differences in others and to build the capacity for intimacy. This development makes one better able to engage in relationships based on interdependence and equality.

5. *Establishing identity:* Involves the development of a stable sense of self that includes being comfortable with one's body, sexual orientation, cultural heritage, self-concept, self-esteem, and personal stability.

6. *Developing purpose:* After clarifying who they are, students need to develop a sense of who they want to be. This includes the development of a career plan that takes into account personal interests and familial commitments.

7. *Developing integrity:* Closely related to the previous two vectors, on this vector students humanize and personalize their values and develop congruence, matching their personal values with those of society and engaging in socially responsible behavior.

ONLINE IDENTITY: REAL IDENTITY, PSEUDONYMITY, AND ANONYMITY

The identity development models reviewed thus far focus exclusively on identity development in the offline world—the expression of and interaction within a community that leads to changes and movement along a developmental path. However, the

105

emergence of online social spaces has allowed youth to explore their identities in ways not previously possible. This section reviews the most global levels of expressed online identity, here referred to as *online identification*. Afterward, the concepts of online self-presentation and the online disinhibition effect are discussed in relation to the development of a stable identity.

Three Levels of Expressed Online Identification

Identity can be expressed online at any of three levels:

1. *True identity:* This level of online identity is the most basic unit of self in the offline world—a person's true identity. A true identity online is expressed by creating a profile that includes the person's real name, real demographic information, and real pictures.
2. *Pseudonymity:* This level allows the user a level of anonymity with the ability to accrue a reputation. A user creates a fake name or a "handle" that is used to represent the user and his or her online contributions. The user is free to, and often does, create demographic information that is related to the pseudonym and not to the user's true identity.
3. *Anonymity:* This is the fullest level of true identity obscurity, with users not sharing any type of identifying information, not even a handle. When users are anonymous, they cannot accrue reputation in online spaces, as those who might choose a pseudonym. In other words, reputation is impossible when being anonymous online (Donath, 1999).

Examples of the Three Levels

Imagine an online discussion forum where users may register for an account and post under that account or post anonymously. Users who choose to register with their real name, and therefore

106

their true identity, will accrue reputation. They might answer questions from other forum members or post helpful information. Over time, they might accrue a reputation as someone who is helpful and will be identified by their true identity. Others on the site are free to Google them and learn even more background information about them than what they share in the forum.

While some forums have a culture that encourages (or even requires) registration with a real name, others allow or encourage registration with a pseudonym. A pseudonym in this case can look like a real name, or it can be a nickname or handle. Like users who register with their true name, those who register with a pseud-onym can also accrue reputation in the forum community. The key difference between those using their real name and those using a pseudonym is that those with a pseudonym can choose to disconnect their true identity from their pseudonym. They can share and engage with the community without anyone else knowing who they really are. Using a pseudonym allows online participants to accrue a reputation; after repeated engagement the person behind the pseudonym can become a known member of the community and be seen as a regular contributor, a firebrand, or any other such identity they will convey through their participation.

Finally, some forums allow for anonymous posting and participation. In this case, the user posting anonymously will neither be able to be identified or accrue reputation. Alas, using pseudonyms or being anonymous online is often viewed with suspicion—if people have nothing to hide, then why hide their true identity? As with other issues raised in this book, and almost all issues having to do with student development, taking a binary approach obfuscates the range of possibilities, many of which are very beneficial for student development. As will be discussed later, there are certainly times when people hide behind the mask of anonymity for nefarious reasons; however, there are many times in the regular course of student development when anonymity, pseudonymity, and a perceived disconnection from one's true identity help students more easily move through developmental tasks.

Why Are Levels of Online Identification Important?

Participating online using a pseudonym or a true identity not only allows the user to build a reputation but also to accrue the benefits received by participation in a community. One of these is the accrual of *social capital*—the psychological and physical benefits gained through connections with friends. People with more social capital are generally healthier and more connected to their communities (Adler & Kwon, 2000; Helliwell & Putnam, 2004). Furthermore, research shows that using social media like Facebook for connection and communication leads to increased social capital (Burke, Kraut & Marlow, 2011; DeAndrea, Ellison, LaRose, Steinfield & Fiore, 2011; Ellison, Steinfield & Lampe, 2007; 2011; Ellison, Vitak, Gray & Lampe, 2014). The difference between using a real name and a pseudonym is the most (in)visible—those who use a pseudonym have an added layer of privacy and, therefore, increased social distance. The importance of this distinction will be explored later in the section on the online disinhibition effect.

When users participate anonymously online, they are afforded a great deal of interpersonal privacy—that is, other users cannot tell who they are. The downside is that the users cannot accrue the benefits associated with being identified online, either using their true identity or a pseudonym. The upside is that the users generally do not experience the negatives associated with being identified online. For instance, someone may not feel comfortable posting that they are exploring their sexuality on an

108

online forum. They may be so reticent as to not even want to have a pseudonym associated with their posting. In some communities being gay and out could lead to negative social (and perhaps even physical) consequences for a young person. Those posting anonymously then often feel free to post things they otherwise wouldn't post when their identity is known, a facet of the online disinhibition effect examined later in the chapter.

Mark Zuckerberg, CEO of Facebook, stated, "Having two identities for yourself is an example of a lack of integrity"—exemplifying his belief that nothing good can come of being anonymous online (Helft, 2011). In an interview with Matt Ingram, Nancy Baym pointed out that Zuckerberg's view on identity "indicates just how privileged Zuckerberg as a wealthy, white, heterosexual male really is—in other words, someone who has nothing to fear from being transparent about his life, and no need to maintain two different identities" (Ingram, 2010). The different affordances of social media sites and services impose restrictions on or open up opportunities for levels of online identification. Facebook, for instance, during its early history required that users sign up with their real names and a college or university e-mail address. While individuals may sign up with any e-mail address now, Facebook works to enforce their name policy, which "require[s] everyone to provide their real names" for personal accounts (Facebook, 2013a). Zuckerberg has long expounded his interest in having all users use their real names (as well as his interest in having users share as much as they can, a topic raised in chapter 1). Facebook's Statement of Rights and Responsibilities states, "Facebook users provide their real names and information, and we need your help to keep it that way"; "You will not provide any false personal information on Facebook, or create an account for anyone other than yourself without permission" (Facebook, 2013b). In other words, you may not register a pseudonym on Facebook or participate anonymously.

109

The opposing viewpoint is that anonymous participation online is essential, not just for individuals' identity development, but also for their basic democratic and human rights. In a report on free expression online, an independent expert to the United Nation's Human Rights Council stated, "The right to privacy is essential for individuals to express themselves freely. Indeed, throughout history, people's willingness to engage in debate on controversial subjects in the public sphere has always been linked to possibilities for doing so anonymously." The report goes on to state that "the Internet also presents new tools and mechanisms through which both State and private actors can monitor and collect information about individuals' communications and activities on the Internet. Such practices can constitute a violation of the Internet users' right to privacy, and, by undermining people's confidence and security on the Internet, impede the free flow of information and ideas online" (La Rue, 2011).

In his keynote speech at the SxSW Interactive Conference in 2011, Chris "moot" Poole, the founder of 4chan, an image board website popular for its /b/ (random) board, declared that "anonymity is authenticity" and described how being anonymous online helps people take more risks with their creativity because "the cost of failure is really high when you're contributing as yourself." Diametrically opposed to Mark Zuckerberg's ideas about anonymity, Poole's site 4chan embraced, celebrated, and supported anonymous contributions. Users of 4chan have been responsible for many of the early and significant Internet memes such as lolcats and Rickrolling, as well as the hacking of *Time*'s "World's Most Influential Person" poll to declare moot the winner. Also notable is that 4chan is recognized as the birthplace of Anonymous, the decentralized collection of online activists that has become famous for efforts to bring awareness of and foment resistance to corrupt governmental and corporate entities. Poole (2011) cites the success of many of the memes created anonymously on 4chan as evidence that anonymity fuels creativity and experimentation. Critics argue that allowing users to participate anonymously allows them to more easily lie, deceive, and express themselves in ways that are hurtful to others. However, research has found that the opposite is true: when people communicate anonymously online, they are more likely to reveal intimate details about themselves (Whitty & Gavin, 2001) and self-disclose more (Qian & Scott, 2007).

Online anonymity is a powerful force for democratic freedoms, interpersonal growth, and creative expression. Therefore, it is vital for student affairs professionals to support online outlets for expression that allow youth to be anonymous or pseudonymous. It is helpful for us to take a more balanced approach when viewing the merits of online anonymity and not to subscribe to Zuckerberg's ideas about online identity. These ideas reflect not just his personal beliefs but also his company's interest in having users share as much as possible in order to mine their data for advertising purposes. Supporting students' ability to be anonymous and pseudonymous online allows them the freedom and creativity to explore who they are in relative safety and allows them to engage in the experimental identity play that may not occur effectively, if at all, when "the cost of failure is really high" while students are projecting new facets of a developing identity. This freedom is especially important for youth from minority racial and ethnic backgrounds, those who are developing an LGBT identity, and those who are from other disenfranchised groups.

Online Self-Presentation

Self-presentation is the conscious or unconscious process by which people try to influence the perception of their image, typically through social interactions. Self-presentation is a natural process that occurs in the offline world—people have a perceived image of

111

themselves and they expend psychological energy in trying to ensure that others see them the same way. So, if people believe they are generous, for example, they will act outwardly in generous ways; they may also highlight the ways in which they are generous so that others make the same evaluation of them. Self-presentation occurs through conscious processes such as selectively sharing self-relevant information. This process is analogous to what happens online—people do not share all aspects of their personality with the public. Details that they find distasteful, rude, or embarrassing never make it into the public sphere. Self-presentation also occurs through unconscious processes, as when people aren't aware of psychological dynamics they bring to interpersonal interactions. In this case, there is no outward declaration of these intrapsychic phenomena, because people themselves are not aware of these phenomena. Indeed, this is one of the focus areas of psychodynamic psychotherapy—addressing the subconscious drivers of behavior that lead to negative social, career, and interpersonal outcomes.

Through self-presentation (either conscious or unconscious), humans portray a desired image of themselves by controlling social interactions. Online platforms allow for different degrees of self-presentation and impression management. For instance, an online video chat platform allows for transmission of facial features and nonverbal facial expressions, as well as voice tone, accent, and volume. In contrast, a text-based forum may allow the user only one small, static profile picture (which, depending on the culture and mores of the forum, may not actually be an image of the user) and would communicate limited information about the person's identity. A social networking site like Facebook allows users to post multiple pictures, videos, and nuanced information about themselves in the form of not only background information but also the content users share and their comments on the content of others.

Self-presentation then allows youth to construct their identity by outwardly expressing the traits they find more desirable while suppressing those they find distasteful (note that a given individual can only do so to a certain extent, often limited by a person's psychological functioning). The online space is a perfect place for youth to then explore these identities and to receive feedback in measurable ways. Imagine that a student is navigating the process of exiting heterosexual identity; the student may test this new identity online either by posting relevant articles on Facebook under their true identity, by assuming a pseudonym and adopting a different identity and posting as someone who has already come out, or by anonymously discussing concerns about the coming-out process. In all of these ways, the student can garner support for the challenging intrapsychic and social processes he or she is dealing with.

The Online Disinhibition Effect

The *online disinhibition effect* occurs because people feel more comfortable saying something online than they would in a comparable offline (or face-to-face) situation. This effect is in part caused by the fact that there is much greater social distance online than there is in person. Online, there is a barrier between the communicator and the recipients—that barrier being the computer. It is certainly much easier to express a sentiment that would elicit a strong reaction when you do not see that reaction. Imagine how many times you would have loved to say exactly what was on your mind during a professional meeting but didn't for apprehension of what the reactions might be. Now imagine if there was no fear of consequences from your statement—would you have been more likely to share it? That can certainly be the case in online communications.

Almost exclusively, the online disinhibition effect is thought of as a negative process—one used by individuals who are interested in provoking, shaming, or generally bullying others. Indeed, plenty of media reports express how online disinhibition leads only to negative consequences. While media coverage of online disinhibition can often be exaggerated and focused solely on negative aspects, there are certainly plenty of real examples of individuals being bullied or harassed because the perpetrator felt comfortable behind the perceived wall of anonymity afforded through online communications. For instance, Amanda Todd, a fifteen-year-old from Vancouver, British Columbia, committed suicide after being bullied and harassed online. A month before she died, she posted a YouTube video that clearly expressed her torment (Elam, 2012). Amanda's story is reflective of the US teen experience, with 11 percent reporting being the victims of bullying (Nansel et al., 2001); a 2011 Pew Internet Project survey found that 88 percent of social media–using teens have witnessed others being cruel or mean on social media (Lenhart et al., 2011).

What has been missing in the national dialogue about online disinhibition is the need for a more balanced approach to understanding the phenomenon and its effects. My research, for instance, has shown positive effects of online disinhibition. For example, students who are allowed to participate in ongoing class discussions on Twitter are more likely to engage on the platform and share sensitive issues and reactions that they wouldn't share in class. Interestingly enough, this effect carries over to the physical classroom, with students participating in more substantial ways in classroom discussions. In this way, online disinhibition helps students feel that they can share their true feelings about an issue and then helps them develop the ability to more freely share those feelings in front of others in class. Helping students, especially new college students, be more comfortable engaging in class discussions leads to improved academic outcomes. Certainly, this process is exactly one of the goals of higher education—to get students involved in their learning and to have them engage more fully in the learning process. Often, professors are frustrated by the lack of participation in their courses; using an online system intended to engender engagement and communication and engage online disinhibition allows students to feel more free to participate.

It is therefore useful to understand the online disinhibition effect as a process that can result in both positive and negative outcomes. As student affairs professionals, we can take advantage of the online disinhibition effect in order to more fully support our students. Take the example of students who might be struggling with issues of coming out. Such students may not have had much support in their family or previous school. Now in college, they are feeling a little more comfortable because they are in a community that more openly embraces LGBT youth. The Internet is a relatively safe place for LGBT youth to seek information and connections in order to combat the marginalization they experience in their daily lives (Gasser, Cortesi, Malik & Lee, 2012). While LGBT youth might be comfortable exploring their LGBT identity online, they might not yet feel comfortable joining the campus LGBT group or asking questions at group meetings. Indeed, LGBT youth may hesitate even to be associated with such a group given their level of LGBT identity development and the marginalization they have already experienced. Such students benefit from joining online forums or spaces where they can share, receive information, and ask questions. There are many LGBT online forums that encourage users to adopt a pseudonym for this very reason—so that the users can feel freer to express themselves.

How Does Online Disinhibition Relate to Levels of Identification?

The more people are identifiable online, the less likely they will be to share openly. Someone who posts with his or her real name has a true identity for which the person is building a reputation.

115

Because the person is using his or her true identity, it is less likely that the person will take risks with what he or she posts online and engage in identity exploration. People may be concerned about the potential career and educational consequences of what they post—for instance, not getting a job because of what a potential employer finds out about them online. Many educators are often surprised to find out that college students are indeed concerned with online reputation and take active steps to manage that reputation. Even before they get to college, some students are aware that they must present themselves a certain way online in order to have the best possible college and career opportunities. Some students even go so far as to create idealized profiles—fake Facebook profiles that portray them in a way that they think adults *want* students to be, instead of showing their true identity.

SOCIAL MEDIA, IDENTIFICATION, DISINHIBITION, AND IDENTITY DEVELOPMENT

College students are in the process of developing an identity, a stable sense of self that is both internally consistent and externally validated (Chickering & Reisser, 1993; Erikson, 1968). Participating in social media allows students to test out or "try on" different facets of their identity through their online self-presentation. Because of online disinhibition, social media give youth the impression that these sites and services are safer places to understand who one is in the context of a social environment. Youth can receive almost-instant feedback about how they are presenting themselves and make just as instant adjustments. Social media help youth move toward consistency in their identity across situations and help them express this consistency publicly and have it recognized by others. Over time, young people begin to settle into a stable sense of online identity expression, as evidenced by the consistency of what they post, how they behave, and their reactions toward others. There are three main affordances of doing such identity work online: first, youth are able to have more experiences to test (or "try on") their developing identities than they can in offline interactions, which happen with less frequency; second, because of the online disinhibition effect, youth are more comfortable taking creative risks and exploring aspects of their identity that they would not wish to or be able to risk or explore offline; and third, exploration of identity online not only seems safer, it is safer, because there is less ego investment by students and their audience.

The extent to which entering college students can develop their identity is directly related to their academic and interpersonal success. Youth who don't successfully pass through the stage of identity formation have much more difficulty in college environments. They don't have strong interpersonal connections, which are necessary for feeling a sense of connection to the college environment and for developing academic and social integration, which in turn are related to their motivation to be successful (Tinto, 1993). Furthermore, building strong connections on social media help students develop greater social capital and have a supportive network of peers when they need assistance (Ellison, Steinfield & Lampe, 2007; 2011; Ellison, Vitak, Gray & Lampe, 2014). In these ways, students who have not successfully engaged in the process of identity formation have more difficulty adapting to college environments (Kroger, 2008). Learning about oneself but also about other's reactions to that constructed self on social media is a skill that transfers to the offline environment. While the content and environments are different, the *process* remains the same—youth test out and learn who they are, learn about how others react to facets of their identity, and build significant interpersonal bonds. Indeed, the process of identity formation online helps students build true intimacy in the offline world (Erikson, 1968).

Racial and ethnic identity development is an important part of the development of a sense of self. The development of racial and ethnic identity happens through an awareness of and interaction with the cultural environment in which an individual is situated. Minority youth in the *conformity* stage may prefer to interact with those in the majority group culture on social media; they may also post content (such as status updates, memes, and jokes) that express negative attitudes toward people of their own race or ethnicity. By interacting on these sites, minority youth may experience an event that precipitates their movement into the *dissonance* stage. They might be the target of racial epithets or witness a conversation that challenges their notion of their identification with the majority culture. For example, a young African American at the conformity stage might have witnessed the racist tweets in reaction to Barack Obama's reelection (for examples, see Morrissey, 2012); such a young person might have been shocked by how majority group members were reacting to African Americans, which might have led to dissonance about identifying with the tweeters and majority culture. If the dissonance was powerful enough, the young person would enter the *resistance and immersion* stage by engaging almost exclusively with African Americans online and participating in forums, groups, and pages supporting Afro-centric world views. After a period of time in this polarity, the young person might realize these views are too extreme, in the *introspection* stage. The young person might develop a more balanced view of the good and bad things about majority and minority cultures and ultimately move to the *synergistic articulation and awareness* stage, in which the young person can interact more fully online with members of all groups and have a more objective and balanced viewpoint about them.

Social media are relatively safe spaces for youth to examine their LGBT identities, especially when using a pseudonym. Youth may explore the differences in their attractions on social media and reach out to others who have self-identified as LGBT for more information. They may *lurk*, read postings about the coming-out process, and eventually use social media for *exiting heterosexual identity*. Again, through their interactions and information seeking online, they begin to *develop their LGBT identity status* by *entering (and participating in) an LGBT online community*. The affordances of the online space allow youth to develop these community connections first and to build social capital within, for instance, a forum dedicated to teens that are going through the coming-out process. Through these affordances, youth can build a community in relative privacy and explore healthy ways of coming out and engaging an LGBT identity. Before social media, it was very difficult if not impossible to join an LGBT community and still maintain a sense of anonymity; however, with social media and the ability to participate online via pseudonyms, as well as the inclination to share more because of the online disinhibition effect, youth are more likely to form connections that can help guide them through a difficult transition time. This holds especially true for youth from families and communities that discriminate against those from LGBT backgrounds. In this sense, the online space is a safe environment for the often-private identity work that comes along with being LGBT.

Examining identity development through the lens of Chickering and Reisser's (1993) vectors, we see that the online space can be a very healthy and productive medium by which to support student development through these stages. Students *develop interpersonal competence*, in part, through the act of interacting with their peers online. Facebook is as important a social space for college students as is the student union (and perhaps even more important than the student union, for more students use Face-book every day than pass through the doors of the student union). Well before their first day of college, students have started the process of *managing emotions*, by testing out their emotional communication online. In subtle and not-so-subtle ways they are able to express their frustrations, concerns, and elations online on sites like Facebook. The online disinhibition effect contributes to the facility with which students can express emotions online, because the expression of strong emotions in offline social interactions is almost regarded as a taboo in North American culture. Therefore, students are freer to explore their emotions and the impact of these expressions and begin to figure out how to regulate these feelings.

Students *move through autonomy toward interdependence* by first realizing their freedom from dependent relationships of their past and engaging in more self-sufficient behaviors. Eventually, they realize that, while they are perfectly comfortable being independent, dependence on others as equals is essential to success. The move from dependence may be expressed online as limiting content shared with parents who may be online friends or followers. Once students become independent, they use social spaces to build social capital but also to seek valuable information about their new college environment. The more students do so, the more they begin to realize that their social network plays an essential role in their continued success in college and beyond. The interaction between the online and offline is much tighter as students begin *developing mature interpersonal relationships*. On Facebook, students begin to realize individual differences in their peer group and begin to see an appreciation for these differences. Students test out forms of relating that go beyond the primary narcissism of earlier stages and reach to the more mature interpersonal processes.

Through the culmination of moving through and resolving the aforementioned vectors, students *establish identity*. They have interacted with their peers in the offline and online worlds and taken advantage of the affordances of social media like Facebook. Because of online disinhibition, they are more likely to take creative risks and explore their identity online than they are in person, leading to more rapid movement through these stages. Furthermore, if students are exploring their identity by adopting a pseudonym or interacting anonymously, they may reap additional affordances of such processes—namely, they are freer to explore facets of their identity that they fear may be found "distasteful" by their peer group or by society at large. In these circumstances, the exploration of racial and cultural and LGBT identities shifts from being a potentially hazardous experience to one that is shrouded in safety and privacy. In some ways, interacting anonymously or with a pseudonym when testing out these minority identities is the equivalent of testing them in the safety of a social vacuum but actually being able to engage in social interactions. In this sense, interacting online becomes the "best of both worlds."

A great example of students constructing identities online is through the creation and presentation of *idealized-self profiles*, which are often developed by high school students to dupe admissions officers and potential employers. Even before Kaplan released survey results showing that 26 percent of admissions officers check applicant Facebook profiles and that 35 percent of those said that they had discovered something online that negatively impacted an application, youth knew about these practices (Kaplan, 2012). Students who have stronger Internet skills engage in a wide variety of techniques to hide their real identity Facebook profiles. For instance, they might use their middle name as their last name, activate privacy preferences to the strictest degree, or delete their real identity Facebook profile every time they log off (which can then be easily reactivated the next time they log on). In addition to hiding their real identity profiles, they create an *idealized-self profile*, which is an extremely sanitized version of their

121

identity. Such profiles include only positive attributes, "safe for work" pictures and posts, and even status updates about nonexistent volunteer activities ("I just visited the nursing home for the fourth time this week and this feels great"). Unfortunately, it is those students with greater skill and perhaps even more parental input into their online behaviors that are savvy enough to engage in these practices, leaving those from minority racial and ethnic backgrounds and those of lower socioeconomic status at a disadvantage.

CONCLUSION

Youth engage in the process of identity development before, in their transition to, and throughout their college careers. Understanding that youth are exploring their identities in online social spaces allows student affairs professionals and other educators to move away from the adult normative perspective and see the benefits of using these technologies for positive psychological growth. Indeed, there are vast affordances for exploring identity through social media, especially for students from disenfranchised backgrounds. Specifically, youth can explore and "try on" new facets of their identities and engage in interpersonal interactions that either solidify or modify their perceptions of self. The online disinhibition effect allows students to take creative risks with identity play that they otherwise wouldn't do in offline situations. Indeed, identity formation is enhanced through online interactions on social media, and such identity development is essential for student success. If a student does not form a solid identity, the student will not have strong connections to the institution and peer group and will be less likely to persist. Exploring identity online is especially powerful for students who are from minority racial or ethnic backgrounds or who are LGBT as they need to develop a sense of identity that is often separate from the majority culture that dominates most college campuses. For some, it is only in online social spaces that they can find a critical mass of individuals with similar identities who can support their transition through these important developmental stages. Student affairs professionals are encouraged to support students in their engagement on these sites and to validate their exploration of their identities online. For without these safer online social spaces, identity aspects essential to healthy student growth might not ever be achieved.

Practical Tips

1. Consider your perspective when working with students and whether a shift to a youth normative perspective might be warranted.
2. Ask your students to teach you about how they use social media and how these technologies affect their lives.
3. Understand how students use social media to develop their identity.
4. Support freedom in online expression and encourage students to explore the benefits of the different levels of online identification.
5. Leverage online disinhibition to promote creative risk taking and exploration of identity.

REFERENCES

Adler, P. S., & Kwon, S. W. (2000). Social capital: The good, the bad, and the ugly. In E. Lesser (ed.), *Knowledge and social capital: Foundations and applications* (pp. 89–115). Boston: Butterworth-Heinemann.

Astin, A. W. (1984). Student involvement: A developmental theory for higher education. *Journal of College Student Personnel, 25,* 297–308.

Atkinson, D. R., Morten, G., & Sue, D. W. (1998). *Counseling American Minorities.* Boston: McGraw-Hill.

Bachrach, Y., Kosinski, M., Graepel, T., Kohli, P., & Stillwell, D. (2012). Personality and patterns of Facebook usage. *Proceedings of the 3rd Annual ACM Web Science Conference, 24–32.*

Bilodeau, B. (2005). Beyond the gender binary: A case study of transgender college student development at a Midwestern university. *Journal of Gay and Lesbian Issues in Education, 2*(4), 29–44.

Burke, M., Kraut, R., & Marlow, C. (2011). Social capital on Facebook: Differentiating uses and users. *Proceedings of the SIGCHI Conference on Human Factors in Computing Systems.*

Chickering, A. W., & Reisser, L. (1993). *Education and Identity.* San Francisco: Jossey-Bass.

D'Augelli, A. R. (1994). Identity development and sexual orientation: Toward a model of lesbian, gay, and bisexual development. In E. J. Trickett, R. J. Watts, & D. Birman (eds.), *Human Diversity: Perspectives on People in Context* (pp. 317–318). San Francisco: Jossey-Bass.

DeAndrea, D. C., Ellison, N. B., LaRose, R., Steinfield, C., & Fiore, A. (2011). Serious social media: On the use of social media for improving students' adjustment to college. *The Internet and Higher Education, 15*(1), 15–23.

Donath, J. S. (1999). Identity and deception in the virtual community. In M. Smith and P. Kollock (eds.), *Communities in Cyberspace* (pp. 29–59). London: Routledge.

Elam, J. (2012). Bullied to death: The tragic story of Amanda Todd. *The Washington Post,* October 17, 2012. Retrieved February 2, 2014, from http://communities.washingtontimes.com/neighborhood/heart -without-compromise-children-and-children-wit/2012/oct/17/ bullied-death-tragic-story-amanda-todd/.

Ellison, N. B., Steinfield, C., & Lampe, C. (2007). The benefits of Facebook "friends:" Social capital and college students' use of online social network sites. *Journal of Computer-Mediated Communication, 12*(4), 1143–1168.

Ellison, N. B., Steinfield, C., & Lampe, C. (2011). Connection strategies: Social capital implications of Facebook-enabled communication practices. *New Media & Society, 13*(6), 873–892.

Ellison, N. B., Vitak, J., Gray, R., & Lampe, C. (2014). Cultivating social resources on social network sites: Facebook relationship maintenance behaviors and their role in social capital processes. *Journal of Computer-Mediated Communication.* DOI: 10.1111/jcc4.12078.

Erikson, E. H. (1968). *Identity: Youth and Crisis.* New York: W. W. Norton & Company.

Evans, N. J., Forney, D. S., Guido, F. M., Patton, L. D., & Renn, K. A. (2009). *Student Development in College: Theory, Research, and Practice.* San Francisco: Jossey-Bass.

Facebook. (2013a). Facebook's name policy. Retrieved August 27, 2013, from https://www.facebook.com/help/292517374180078.

Facebook. (2013b). Facebook statement of rights and responsibilities. Retrieved August 28, 2013, from https://www.facebook.com/legal/terms.

Gasser, U., Cortesi, S. C., Malik, M., & Lee, A. (2012). Youth and digital media: From credibility to information quality. *SSRN Electronic Journal.* Retrieved February 2, 2014, from http://papers.ssrn.com/sol3/papers.cfm?abstract_id=2005272.

Helft, M. (May 13, 2011). Facebook, foe of anonymity, is forced to explain a secret. *New York Times.* Retrieved April 12, 2014, from http://www.nytimes.com/2011/05/14/technology/14facebook.html.

Helliwell, J. F., & Putnam, R. D. (2004). The social context of well-being. *Philosophical Transactions of the Royal Society of London, 359* (1449), 1435–1446.

Ingram, M. (2010). Are Facebook's views on privacy "naive and utopian"? *GigaOm.* Retrieved August 28, 2013, from http://gigaom.com/2010/06/01/facebooks-views-on-privacy-are-naive-and-utopian-prof-says/.

Junco, R. (2012). Too much face and not enough books: The relationship between multiple indices of Facebook use and academic performance. *Computers in Human Behavior, 28*(1), 187–198.

125

Kaplan. (2012). *Kaplan Test Prep's 2012 Survey of College Admissions Officers*. Retrieved January 31, 2014, from http://press.kaptest.com/httppress-kaptest-comresearch/kaplan-test-preps-2012-survey-of -college-admissions-officers.

Kroger, J. (2008) Identity development during adolescence. In G. R. Adams & M. D. Berzonsky (eds.), *Blackwell Handbook of Adolescence* (pp. 205–226). Oxford, UK: Blackwell.

La Rue, F. (2011). Report of the Special Rapporteur on the promotion and protection of the right to freedom of opinion and expression. *United Nations Human Rights Council Freedom of Opinion and Expression Annual Reports.* Retrieved August 28, 2013, from http://www.ohchr .org/EN/Issues/FreedomOpinion/Pages/Annual.aspx.

Lenhart, A., Madden, M., Smith, A., Purcell, K., Zickuhr, K., & Raine, L. (2011). *Teens, Kindness and Cruelty on Social Network Sites.* Pew Internet and American Life Report. Retrieved February 2, 2014, from http://pewinternet.org/Reports/2011/Teens-and-social -media.aspx.

Morrissey, T. E. (2012, November 7). Twitter racists react to "that nigger" getting reelected. *Jezebel.* Retrieved August 27, 2013, from http:// jezebel.com/5958490/twitter-racists-react-to-that-nigger-getting -reelected/.

Nansel, T., M. Overpeck, R. Pilla, W. Ruan, B. Simons-Morton, & P. Scheidt (2001). Bullying behaviors among US youth: Prevalence and association with psychosocial adjustment. *Journal of the American Medical Association, 285*(16), 2094–2100.

Ong, E., Ang, R., Ho, J., Lim, J., & Goh, D. (2011). Narcissism, extraversion, and adolescents' self-presentation on Facebook. *Personality and Individual Differences, 50*, 180–185.

Poole, C. (2011). Keynote address to the SxSW Interactive Conference. Austin, TX. Retrieved August 28, 2013, from http://schedule .sxsw.com/2011/events/event_IAP000001.

Qian, H., & Scott, C. R. (2007). Anonymity and self-disclosure on weblogs. *Journal of Computer-Mediated Communication, 12*(4), 1428–1451.

Roblyer, M. D., McDaniel, M., Webb, M., Herman, J., & Witty, J. V. (2010). Findings on Facebook in higher education: A comparison of college faculty and student uses and perceptions of social networking sites. *The Internet and Higher Education, 13*, 134–140.

Ross, C., Orr, E. S., Sisic, M., Arseneault, J. M., Simmering, M. G., & Orr, R. R. (2009). Personality and motivations associated with Facebook use. *Computers in Human Behavior, 25*(2), 578–586.

Seidman, G. (2012). Self-presentation and belonging on Facebook: How personality influences social media use and motivations. *Personality and Individual Differences, 54*(3), 402–407.

Sue, D. W., & Sue, D. (2003). *Counseling the Culturally Diverse: Theory and Practice* (4th ed.). Hoboken, NJ: Wiley.

Tinto, V. (1993). *Leaving College: Rethinking the Causes and Cures of Student Attrition* (2nd ed.). Chicago: The University of Chicago Press.

Whitty, M., & Gavin, J. (2001). Age/sex/location: Uncovering the social cues in the development of online relationships. *Cyberpsychology & Behavior, 4*(5), 623–630.

CHAPTER 4

Informal Learning Using Social Media

Before discussing social media's use in formal learning, this chapter reviews the ways students use social media for informal learning. *Informal learning* is the learning that happens through processes and in contexts not related to teaching, training, or research in educational institutions. Learning the dominant community language and the mores and values of society, for instance, occurs through informal learning. Student affairs professionals promote informal learning by supporting students' integration into the institution. *Implicit learning* is learning that happens without the person being aware that he or she is learning. Implicit learning is often discussed in reference to physical activities like riding a bicycle, jumping rope, gymnastics routines, or swimming; however, implicit learning can also occur in social contexts. By contrast, *formal learning* is learning that happens in formal learning environments, such as a classroom, via formal instruction.

Student affairs professionals are interested in supporting students during their transition to, throughout their time in, and in their transition out of college. As a result, student affairs professionals often focus on promoting informal learning to enhance student psychosocial development, engagement, and social and academic integration (Evans, Forney, Guido, Patton & Renn, 2009). While most of what student affairs professionals do is related to informal learning—such as helping students learn about the culture of being a student—there are times when student affairs professionals also engage students in formal learning. For instance, cocurricular alcohol awareness programs, which are usually delivered as lectures in classroom-like settings, might be classified as formal learning. The use of social media for formal learning, such as that which takes place through degree programs and formal programming conducted by student affairs professionals, will be covered in the next chapter.

Student affairs professionals have traditionally focused on *meeting students where they are*; in other words, to maximize the impact of their work with students, student affairs professionals try to address students at their current developmental level, being careful to not adopt an adult-normative perspective when attempting to understand students' experiences and needs. To meet students where they are, educators need an appropriate understanding of how each individual is situated within his or her cultural environment, taking care to understand the idiosyncrasies of the individual's worldview. To meet students where they are is to enlist students as collaborators in their developmental process and to work to help them grow in that collaborative spirit. Student affairs professionals must also be interested in their own growth and understand how they themselves are situated in the college and broader cultural milieu and how their situation affects their work with students.

Since student affairs professionals are interested in meeting students where they are and because of the popularity of social media among students, it is imperative that educators understand and hopefully even leverage these tools to improve their work with students.

Social media use is related to many facets of the college student experience, including the following:

1. Self-esteem (Gonzales & Hancock, 2011; Mehdizadeh, 2010; Tazghini & Siedlecki, 2013)
2. Shyness (Orr et al., 2009)
3. "Big Five" personality traits such as Extraversion and Neuroticism (Bachrach, Kosinski, Graepel, Kohli & Stillwell, 2012; Gosling, Augustine, Vazire, Holtzman & Gaddis, 2011; Moore & McElroy, 2012; Ong, Ang, Ho, Lim & Goh, 2011; Ross et al., 2009; Seidman, 2012)
4. Political participation (Kim & Khang, 2014; Vitak et al., 2011)
5. Life satisfaction, social trust, civic engagement, and political participation (Valenzuela, Park & Kee, 2009)
6. Development of identity and peer relationships (Pempek, Yermolayeva & Calvert, 2009)
7. Relationship building and maintenance (Ellison, Steinfield & Lampe, 2007; 2011; Ellison, Vitak, Gray & Lampe, 2014; Manago, Taylor & Greenfield, 2012; Valenzuela, Park & Kee, 2009)
8. Perceptions of social support (DeAndrea, Ellison, LaRose, Steinfield & Fiore, 2011; Manago, Taylor & Greenfield, 2012)
9. Student engagement (Heiberger & Harper, 2008; HERI, 2007; Junco, 2012; Junco, Elavsky & Heiberger, 2012; Junco, Heiberger & Loken, 2011)
10. Social and academic integration (Selwyn, 2009; Yu, Tian, Vogel & Kwok, 2010)

131

The list, while not exhaustive, illustrates the student learning and developmental outcomes of interest to student affairs professionals, encompassing many of the desired outcomes of a college education. This research shows that there may be great benefit in using social media to promote informal learning.

There is scant research on the outcomes of using social media in formal learning environments, and unfortunately there is even less research on the outcomes of using social media for informal learning. That being said, this chapter will draw upon what research has been done relevant to informal learning and also provide examples of effective uses of social media in student affairs functional areas.

INFORMAL AND IMPLICIT LEARNING USING SOCIAL MEDIA

Informal and *implicit learning* both happen when college students use social media. As was explained in chapter 3, youth engage in constructing identity both online and offline. The psychological tensions experienced by teens in the offline world are mimicked in the online world. Teens are developing a sense of self in the context of a teenage peer group; they want to be accepted and be seen as part of an in-group. Their behaviors on social media like Facebook help them understand the norms and mores of their peer group, not just on the site but offline as well. Indeed, each site has its own cultural norms to which students eventually adhere. For example, boyd (2007) described youth culture on MySpace and what was required to be "cool" on the site, which included having friends (but not too many) and sharing wall posts that were satirical or mocking of people with status. These norms are learned only through participation on the site, much like social norms in the offline world (such as "stand close to the person you are talking to, but not too close").

Youth learn the cultural norms of sites and of their peer group through participation in social media; however, through implicit learning, they also learn the process of social interactions. For instance, young people learn how to communicate with their peer group, discuss difficult issues, share successes without seeming to brag, and so on. Of course, this is a developmental process that occurs over time and by "messing around." Ito and colleagues (2009) describe *messing around* as a multifaceted process by which youth experiment and learn about technologies; however, I extend this idea further to the social aspects of technology use. In other words, youth also learn about how to be members of society by messing around, a process of trial and error that lets them learn what is culturally appropriate and acceptable and what isn't, within the context of their peer group. They "test the waters" with interactions by posting content and evaluating the reactions of their peers. Indeed, "likes" on Facebook are a "strong proxy for social status," and youth try to post photos that garner the maximum number of likes and go so far as to delete photos that don't get enough likes (Madden et al., 2013).

As they transition to college, youth use social media to maintain their former network of high school friends and also to build and sustain bonds with new friends at their campus (Ellison, Steinfield & Lampe, 2007; 2011; Ellison, Vitak, Gray & Lampe, 2014; Junco & Mastrodicasa, 2007). Recall from chapter 2 that such social integration is a powerful force in student success. Students who interact a great deal with their peers, who have broad social ties and reciprocated relationships, and who have strong bonds in their social network are more socially integrated and more likely to persist (Eckles & Stradley, 2011; Pascarella & Terenzini, 2005; Thomas, 2000). Students use Facebook to learn the norms of their new peer group—a task that was more difficult before the advent of Facebook, as Facebook affords a faster communication of norms through consistent micro-interactions. Indeed, Yu and colleagues (2010) showed that Facebook use had a direct impact on student self-esteem, satisfaction with university life, and performance proficiency. Additionally, Facebook use was directly related to developing relationships and gaining acceptance from peers and to students' acculturation to the university, and these two variables mediated the relationship between Facebook use and self-esteem, satisfaction with university life, and performance proficiency (Yu, Tian, Vogel & Kwok, 2010).

To use Tinto's (1993) terminology, Yu and colleagues (2010) found that using Facebook improved students' academic and social integration and that these variables mediated student success by improving students' self-esteem, satisfaction with life at the university, and views of their own performance. As Selwyn (2009) described in his analyses, students used Facebook to shape their identities as students and to learn academic cultural norms and mores. These processes occurred through informal interactions that might simply be dismissed as socializing; however, these uses of Facebook show students using the site for implicit and informal learning—for instance, by posting about their academic experiences. Additionally, students who spent more time on Facebook and who more frequently commented on their friends' posts and pictures, created or RSVP'd to events, and viewed their friends' photos were more engaged and involved in campus activities (Junco, 2012). In other words, students engage in social information-seeking activities and communication with friends and through implicit and informal learning improve their social and academic integration.

Lurking can be conceptualized as a way in which students engage in implicit learning. *Lurking* is defined as observing online communities, such as discussion boards in an academic context, but not actively participating. Almost exclusively, online course participation is graded based on student activity. Interestingly, there is research to show that lurking can also be a measure of student engagement—indeed, Dennen (2008) found that students who read messages to find a point of entry into the discussion and who returned to review ideas raised in earlier discussions were more likely to report that the discussion activity was worthwhile compared to students who only read the minimum number of posts and who only posted to meet course requirements. By lurking in order to find an appropriate message to which to respond or a model to follow, or to avoid making a redundant response, these students were learning about course content, following along with peers, and learning about the cultures and norms of the course discussion environment. Therefore, active participation that can be "seen" is not the only way that students can benefit from the use of social media to improve social and academic outcomes.

EFFECTIVE USES OF SOCIAL MEDIA IN STUDENT AFFAIRS

Research on students' uses of social media and how those uses relate to informal learning give us some idea of how student affairs professionals can use social media effectively. For instance, my colleagues and I conducted a controlled study (Junco, Heiberger & Loken, 2011) and found that using Twitter in educationally relevant ways can improve in-class and cocurricular student engagement as well as academic and social integration. We can also use student development theory and information about how student affairs professionals are using social media to develop practices congruent with the goals of the profession. Take our Twitter and student engagement study as an example (Junco, Heiberger & Loken, 2011). Because there was no research on implementing social media interventions in the classroom when we designed our study, we decided to use a theoretical model of student engagement (Astin, 1984; Chickering & Gamson, 1987) to guide how we would use social media in the classroom (Junco, Heiberger & Loken, 2011). In a follow-up study, we concluded that using such theoretical models helps educators have an appropriate guide for using social media in ways that will improve student outcomes (Junco, Elavsky & Heiberger, 2012). Student affairs professionals can do the same thing combining theoretical models of student engagement, academic and social integration, identity development, and academic performance into their work with social media.

A few factors have emerged from the research on social media that help inform how student affairs professionals can use social media to promote informal learning. Here they are organized under the framework of Chickering and Gamson's (1987) principles for good practice in undergraduate education:

1. *Contact between students and student affairs professionals.* We know from the research that using social media as part of a course increases the number and the quality of student-faculty interactions (Bosch, 2009; Junco, Heiberger & Loken, 2011; Schroeder & Greenbowe, 2009). Using social media with students can also help student affairs professionals have more, better-quality interactions with their students.

2. *Cooperation among students.* In courses, social media can be used to foster and support student cooperation (Hollyhead, Edwards & Holt, 2012; Junco, Elavsky & Heiberger, 2012; Schroeder & Greenbowe, 2009). In the cocurriculum, student affairs professionals can use social media to support student groups that by their very nature require students to work together to reach common goals.

3. *Active learning.* Students can use social media to reflect on how what they learn outside the classroom relates to formal

learning. For instance, students can reflect on their internship experiences and discover how the experiences are linked to what they are learning in class (Junco, Elavsky & Heiberger, 2012; Junco, Heiberger & Loken, 2011).

4. *Prompt feedback.* In formal learning settings, social media can provide students with prompt feedback about their course-work from their peers and instructors; however, in student affairs, students can receive prompt feedback about anything, ranging from questions about when financial aid applications are due to learning how to better market themselves online (Junco, Elavsky & Heiberger, 2012; Junco, Heiberger & Loken, 2011).

5. *Communicating high expectations.* Student affairs professionals can communicate high expectations via social media through direct statements about what behaviors and types of communications are expected from students but also through modeling appropriate and professional uses of the sites and services. Since many students will continue on in workplaces where social media might be used, students need to build these skills to support their career advancement.

6. *Respecting diverse ways of learning.* The use of social media helps communicate to students that student affairs professionals are interested in meeting them where they are through more expansive methods of student engagement. Often, students who interact with faculty via social media learn that faculty are approachable and indeed approach those faculty members with greater frequency than students who don't interact with faculty online (Bosch, 2009; Junco, Heiberger & Loken, 2011).

When thinking about using social media to promote informal learning, student affairs professionals must match their learning outcomes to a technology with appropriate affordances. A vital question to ask is this: Is there a process by which you can reach the same learning outcomes more effectively without technology? If the answer is yes, then proceed with the nontechnology solution. As has been stated many times in this book so far, social media are just tools, whose outcomes depend on how they are used. I've been in (or heard about) way too many meetings where someone will say, "Let's use social media!"—but if someone else asks why, the answer often boils down to "Students use social media, and it would be cool." If you've ever been in one of these meetings, you have my sympathy. If you've been the person saying such a thing, please stop.

Here are some questions for evaluating whether the use of social media is an appropriate intervention strategy.

- *What are the desired learning outcomes?* As with any student affairs intervention, identifying learning outcomes in advance will have a profound effect on the intervention's success.
- *How will success be measured?* This is an area where the field of student affairs often falls short—measuring the effects of an intervention on a learning outcome. Chapter 6 reviews how we can collect data to evaluate the effectiveness of our interventions. Student affairs professionals should be collecting data on all types of interventions, not just those involving social media.
- *What do results of research studies say about effective interventions for the selected learning outcomes?* This question is the research version of the practical question, "What's being done at similar institutions?" While learning what others are doing is important, it's even more important to understand what types of interventions work, how they work, and how they can be adapted to your goals.

- *Are social media appropriate to use to reach these learning outcomes?* If learning outcomes can be attained through the use of either social media or nontechnology interventions, what is the benefit of using social media? Typically the reason to use social media will be some form of *efficiency*: in a particular case, using social media might make it easier to reach the desired learning outcomes, or you'll be able to help more students reach the outcomes with the same resource investment as the nontechnology intervention.
- *Which social media sites have affordances that match the goals of the intervention?* The affordances of some sites make them better educational tools than others (an issue explored further in chapter 5). For instance, you wouldn't use Instagram as a tool to continue class discussions, although you might use Instagram as a way for the student sustainability club to document their progress in developing a bike share program.

HOW ARE SOCIAL MEDIA BEING USED IN STUDENT AFFAIRS?

The NASPA Technology Knowledge Community conducted a survey of social media users in student affairs (Valliere, Endersby & Brinton, 2013). The survey was advertised on Facebook and Twitter, and as such represents a sample of those in student affairs already using social media. Indeed, 78 percent of respondents reported that they were either "above average" or "well above average" in their technology skills. Since the survey sampled only social media users with strong technology skills, the results likely reflect more positive attitudes about social media than are actually held in the greater student affairs population. However, the survey is useful in understanding how these individuals are using and thinking about social media. Of the 315 respondents, 42 percent reported being mid-managers, 25 percent new professionals, 20 percent graduate students, 8 percent senior student affairs officers, and 5 percent faculty. Valliere and colleagues (2013) asked about personal and professional uses of social media. They found that 96 percent of respondents reported using Facebook, 82 percent reported using Twitter, 81 percent reported using YouTube, and 39 percent reported using blogs for personal uses (see figure 4.1). The researchers also found that 71 percent used Facebook, 63 percent used Twitter, 49 percent used YouTube, and 25 percent used blogs in their jobs as student affairs professionals. A full 95 percent of respondents believed that Facebook was important for student engagement, and 93 percent reported the same for Twitter. When asked about skills for new professionals, 99 percent of the respondents believed that new professionals should have Microsoft Word skills, while 96 percent believed they should have social media skills.

Two student affairs functional areas have been most influenced by social technologies: admissions and career services.

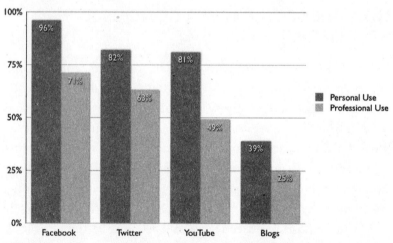

Figure 4.1. Use of social media by student affairs professionals for personal and professional purposes, as reported in the NASPA Technology Knowledge Community Survey (Valliere, Endersby & Brinton, 2013).

140

Admissions offices have recognized the need to use social media to recruit students, while career services offices have recognized the need to help students use social media effectively in their job searches. Barnes and Lescault (2011) found that 100 percent of the colleges and universities they surveyed were using social media in admissions. Facebook was the most common site used, with 98 percent of schools having a page, while 84 percent had a Twitter account and 66 percent had a blog. The National Association of Colleges and Employers (NACE) (2013) conducted a survey of career services directors, associate directors, and counselors and found that Facebook (92 percent), LinkedIn (88 percent), and Twitter (72 percent) were the most used by respondents. Furthermore, 77 percent of respondents reported that their career center provided social media training to students. Although the NACE survey reported that most career centers use social media with students, the researchers pointed out that social media were only used with students for one-way transmission of information like messages about upcoming events. (See figure 4.2 for a graphic representation of the results of these two surveys.)

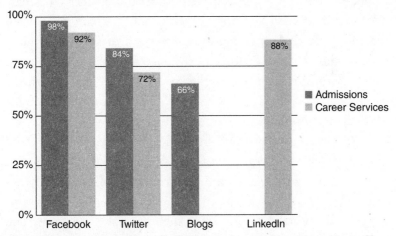

Figure 4.2. Use of social media by admissions and career services offices as reported in the Barnes and Lescault (2011) and NACE (2013) surveys.

The NASPA (Valliere, Endersby & Brinton, 2013), NACE (2013), and Barnes and Lescault (2011) surveys suggest several interesting trends in the field of student affairs; however, keep in mind that the NASPA survey sampled only student affairs professionals who likely already recognized the value in social media. Given that caveat, the NASPA survey suggests that student affairs social media users see the value of these technologies in order to support student engagement. Many of the respondents to the NASPA survey reported using social media as part of their jobs. Interestingly, the use of blogs was less than what might be expected given the results of a Pearson faculty social media survey, suggesting a move away from blogs and to more interactive social technologies in student affairs (Seaman & Tinti-Kane, 2013). Lastly, and of particular interest to graduate students in student affairs, 96 percent of respondents to the NASPA survey believed that new professionals should have social media skills, indicating that more applicants will be evaluated on their ability to use these technologies effectively to engage students. This finding presents an interesting dilemma in that these skill sets are rarely taught in student affairs graduate programs but are of great importance to at least the functional areas of career services and admissions and are becoming of even greater importance to the profession as a whole. Compounding this dilemma is the fact that those serving on search committees evaluating new professionals may not themselves have the requisite skills to evaluate how an applicant might use these technologies to effectively engage students.

This is a major weakness in the field of student affairs. Most college students are connected through social media and have an interest in using these sites and applications in educationally relevant ways; however, student affairs professionals are not obtaining the requisite skills to do so in their graduate programs. The next section discusses a selection of effective uses of social media in student affairs in order to serve as a framework for more effective practices. Because of the lack of research and written work on effective social media practices in the field, I leveraged my social media network to find out what student affairs professionals were doing in their functional areas. I put out a call for examples by posting an entry on my blog, tweeting a request for help with a link to my blog post, and posting on Facebook. I received a great number of responses, many of which are summarized in the next section.

Functional areas in student affairs are using social media for the following overarching informal learning goals:

· *Reaching and deepening relationships with individual students.* Much as we do in the offline context, we can use social media to build and strengthen relationships with our students. However, we can reach more students by participating in online social spaces.
· *Engaging in community building.* In offline settings, community building is often accomplished through connections in residence halls and campus activities. Social media allow for building and strengthening these connections and are very helpful for students who don't live on campus.
· *Guiding student sentiment.* Before social media, it was difficult to assess the sentiments held by the student community; however, with social media, student affairs professionals can not only learn about students' reactions to what we do, but also address issues that might cause these sentiments to change.
· *Promoting networking skills.* Teaching students how to network with those in their chosen field happens almost exclusively through informal learning. It's rarely the case that an undergraduate class is available on networking for one's

major. However, social media can be used to model, teach, and refine student professional networking skills.

- *Modeling appropriate online behavior.* Through the process of interacting with students on social media, student affairs professionals teach them how to engage civilly in their community.

These goals are being accomplished in the following ways:

- *Sharing content*—using social media for one-way communication of information such as posting about campus events, news items, and academic deadlines. Although important from an information-sharing perspective, engaging in sharing content alone or for the majority of social media interactions negates the affordances of these newer media, instead mimicking a broadcast technology like e-mail.
- *Social media listening*—conducting keyword searches and other methods of reviewing what students are talking about. This allows student affairs professionals to engage in an unobtrusive method of "keeping their finger on the pulse" of what is important to students.
- *Direct engagement*—participating in existing conversations or engaging students in new conversations. This is a way to further engagement with university social media accounts and also a way to help students build social and academic integration.

Reaching and Deepening Relationships with Individual Students

The financial aid office at the University of Missouri has a staff position dedicated to maintaining social media accounts and working with online students. The office maintains both a Facebook page and a Twitter account with the stated goals of meeting students where they are most comfortable, decreasing lines and phone calls, enhancing the office's reputation and credibility, and increasing transparency, access, and financial literacy. The office engages in *social media listening* by monitoring instances of student references to "financial aid" at "mizzou," *participating in conversations* by responding to students who tweet about inferred needs (the office responded to a tweet containing "hate being broke" by inviting the student to visit the Office for Financial Success), *answering direct questions* that are sent to the office Twitter account or posted on the office Facebook page, and *posting bulletins* about upcoming deadlines. In these ways, the office supports student informal learning about financial aid procedures at the University of Missouri.

The Office for Retention and Student Success at Southern Illinois University Edwardsville (SIUE) works with offices such as academic advising, disability services, career services, counseling and health services, international programs, and student government. The office created a Twitter account to engage with SIUE students. Office staff intentionally search for and follow students, campus offices, and local area resources. However, Director of Retention and Student Success Kevin P. Thomas reported that the office's biggest successes have come when conducting Twitter searches for "SIUE." About twice a week, the office conducts a search in order to respond to student questions, provide feedback, or offer phone numbers to help students with whatever they are posting about. Through Twitter, the office has helped students with advising, financial, and other concerns to enhance student success. The office also engages in social media listening not just to reach out to students but also to monitor the successes and struggles of the SIUE student body.

Kevin provided a typical example of how his office's use of Twitter supports student success. A first-year student was not going

145

to be allowed into the nursing program due to an error in course selection. She vented her frustration and strong disappointment on Twitter. Monitoring instances of the use of "SIUE" on Twitter allowed the office to see that the student was frustrated and to intervene. The office staff clarified the steps she needed to take to appeal the decision, and as part of the process they became advocates for the student. Because of the help obtained through this office, the student's appeal was granted, and she was admitted to the nursing program. Indeed, social media listening can be a powerful way to learn about and address student concerns and to engage informal learning.

Both of these examples also show how social media can be used to help support informal learning of university policies and procedures necessary for student success. The financial aid office at the University of Missouri and the Office for Retention and Student Success at SIUE used social media to reach students and help them feel a sense of connection at the institution by offering support with essential university services.

Engaging in Community Building

Jessica Fantini described how she integrated the use of Facebook into her work as a residence director at Southern Maine Community College. She began by using a private Facebook group with her resident assistant staff. She indicated in the group description that it was "to be used for important information, such as duty schedules and programming ideas." To her surprise, her staff were very engaged with the group and started using it as a "virtual RA lounge." Jessica reported that her staff posted content such as "pick-me-ups (messages or images such as memes intended to be humorous and lighten other RAs' moods and statements intended to praise one another), dates they needed duty coverage, and program ideas." In her conversations with staff, Jessica reported that they really appreciated the ability to reach other staff members easily without having to send individual text messages. She also reported a negative: some staff members who were more active in the group were frustrated with those who were not as active and not as easily reachable.

Because of the group's quick uptake and success with her RAs, Jessica created another group for the front desk clerk staff to be used in the same way as the RA group, as well as another group for her residents (see figure 4.3). Again, the group for her residence hall has been well received by students and has been used as a virtual lounge, with residents "asking for assistance with rides, borrowing books, or inviting people to events." She has also used the group to monitor complaints and to inform residents of important information. Jessica reported that while they still use posters and flyers to convey information, residents receive updates much more quickly through the Facebook group because most of them have smartphones. Interestingly, residents from the previous academic year remained active in the summer, connecting with the incoming summer residents. When Jessica shared her story, she was getting many questions in the group about housing assignments for next year (obviously a hot topic for students as the academic year draws near).

The Facebook group for residents fostered informal and implicit learning about the residence hall community, promoting social and academic integration. As has been found with students who use social media in courses and then bring their online conversations into the classroom, Jessica noted the connections between what was posted in the resident's group and offline discussions (Junco, Heiberger & Loken, 2011).

Jessica reported that residents could often be heard in the hallways and commons areas discussing a complaint that was

147

Figure 4.3. Screen capture of Southern Maine Community College Residence Hall page created by Jessica Fantini.

shared in the Facebook group; additionally, residents could be heard talking about events that were posted in the group. Jessica and her staff would create events on Facebook and post them to the page, while residents would encourage others in the group to attend the events via the group wall.

While Jessica considered using other social media tools, she realized that Facebook was most appropriate not only because many of her residents were already users but also because of its affordances. For instance, she was able to collect feedback to support formative assessment, and in addition her monitoring of student complaints allowed her to respond to students individually. Selwyn (2009) found that students were prone to complain about their faculty and their academic "condition" on Facebook; however, addressing these complaints meets students where they are in experiencing university services and helps them feel heard, which improves their sense of connection to the institution. In the terminology of psychologists, complaints are material with which student affairs professionals can work in order to connect with students who may be dissatisfied and who are in danger of becoming disengaged, as seen with the students in Selwyn's (2009) study. Additionally, creating and posting events on Facebook was one of the activities found to be strongly predictive of student engagement (Junco, 2012). Jessica leveraged this affordance of Facebook to help support student engagement and leveraged social media listening to help improve student academic integration.

TJ Logan and his team in the University of Florida's Department of Housing and Residence Education engaged in an innovative strategy to match roommates. Unlike many institutions around the country, the University of Florida (UF) does not have a mandatory housing requirement for any student. Coupled with the challenge of competing in the most overbuilt off-campus student housing market in the country, the Department of

Housing and Residence Education is always looking for opportunities to better serve students and to attract them to on-campus housing. In the past, roommate matching was done using the traditional application system and asking students questions about their likes and dislikes. However, UF students consistently reported the importance of having a good roommate and asked for more control over their roommate match. UF tried a myriad of popular matching methods, including surveys and random matching, in an effort to identify effective ways to make good roommate matches that would leave students satisfied. Unfortunately, none of these strategies helped reduce student complaints and roommate conflicts.

Understanding that incoming students used Facebook to "check out" their assigned roommates, TJ and his team decided to try RoomSync, a Facebook app designed to help students choose their own roommates (Farrell, 2006; Junco & Mastrodicasa, 2007). RoomSync uses the affordances of Facebook—student profile information—to develop suggested matches. Then the students themselves can evaluate their matches' Facebook profiles to see who might be a good fit. In just two years of using the application, TJ and his team had the following results:

- A substantial decrease in staff hours to conduct the roommate matching/assignment process.
- A progressive increase in users each year, leading to dramatic increases in mutually requested roommates.
- More diverse (in terms of racial and ethnic background) roommate matches than the formerly used "random matching" process.
- Increased retention of students who utilized RoomSync.
- Higher satisfaction among students who utilized RoomSync.
- A considerable decrease (67 percent) in documented roommate conflicts.

150

At the University of Michigan, Eric Heilmeier and his colleagues in Central Communications created the #askumich Twitter hashtag for incoming students to get information before or when arriving on campus, purposefully using Twitter as a platform for informal learning about the campus environment. Campus Information partnered with the university's central communications and social media team to develop a social media listening strategy in order to answer student and parent questions and make referrals to university resources. Staffers started the process by meeting with the central communications team and enlisting their help early in their planning. The main University of Michigan Twitter account was used to assist in promoting the hashtag in the run-up to orientation, while the Campus Information account was used to answer questions directly. Eric and his colleagues created a management group in Hootsuite (a service to manage and measure multiple social media accounts) that included him, the university social media manager, her interns, and Eric's information attendants (student employees at the university Information Center). With this group, the team could assign tweets to each other and ensure they were all answered within an appropriate time frame. This setup also allowed the central communications team to assign to Eric tweets directed to the main University of Michigan Twitter account that did not necessarily use the hashtag but that did have questions related to orientation.

Eric reported that he and his colleagues trained students who were going to tweet from the Campus Information account in order to maintain consistency and congruence in using the "voice" of the account. Training consisted of an in-person training session, followed up with a link to a short Google+ video after the training as a refresher. Additionally, Eric and his team created prepared responses for common questions to help reduce the cognitive load of those monitoring the hashtag. Indeed, Eric reported the most difficult training topic was helping his information assistants (student employees) figure out how to answer questions within the short Twitter character limit. Each response needed to provide an answer as well as a link to a helpful university site so the user could reference it in the future. At the time of this writing, Eric and his colleagues had been using the hashtag for one year and were planning on promoting and using the hashtag in future academic years.

Donna Talarico-Beerman reported that Elizabethtown College designed an acceptance letter intended to make students' admission an "experience" by asking them to share their acceptance on social media. Students shared their acceptance on Instagram, Twitter, and Facebook and used the suggested hashtag #etown2017. In all, more than 176 students (7 percent of the incoming class) shared their moment on Instagram or Twitter (see figure 4.4). Donna's team could not collect accurate data on Facebook because there was no way to monitor student wall posts.

Figure 4.4. Example of a student Facebook post from the Elizabethtown College Share Your Acceptance campaign.

This is a creative and efficient way to help incoming students informally and implicitly learn about their new community and to build a sense of social and academic integration.

The University of Michigan and Elizabethtown College encouraged students to build community and institutional commitment (and by extension to enhance their social and academic integration) even before arriving on campus. Through informal learning, students learned about the campus environment and also had a chance to build community through implicitly learning about the campus norms being communicated on social media. Southern Maine Community College, on the other hand, used social media to build and strengthen community in residence halls. Again, through informal and implicit learning, Jessica Fantini promoted student engagement in the hall community. Lastly, the University of Florida used RoomSync to build community at an early step of the college transition process—during roommate selection. Those roommates who matched with Room-Sync tended to have less conflict, building a more supportive environment throughout the institution, which would lead to increased academic and social integration.

Guiding Student Sentiment

Not all content has to be academic or directly related to a functional area in order to engage students. TJ Willis, associate director of University Student Centers at North Carolina State University, provided an example of a viral post he shared on the student union's Facebook page. In February 2013, the temperature and weather fluctuated wildly in Raleigh. Given that conversations about the weather are usually deemed safe for casual conversations, especially with people you don't know well, TJ realized an opportunity for engagement (as well as an opportunity to show off his wicked Photoshopping skills). He created the picture

153

Figure 4.5. North Carolina State Student Union weather montage created by TJ Willis.

shown in figure 4.5 by downloading screenshots from a live student union construction webcam.

The post was a huge success, based on previous engagement metrics. More than 3,000 people engaged with the post. It was liked 226 times and shared 210 times. You may wonder how such a viral picture, with no clear connection to academics or student development, might help students. There are a number of possibilities. First, research shows that engaging students with social media can translate to offline engagement both in the classroom and on campus (Bosch, 2009; Hurt et al., 2012; Junco, Heiberger & Loken, 2011; Schroeder & Greenbowe, 2009). Engagement with social media does not have to solely focus on professional or academic matters. As in the offline world, people under stress respond well to breaks from that stress, and social media can help by allowing professional content to be interspersed with levity and curiosity. Second, the widespread sharing of TJ's post helped publicize two things: the student union construction project and the union's new Facebook account. The student union did not have a Facebook account before the construction, and therefore the only account that existed was one documenting the construction progress. In a sense, this viral post encouraged student implicit learning and informal learning as students learned that the broader university community was also discussing the wildly fluctuating weather. Third, learning about the culture of the broader university community helped support student academic and social integration.

James McHaley shared how he and his team turned "bad publicity" into continued engagement at Northwestern University. In the summer of 2012, the university closed three popular restaurants at the Norris University Center. Unfortunately, students found out via Twitter before there was an official announcement, and reactions were mostly negative, which forced James and his team to take a reactive stance. However, instead of reacting defensively, they responded to students with humor (see figure 4.6). They didn't stop there—although the team couldn't announce

Figure 4.6. Northwestern University Norris Center tweets about restaurant closures.

what the new restaurant would be because the contract wasn't signed yet, they reassured students they would be pleased with the new food options. Furthermore, the team ran a contest asking students to guess the new restaurant from hints such as small portions of the logo. The first to guess correctly on Facebook and Twitter were awarded a forty-dollar gift card to the new restaurant. Even though this happened while Northwestern was still in summer mode, engagement was strong, with both positive and negative online feedback from students. Once it was announced that Rick Bayless's Frontera Fresco was opening in the fall, the reactions were positive. Through this process, James and his team went from having to engage in a reactive stance to becoming proactive, guiding the conversation and engaging students in the unveiling process. Before social media, students would have had to wait for the restaurant to open, and there would have been time to build negative sentiment about being "out of the loop." However, with social media, James and his staff were able to help guide the initial "back-channel" disappointment and generate excitement about the new restaurant.

In ways that we couldn't do before the advent of social media, North Carolina State University and Northwestern University were able to guide student feelings about changes happening on their campuses. Through the use of social media, students felt more involved in the process, leading to more positive sentiments about their institutions. These examples show how student affairs professionals not only can learn about student sentiment through social media listening but also can change sentiment through informal learning. Changing sentiment in the ways shown in Northwestern example can go a long way toward improving students' feelings of connection to their institutions, and by extension improving their academic and social integration.

Promoting Networking Skills

Jeff Pelletier, the associate director of Ohio Union events at the Ohio State University, reported: "Unlike many of my colleagues, I am comfortable initiating contact with students on social media (which for me is primarily Twitter, then Facebook, with LinkedIn making a more recent charge). I will connect with men in the fraternity I advise, students who work in our union, or students I have a face-to-face connection with as the result of a program or presentation." Jeff explained that through his interactions on Twitter, he has helped students either get a job or advance professionally. He also shared three specific examples: (1) He retweeted a job posting for a beverage distributing company; one of the students who follows him saw it, applied, and ended up getting the position. Interestingly, the student was not following the original account that the tweet came from, so without the connection to Jeff, she might not have come across the posting. (2) Jeff posted a tweet about an intern position with Coca-Cola; one of his students (who happened to be a student in the fraternity he advises) saw the tweet, spoke to Jeff about the position in person, and ended up getting hired. (3) Another student saw a job posting Jeff retweeted from the city's leadership team, and because they had built a relationship that included contact on social media, she asked him to be a reference. The student got the position and ultimately became the social media manager for the city.

In very effective ways, Jeff leveraged social media to build and maintain his relationships with students, and these relationships have been very beneficial for students. It is exactly through such informal learning that students feel both academically and socially connected to their institution—learning that there is someone at the institution who cares about students as individuals. These staff-student connections can be very powerful in supporting student persistence and also, as Jeff's examples show, in helping students to be successful beyond college. Jeff's third example suggests that his connection to the student via social media may have helped her to learn informally (and perhaps even implicitly) about appropriate professional uses of social media that she was then able to transfer to her position managing social media use for the city.

Josh Kohnert at Western Michigan University described how he and his colleagues used social media for a "Michigan Industry Road Trip" sponsored by Career Services. Students were already prepared for networking with professionals during these company visits, but Josh and his colleagues were interested in incorporating Twitter into the experience, so students could learn about online networking and how to maintain a professional online presence. Josh and his colleagues thought it a good idea to help students start to build a positive online presence, as more and more companies are searching online for candidates and evaluating them based on their social media profiles (CareerBuilder.com, 2012). There were two informal learning objectives for the road trip that influenced the use of Twitter: for students to be able to communicate their skills and to learn networking techniques. Josh and his colleagues considered other social media tools but decided on Twitter because of the ability to interact with company Twitter accounts and network publicly. Specifically, they chose Twitter because it was available on mobile platforms, it was easy to teach, and its required brevity compelled students to think about what they wanted to say. Josh and his colleagues developed the #MIRoadTrip(Year) hashtag in order to aggregate the conversations about the trip. In the first year of the trip they did not require Twitter use, nor did they provide guidance about what to post. Even so, eight of the fourteen students participated and engaged with company accounts, discussed the experience with each other, and provided "valuable and concise insight about how the trip was impacting them as future engineers."

Given the success of the intervention (based on their review of Twitter activity), Josh and his team decided to integrate Twitter into the second year of the trip. As a separate matter from the trip objectives, the strategic planning committee in Student Affairs, of which Josh is a member, was tasked with "designing, implementing, and assessing" a social media intervention. They used the road trip as their evaluation project, with this learning objective: "Students will be able to define a professional online identity as well as describe their identity development plan." This time, Josh and his team made Twitter a requirement and taught students how to use it as part of the pre-trip training session. Josh reported that while each of the eighteen students had posted at least one tweet during the trip, more than 50 percent had posted at least twenty tweets. Again, Josh reported the students had great interactions with company Twitter accounts and were very engaged with each other. Josh and two other staff members were directly engaged and participated in the conversations with students on Twitter by retweeting, sending replies to questions, and asking questions to help students reflect on their experiences. Furthermore, the staff members provided a model by also posting their own reflections about the trip. The second year saw a substantial increase in students posting photos of the trip and of their evening activities, which Josh planned to use to market the trip for the next year.

Josh identified two major informal learning outcomes of Twitter use during the road trip: (1) Even though many of the students didn't have Twitter accounts before the road trip, the group continues to stay active on Twitter communicating with each other. (2) Students have been interested in talking about their online professional self-presentation and how they can leverage it to their advantage. In this context, students defined online self-presentation as creating "an identity suitable for prospective employers" that conveyed their "brand" in a professional manner (Kohnert, 2013). An examination of the tweet archive for the road trip found that students posted reflections of their experiences, interactions with the companies they visited (for instance, tweets thanking the companies for hosting them), and tweets and pictures sharing what they were doing in their free time. Evaluation of the intervention found that students either enjoyed their ability to "reflect and keep track" of their experience or were disappointed that they could not participate because of Internet connectivity issues. Unsurprisingly, students who had good experiences reported they would continue to use Twitter for professional networking and to obtain information about their field. Overall, students wanted to learn more and receive education about how to use other social media sites professionally.

This example illustrates an effective process by which the social media intervention was planned, instituted, and assessed. Josh and his colleagues decided on a priori learning objectives, chose a social media service based on the learning objectives and the affordances of the tool, assessed the intervention, and made refinements to the intervention in the following year based on assessment results from the previous year. The activities engaged in on Twitter were directly related to the purposes of the road trip—communicating in a professional manner and presenting oneself and one's skills effectively to employers. Furthermore, incorporating Twitter in these ways allowed students to learn how to interact with potential employers online. In today's work environment, many job searches are fueled by social media (as is evident in the previous examples shared by Jeff Pelletier), and this intervention allowed students to interact with potential employers and to learn the cultural norms and values of the Twitter platform (which are decidedly different from the cultures and norms of other forms of social media and which might be an emerging literacy practice (Greenhow & Gleason, 2012)). As has

160

been shown by our research on Twitter, interacting with students on the platform leads to increases in engagement and increases in staff-student offline interactions (Junco, Heiberger & Loken, 2011).

Through informal learning, Jeff Pelletier taught his students the value of networking through social media, while Josh Kohnert taught students the power of using Twitter for networking. Josh and Jeff took what typically happens through implicit learning and created deliberate informal learning experiences, in which learning how to connect with other professionals was made intentional. While networking is important for career development, networking skills are rarely taught at universities, formally or informally, signaling an important role student affairs professionals can play.

Modeling Appropriate Online Behavior

In these examples, those responsible for social media use modeled appropriate interactions and communication. For instance, Jessica Fantini showed her RAs, desk staff, and residents that her hall was a welcoming environment and open to discussing student concerns in productive ways. Eric Heilmeier's team answered questions for incoming students and, in doing so, modeled a professional yet helpful online tone. TJ Willis modeled appropriate online interactions about the weather, while James McHaley and his team reshaped student's negative online conversations into more constructive positive dialogue. James and his team also used humor in professional ways to lighten the mood of the conversation and in doing so modeled a way for students to defuse potentially problematic online interactions. Lastly, Jeff Pelletier in the Ohio Union and Josh Kohnert at Western Michigan modeled the power of positive online interactions in both supporting students and in professional networking.

Typically, students learn how to interact with others through implicit and informal learning of communication norms. However, development of interpersonal communication skills can be made more explicit through the use of social media. While traditionally we've been able to directly guide some students in learning these skills, social media allow us to widen our reach to encompass more students and to teach these skills more directly. Helping students learn about how to communicate online helps them discover ways that they can improve their online professional self-presentation (discussed in chapter 7). As more employers are using social media to research candidates and are making hiring decisions based on what they find, students need to understand not only how their online self-presentation is viewed by others, but also how to engage in these spaces in ways that help their career development rather than hindering it (CareerBuilder.com, 2012).

Student affairs professionals have an opportunity and an obligation to help students learn how to be good online citizens. As explained in the next chapter, faculty are not using social media much in formal learning settings, missing an opportunity to teach students how to interact effectively online. As we have helped students engage with their campus community offline, student affairs professionals are the higher education professionals perhaps best suited to help students engage with their campus and the broader international community online. In so doing, we can help them learn about diverse ways of thought and other cultures—for social media are generally without national boundaries.

In order to help students learn how to be successful online citizens, student affairs professionals must themselves learn how to engage in online social spaces effectively. As highlighted in chapter 6, professionals who already use social media must shift from a *social-personal* perspective to a *social-educational* one. That is, they must understand how they have used social media casually (with friends and family) and learn to use social media to convey professional expectations of online communication. Through this process, student affairs professionals can model online civil discourse, important for building community at their institutions and for helping students be successful more broadly in society (Junco & Chickering, 2010).

CONCLUSION

These examples are a great start in showing how to use social media successfully to promote informal learning in student affairs, but we must continue to collect data on effectiveness. Social media allow student affairs professionals to collect data on student participation with the technology. Platforms like Facebook and HootSuite provide data on student interaction with content. Although those data are helpful in evaluating how the technologies are used, it is essential to evaluate data beyond simple usage statistics: for instance, how TJ Logan evaluated student retention and roommate conflicts between students who used the roommate matching service and those who didn't, or how Josh Kohnert evaluated students' reactions to using Twitter as part of their industry road trip.

As universities continue to adopt social media as tools for academic good, more data need to be collected and disseminated about effective practices. It's not enough to know that incoming students want to interact with university social media accounts and to offer sites that just "push" information (Noel-Levitz, 2012). In fact, it's necessary to learn how to engage in social media practices that will effectively help students transition to college; feel connected to their institution, faculty, and peer group; and develop important academic skills such as information literacy, critical thinking, digital identity development, and self-advocacy. There is hope that in the years to come, student affairs professionals will document and add to the body of literature to show how what they do with social media impacts these desired outcomes of a college education.

Practical Tips

1. If you are going to use social media for informal learning, it is important to do the following:
   a. Consider whether social media are the appropriate tool for your intervention.
   b. Identify learning outcomes for your intervention.
   c. Match the affordances of the social media tool to your learning outcomes.
   d. Use a theoretical model to integrate social media in educationally relevant ways.
   e. Review research and practical examples to discover effective uses of social media for informal learning.
   f. Engage with students on the platform.
   g. Engage in activities on the sites or services that lead to more positive learning outcomes.
   h. Model appropriate online behavior.
   i. Evaluate the outcomes of your intervention.
2. Use social media to encourage these outcomes:
   a. Student-student affairs professional contact.
   b. Cooperation among students.
   c. Active learning.
   d. Prompt feedback.
   e. Communication of high expectations.
   f. Respect for diverse ways of learning.

REFERENCES

Astin, A. W. (1984). Student involvement: A developmental theory for higher education. *Journal of College Student Personnel, 25*(4), 297–308.

Bachrach, Y., Kosinski, M., Graepel, T., Kohli, P., & Stillwell, D. (2012). Personality and patterns of Facebook usage. *Proceedings of the 3rd Annual ACM Web Science Conference,* 24–32.

Barnes, N. G., & Lescault, A. M. (2011). *Social Media Adoption Soars as Higher-Ed Experiments and Reevaluates Its Use of New Communications Tools.* University of Massachusetts Dartmouth Center for Marketing Research Report.

Bosch, T. E. (2009). Using online social networking for teaching and learning: Facebook use at the University of Cape Town. *Communicatio: South African Journal for Communication Theory and Research, 35*(2), 185–200.

boyd, d. (2007). *Why Youth (Heart) Social Network Sites: The Role of Networked Publics in Teenage Social Life.* MacArthur Foundation Series on Digital Learning: Youth, Identity, and Digital Media Volume (ed. David Buckingham). Cambridge, MA: MIT Press.

CareerBuilder.com. (2012). Thirty-seven percent of companies use social networks to research potential job candidates, according to new CareerBuilder Survey. Retrieved February 2, 2014, from http://www.careerbuilder.com/share/aboutus/pressreleasesdetail.aspx?id=pr691&sd=4%2F18%2F2012&ed=4%2F18%2F2099.

Chickering, A. W., & Gamson, Z. F. (1987). Seven principles for good practice in undergraduate education. *AAHE Bulletin,* 3–7.

DeAndrea, D. C., Ellison, N. B., LaRose, R., Steinfield, C., & Fiore, A. (2011). Serious social media: On the use of social media for improving students' adjustment to college. *The Internet and Higher Education, 15*(1), 15–23.

Dennen, V. P. (2008). Pedagogical lurking: Student engagement in non-posting discussion behavior. *Computers in Human Behavior, 24*(4), 1624–1633.

Eckles, J. E., & Stradley, E. G. (2011). A social network analysis of student retention using archival data. *Social Psychology of Education, 15*(2), 165–180.

Ellison, N. B., Steinfield, C., & Lampe, C. (2007). The benefits of Facebook "friends:" Social capital and college students' use of online social network sites. *Journal of Computer-Mediated Communication, 12*(4), 1143–1168.

Ellison, N. B., Steinfield, C., & Lampe, C. (2011). Connection strategies: Social capital implications of Facebook-enabled communication practices. *New Media & Society, 13*(6), 873–892.

Ellison, N. B., Vitak, J., Gray, R., & Lampe, C. (2014). Cultivating social resources on social network sites: Facebook relationship maintenance behaviors and their role in social capital processes. *Journal of Computer-Mediated Communication,* DOI: 10.1111/jcc4.12078.

Evans, N. J., Forney, D. S., Guido, F. M., Patton, L. D., & Renn, K. A. (2009). *Student Development in College: Theory, Research, and Practice.* San Francisco: Jossey-Bass.

Farrell, E. F. (2006). Judging roommates by their Facebook cover. *Chronicle of Higher Education, 53*(2), A53.

Gonzales, A. L., & Hancock, J. T. (2011). Mirror, mirror on my Facebook wall: Effects of exposure to Facebook on self-esteem. *Cyberpsychology, Behavior and Social Networking, 14*(1–2), 79–83.

Gosling, S. D., Augustine, A. A., Vazire, S., Holtzman, N., & Gaddis, S. (2011). Manifestations of personality in online social networks: Self-reported Facebook-related behaviors and observable profile information. *Cyberpsychology, Behavior and Social Networking, 14*(9), 483–488.

Greenhow, C., & Gleason, B. (2012). Twitteracy: Tweeting as a new literacy practice. *The Educational Forum, 76*(4), 464–478.

Heiberger, G., & Harper, R. (2008). Have you Facebooked Astin lately? Using technology to increase student involvement. In R. Junco & D. M. Timm (eds.), Using emerging technologies to enhance student engagement. *New Directions for Student Services,* Issue 124, pp. 19–35. San Francisco: Jossey-Bass.

Higher Education Research Institute (HERI). (2007). College freshmen and online social networking sites. Retrieved February 2, 2014, from http://www.heri.ucla.edu/PDFs/pubs/briefs/brief-091107 -SocialNetworking.pdf.

Hollyhead, A., Edwards, D. J., & Holt, G. D. (2012). The use of virtual learning environment (VLE) and social network site (SNS) hosted forums in higher education: A preliminary examination. *Industry and Higher Education, 26*(5), 369–379.

Hurt, N. E., Moss, G. S., Bradley, C. L., Larson, L. R., Lovelace, M. D., Prevost, L. B., Riley, N., et al. (2012). The "Facebook" effect: College students' perceptions of online discussions in the age of social networking. *International Journal for the Scholarship of Teaching and Learning, 6*(2), 1–24.

Ito, M., Baumer, S., Bittanti, M., Boyd, D., Cody, R., Herr, B., et al. (2009). *Hanging Out, Messing Around, Geeking Out: Living and Learning with New Media.* Cambridge: MIT Press.

Junco, R. (2012). The relationship between frequency of Facebook use, participation in Facebook activities, and student engagement. *Computers & Education, 58*(1), 162–171.

Junco, R., & Chickering, A. W. (2010, September/October). Civil discourse in the age of social media. *About Campus, 15*(4), 12–18.

Junco, R., Elavsky, C. M., & Heiberger, G. (2012). Putting Twitter to the test: Assessing outcomes for student collaboration, engagement, and success. *British Journal of Educational Technology, 44*(2), 273–287.

Junco, R., Heiberger, G., & Loken, E. (2011). The effect of Twitter on college student engagement and grades. *Journal of Computer Assisted Learning, 27*(2), 119–132.

Junco, R., & Mastrodicasa, J. (2007). *Connecting to the Net.Generation: What Higher Education Professionals Need To Know about Today's Students.* Washington, DC: NASPA.

Kim, Y., & Khang, H. (2014). Revisiting civic voluntarism predictors of college students' political participation in the context of social media. *Computers in Human Behavior, 36*, 114–121.

Kohnert, J. (2013). *Using Twitter on the Michigan Industry Road Trip.* 4C–Social Media Committee Report, University of Michigan.

Madden, M., Lenhart, A., Cortesi, S., Gasser, U., Duggan, M., & Smith, A. (2013). *Teens, Social Media, and Privacy.* Pew Internet and American Life Project Report. Retrieved July 7, 2013, from http://

www.pewinternet.org/Reports/2013/Teens-Social-Media-And-Privacy.aspx.

Manago, A. M., Taylor, T., & Greenfield, P. M. (2012). Me and my 400 friends: The anatomy of college students' Facebook networks, their communication patterns, and well-being. *Developmental Psychology, 48*(2), 369–380.

Mehdizadeh, S. (2010). Self-presentation 2.0: Narcissism and self-esteem on Facebook. *Cyberpsychology, Behavior and Social Networking, 13*(4), 357–64.

Moore, K., & McElroy, J. C. (2012). The influence of personality on Facebook usage, wall postings, and regret. *Computers in Human Behavior, 28*(1), 267–274.

National Association of Colleges and Employers. (2013). *Career Services Use of Social Media Technologies*. Career Advisory Board Report. Retrieved February 2, 2014, from: http://www.careeradvisoryboard .org/public/uploads/2013/05/Career-Services-Use-of-Social -Media-Technologies-Report.pdf.

Noel-Levitz. (2012). *2012 E-Expectations Report*. Retrieved August 20, 2013, from https://www.noellevitz.com/documents/shared/ Papers_and_Research/2012/2012_E-Expectations.pdf.

Ong, E., Ang, R., Ho, J., Lim, J., & Goh, D. (2011). Narcissism, extraversion, and adolescents' self-presentation on Facebook. *Personality and Individual Differences, 50*(2), 180–185.

Orr, E. S., Sisic, M., Ross, C., Simmering, M. G., Arseneault, J. M., & Orr, R. R. (2009). The influence of shyness on the use of Facebook in an undergraduate sample. *Cyberpsychology & Behavior, 12*(3), 337–340.

Pascarella, E., & Terenzini, P. (2005). *How College Affects Students: A Third Decade of Research*. San Francisco: Jossey-Bass.

Pempek, T. A., Yermolayeva, Y. A., & Calvert, S. L. (2009). College students' social networking experiences on Facebook. *Journal of Applied Developmental Psychology, 30*(3), 227–238.

Ross, C., Orr, E. S., Sisic, M., Arseneault, J. M., Simmering, M. G., & Orr, R. R. (2009). Personality and motivations associated with Facebook use. *Computers in Human Behavior, 25*(2), 578–586.

Schroeder, J., & Greenbowe, T. J. (2009). The chemistry of Facebook: Using social networking to create an online community for the organic chemistry laboratory. *Innovate: Journal of Online Education, 5*(4). Retrieved February 2, 2014, from http://gator.uhd.edu/~williams/AT/ChemOfFB.htm.

Seaman, J., & Tinti-Kane, H. (2013). *Social Media for Teaching and Learning*. Pearson Annual Survey of Social Media Use by Higher Education Faculty. Retrieved February 2, 2014, from http://www.pearsonlearningsolutions.com/higher-education/social-media-survey.php.

Seidman, G. (2012). Self-presentation and belonging on Facebook: How personality influences social media use and motivations. *Personality and Individual Differences, 54*(3), 402–407.

Selwyn, N. (2009). Faceworking: Exploring students' education-related use of Facebook. *Learning, Media and Technology, 34*(2), 157–174.

Tazghini, S., & Siedlecki, K. L. (2013). A mixed method approach to examining Facebook use and its relationship to self-esteem. *Computers in Human Behavior (29)*3, 827–832.

Thomas, S. L. (2000). Ties that bind: A social network approach to understanding student integration and persistence. *Journal of Higher Education, 71*(5), 591–615.

Tinto, V. (1993). *Leaving College: Rethinking the Causes and Cures of Student Attrition* (2nd ed.). Chicago: The University of Chicago Press.

Valenzuela, S., Park, N., & Kee, K. F. (2009). Is there social capital in a social network site? Facebook use and college students' life satisfaction, trust, and participation. *Journal of Computer-Mediated Communication, 14*(4), 875–901.

Valliere, K., Endersby, L., & Brinton, M. (2013). *Student Affairs Technology Competencies Survey*. NASPA Technology Knowledge Community.

Vitak, J., Zube, P., Smock, A., Carr, C. T., Ellison, N., & Lampe, C. (2011). It's complicated: Facebook users' political participation in the 2008 election. *Cyberpsychology, Behavior and Social Networking, 14*(3), 107–114.

Yu, A. Y., Tian, S. W., Vogel, D., & Kwok, R. C.-W. (2010). Can learning be virtually boosted? An investigation of online social networking impacts. *Computers & Education, 55*, 1495–1503.

CHAPTER 5

Formal Learning Using Social Media

Review these two pictures of college classrooms—one from the 1900s and one from today (figures 5.1a and 5.1b). You'll no doubt notice many differences, such as the typewriters versus computers, or the fact that today's students are much more casually dressed, or the hairdos (oh, those hairdos!). What you might not notice are the similarities—college classrooms are still places where students sit and *receive* knowledge. The only active participation necessary is for students to take notes (and many don't even do that). To the disservice of our students, very little engagement will take place in a 60-, 90-, or 120-minute lecture course. For student affairs professionals who teach as faculty as well as for those who support students as learners both in and out of the classroom, there is ample opportunity to engage students through the use of social media both in their formal and informal learning environments.

Figure 5.1a. A college classroom from the 1900s.

Figure 5.1b. A college classroom today.

Within the past ten to fifteen years and with the advent of more wired campuses, classrooms have expanded beyond the physical. Specifically, many college classrooms are now *hybridized*, having both offline and online components. The mix of hybridization varies by course, with either few or many assignments being completed online. Online assignments in hybrid or *blended* courses are typically organized, handled, completed, and graded through learning or course management systems (LMSs or CMSs). LMSs and CMSs both have online discussion boards, support for quizzes, course materials, and a grade book. LMSs, however, are more comprehensive and broad allowing for administrative functions like enrollment-related tasks. For the purposes of this discussion, the terms are used interchangeably as they are in the literature to denote the course management features of the applications— namely, the online discussion boards. Higher education institutions rely primarily on these traditional platforms for their online course support (Dabbagh & Kitsantas, 2011). Students have shown a preference for using social media over CMSs and will often create course-related groups without input from faculty (Bosch, 2009; Hollyhead, Edwards & Holt, 2012; Hurt, Moss, Bradley, Larson & Lovelace, 2012; Schroeder & Greenbowe, 2009). CMSs are not (and were not intended to be) engaging platforms like social media sites. Indeed, Facebook is determined to be an engaging platform, going so far as to measure its success in terms of user engagement (Heiberger & Harper, 2008; Morrin, 2007). As we know from the review in chapter 2, student engagement is a powerful force for student growth both inside and outside of the classroom.

Student affairs professionals recognize the importance of student engagement in supporting student development. While some student affairs professionals engage in classroom teaching, all student affairs practitioners have a great deal of experience both in and out of the classroom and provide important support for students in all of their learning contexts. For instance, a residence hall director might help a student who is having difficulty organizing time to study effectively for a difficult course; a career services professional might recognize that a student who is struggling might need a referral to the counseling center; during orientation, a staff member might identify and follow up with a student who is at risk academically by discussing the student's

173

motivation for being in college. Furthermore, student affairs professionals engage in formal learning by providing programming that takes place in formal learning environments (for instance, orientation programs).

These examples illustrate how student affairs professionals directly influence formal learning, even without participating in classroom instruction. In order to best support student learning, it is helpful for student affairs professionals to understand how social media influence both informal and formal learning. While the previous chapter explored *implicit* and *informal* learning, we now turn to how social media can be used for *formal* learning.

FORMAL LEARNING USING SOCIAL MEDIA

As discussed in the previous chapter, *formal learning* is learning that happens in formal learning environments like a college classroom. Almost all of the research conducted on using social media for formal learning has focused on Facebook and Twitter; therefore, this section will focus on those social media as well. It is possible and highly probable that other social technologies can be used for engaging students in the learning process as effectively as these sites—and perhaps even more effectively. The goal here is to review processes for effective learning using these tools in the hope that the reader can transfer these processes to newer technologies as they become more relevant to the student experience. For example, it is possible that in the near future educators will use Instagram or Vine for students to document learning objectives.

Encouraging students to use social media not only places more responsibility on students themselves for their learning but also takes some of the responsibility off of the educator. One can clearly see the benefits of such an approach, especially when viewed in the context of developing lifelong learners. However, one can also see the concerns inherent in moving beyond the guided process of the traditional college curriculum. We *can* do both—educators can guide students as well as encourage them to take charge of their learning, and these two facets of learning can remain in balance indefinitely. Take for instance the issue of information literacy reviewed later in this chapter. Students (and many adults) lack the necessary skills to evaluate information they find online. Educators can help students build the critical thinking abilities necessary to refine their evaluations of online information. Ultimately, social media use in courses can help educators teach students how to share, collaborate, and think more critically in a networked society.

EFFECTIVE USES OF SOCIAL MEDIA FOR LEARNING

In chapter 4, we looked at possible uses for social media for informal learning using Chickering and Gamson's (1987) principles for good practice in undergraduate education. Let's use those same principles to examine social media use in formal learning environments, especially as it relates to student engagement.

1. *Student-faculty contact.* Using social media as part of a course can increase the number and the quality of student-faculty interactions (Bosch, 2009; Junco, Heiberger & Loken, 2011; Schroeder & Greenbowe, 2009).
2. *Cooperation among students.* Because of the dynamic nature of social media, their use in courses can help to encourage student cooperation and collaboration (Hollyhead, Edwards & Holt, 2012; Junco, Elavsky & Heiberger, 2012; Schroeder & Greenbowe, 2009).
3. *Active learning.* Using social media to continue class discussions allows students to be active participants in the learning

175

process—extending what they learn in the classroom to personal or professional settings (Junco, Elavsky & Heiberger, 2012; Junco, Heiberger & Loken, 2011).

4. *Prompt feedback.* One of the major benefits of using social media in the classroom is that students can receive prompt feedback from each other as well as from their instructors, allowing them to focus their learning more appropriately (Junco, Elavsky & Heiberger, 2012; Junco, Heiberger & Loken, 2011).

5. *Time on task.* Another affordance of using social media in courses is that when planned appropriately, they can increase the time students spend interacting with course content. This leads not only to content-level knowledge but to further engagement (Junco, Heiberger & Loken, 2011).

6. *Communicating high expectations.* While the use of social media, per se, does not communicate high expectations, as discussed later in this chapter, educators modeling appropriate uses of social media can communicate high expectations for student online work, which translates to offline academic behaviors (Junco, Heiberger & Loken, 2011).

7. *Respecting diverse ways of learning.* The use of social media communicates to students that the educator is willing to engage in learning strategies that encompass the different ways that students learn—especially today's students, who show preferences for using social media in their courses (Hollyhead, Edwards & Holt, 2012; Hurt, Moss, Bradley, Larson & Lovelace, 2012; Junco, 2012c).

EVIDENCE-BASED PRACTICES FOR SUPPORTING FORMAL LEARNING WITH SOCIAL MEDIA

The following outline presents evidence-based ways educators can support classroom instruction with social media.

176

1. How social media are used is important

Integrating social media in relevant ways in the classroom begins with an evaluation of the existing course curriculum.

a. *Are the goals of the course congruent with social media?* Perhaps the instructor is interested in ensuring that there is a great deal of discussion in the course; however, there is also little class time to cover all of the material. In this case, social media can be used to extend class discussion, which increases students' time on task, engagement, and ultimately academic outcomes (Junco, Heiberger & Loken, 2011).

b. *Is the instructor's style congruent with using social media?* The *Web 2.0* mentality is reviewed in chapter 2—educators who are more interested in taking risks with their curricular design and teaching style might do better with integrating social media into their course. This Web 2.0 mentality is often related to constructivist and emergentist philosophies about learning. As Osberg and Biesta (2008) stated, "Knowledge is understood, rather, to 'emerge' as we, as human beings, participate in the world. Knowledge, in other words, does not exist except in our participatory actions" (p. 313). Educators who hold these views are more likely to "let go" of their need to control the learning process and allow students to construct their own learning through various methods, including the use of social media. Furthermore, the reality of using social media in the classroom is that the instructor must expend both physical and psychological energy to engage with students on the platform. Recall our study that found that merely adding Twitter to a course as a conversation tool did not improve student engagement or academic performance (Junco, Elavsky & Heiberger, 2012).

c. *Is the subject matter appropriate to discuss on social media?* Some subjects are better served by the use of social media than

177

others. For instance, a calculus course might not be the best environment in which to use Twitter, for there will be little discussion and much use of symbols and formulas that may be difficult to reproduce online. However, a psychology course would be a great environment in which to use social media, for there can be engaging discussion outside of class time, leaving class time for learning new material and explanation of concepts. In support of this point, Hurt and colleagues (2012) found differential effects of Facebook use in a women's studies course and a philosophy course.

2. Decide on which tool to use

As explored in chapter 1, the design-specific and design-driven affordances of each site make them better or less suited for different uses. Twitter is a great tool for short communications; however, Twitter does not lend itself well to a threaded conversation, as would a Facebook group.

3. Plan assignments

Plan lessons so that online discussions are an integral part of the course. While students will often bring online discussions into the classroom and feel more confident in their face-to-face discussions, educators can facilitate this process by bringing up online discussions during class time. Plan how you will grade student assignments on social media. If you have already used online threaded discussions, you can use a similar grading rubric. If you use a Facebook group, for instance, you can have students earn points by responding to questions you propose and by responding to other students.

178

4. Set aside time to teach students about social media

Chapter 1 reviews the issue of digital inequalities. Some students are not on social media because of socioeconomic inequalities. And some students choose not to use social media. Both of these groups will not be as fluent in the cultural norms of social media; educators must be sure to teach them how the site or sites being used work and what is expected of students. It is important to start these sessions at the most basic level—that is, showing students how to sign up for an account, how to update their profile information, how to post updates, and so on.

5. Engage with students

It is critical that educators engage with students on the social media platform to realize desired educational outcomes (Junco, Elavsky & Heiberger, 2012). The affordances of a site like Facebook in the educational setting will not be realized without input from the educator. Keep in mind that including social media as part of a course is a curricular intervention, and, as such, it should be treated the way one would treat any other curricular intervention—by being engaged and monitoring, assessing, and encouraging student engagement. Such engagement helps to support academic integration. Students who used Facebook (Bosch, 2009) and Twitter (Junco, Heiberger & Loken, 2011) for formal learning activities felt that their professors were more approachable because of students' online interactions with the professors. It is useful to plan how you will engage with students on social media: Will you check the site every day? How will you reach students who are less engaged on the site? Our research has found that there were no benefits in engagement and academic performance for students whose instructors didn't engage with them on Twitter (Junco, Elavsky & Heiberger, 2012). Furthermore, students in a class where instructors contributed more frequently to the course Facebook group had better perceived learning outcomes (Hurt, Moss, Bradley, Larson & Lovelace, 2012). Consistently encourage student interactions on the site, but keep in mind that some students are learning by lurking.

6. *Engage in activities linked to positive outcomes*

We know from the research that certain activities are more predictive of positive student outcomes than others. For instance, sharing links on Facebook was positively related to student grades (Junco, 2012b). From this research, we know that encouraging students to collect and share information on Facebook will lead to more positive outcomes. Other research shows that students who interact with each other on Twitter are more engaged in the classroom and do better academically. Posting campus event reminders on Twitter led to better engagement, while posting course reminders led to better academic performance (Junco, Elavsky & Heiberger, 2012; Junco, Heiberger & Loken, 2011). Support students in using social media for academic and social integration. Make students explicitly aware of the benefits of using social media to make academic and social connections with their peers.

7. *Keep it professional*

The relationship between educators and students is a professional one, and it should be kept that way on social media. Educators are discouraged from sharing sensitive personal information on social media they are using for educational purposes. Students in Mazer and colleagues' (2007) study suggested that as educators

180

you not post about politics or "stuff you think students might make fun of you about" and that you be mindful of what others post on your wall (p. 12). Ensure that you have communicated the boundaries of your social media use with students—that is, how you are using the site or sites for professional purposes and that you expect the same types of community behaviors online as you do offline.

8. Model appropriate uses of social media

Students need guidance to make sure they are using social media in appropriate, ethical, and responsible ways and that they are engaged in productive and civil discourse (Junco & Chickering, 2010). Monitor online discussions to ensure that interactions remain civil and to rectify any academic misinformation that might arise. Educators can guide students directly through formal instruction; however, they can also allow students to *implicitly* and *informally* learn digital citizenship skills by modeling appropriate online behaviors, including civility, restraint, and productive academic and social communication. Furthermore, educators should discuss professional uses of social media in their respective fields. This includes discussing methods of creating effective professional online identities.

9. Plan for problems

Understand that issues will arise, as with any teaching method, that will need to be addressed. When we conducted one of our earlier Twitter studies, a student sent a tweet insinuating that she wanted to commit suicide. Another student communicated with her, and we were able to intervene and refer her to the counseling center. While such extreme cases will be few and far between, this example illustrates that students will share things on social media that they otherwise won't in the classroom as a result of the online disinhibition effect, described in detail in chapter 3.

10. *Leverage the online disinhibition effect*

Luckily, the online disinhibition effect will also help students engage in more rich conversations because students are more likely to share comments, questions, and personal experience they might be too reticent to share in class (Bosch, 2009). Once they share these things online, students are more likely to share in class and to be even more engaged (Junco, Heiberger & Loken, 2011). Knowing this, educators can engage students in more thorough examinations of their thoughts and feelings about critical issues. Educators can bring online discussions back into the classroom and ask students to expand on what they have shared. Indeed, examination of tweets from one of our studies found that first-year students who used Twitter were much more open and allowed themselves to be more vulnerable when discussing the course common reading (Junco, Heiberger & Loken, 2011).

11. *Assess the intervention*

Evaluating the effect of including social media in your courses does not have to be a Herculean effort, but it is fruitful to collect information to make adjustments for future courses. What do you want to know about social media use in your course? Perhaps you will ask students for their opinions and whether they feel that social media use in the course helped or inhibited their learning. Perhaps you will create a structured survey to compare responses across courses. Some variables to consider include student comfort with the technology, frequency of student posts, the extent to which online discussions were transferred offline, student engagement, and course outcomes.

182

EXAMPLES OF USING SOCIAL MEDIA IN COURSES

A survey conducted by Pearson showed that 41 percent of U.S. faculty reported using social media in their courses (Seaman & Tinti-Kane, 2013). However, blogs and wikis were the most used, with 26.9 percent of respondents reporting using them in their courses, podcasts were next with 16.3 percent, then LinkedIn, Facebook, and Twitter, with respectively 11.1 percent, 8.4 percent, and 4.1 percent using them in courses. Younger faculty were more likely to use social media in their courses than older faculty—suggesting that younger faculty are more willing to explore new teaching methods, especially those involving technology, perhaps because younger faculty grew up with social media for much of their lives and are more likely to use the sites personally. Indeed, the Pearson results show that 86.6 percent of faculty under the age of thirty-five engage in personal uses of social media, as compared with 63 percent of those fifty-five and over (Seaman & Tinti-Kane, 2013). While the results from the Pearson report are promising, there are some methodological issues to consider. There was an 8 percent return rate on the survey; because the survey was sent via e-mail, there is a greater probability that respondents had higher levels of Internet skills than those who did not respond and those who might not be able to be reached through e-mail. Internet skills are related to diversity of online site usage, so respondents might have been more likely to use social media than those who did not return the survey (Hargittai, 2010). Even so, the Pearson survey serves as a good starting point for evaluating how social media are being used in the classroom.

If we consider the most popular sites used by students, then the Pearson survey suggests that few educators are using them in their courses. Only 8.4 percent were using Facebook and 4.1 percent Twitter; this was an increase from the 2011 Pearson survey, which found that 4 percent were using Facebook and 2 percent were using Twitter (Moran, Seaman & Tinti-Kane, 2011). There is a long way to go before these sites are used in a substantial way in higher education. The more recent Pearson survey shows that the most often reported barriers to implementing social media were integrity of student submissions (72.4 percent of faculty said this was "very important" or "important"), concerns about privacy (62.7 percent), separate course and personal accounts (58.6 percent), grading and assessment (57.7 percent), inability to measure effectiveness (52.4 percent), lack of integration with LMS (45.3 percent), takes too much time to learn or use (41.4 percent), and lack of institutional support (35.8 percent) (Seaman & Tinti-Kane, 2013). (See figure 5.2 for a graphic representation of these results.)

Data from Pearson and from our research show that some educators interested in using social media like Facebook and Twitter in their courses hesitate to do so because of concerns about privacy, student lack of appreciation for such interventions, evaluation concerns, and lack of institutional support. Institutional support is important: if an institution does not recognize and reward innovative teaching methods, there is little incentive

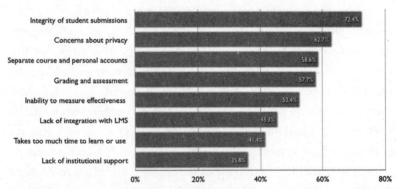

Figure 5.2. Most often reported barriers to the implementation of social media in courses as reported in the Pearson Survey (Seaman & Tinti-Kane, 2013).

184

for educators to develop their teaching skills to include social media use. Younger faculty are more likely to use social media in teaching, and yet they are also the ones most at risk because they have to meet requirements for promotion and tenure. In institutions that emphasize research over teaching, the scholarship of teaching and learning (that is, conducting research on teaching methods and outcomes) may not count as much as the scholarship of discovery in a discipline. In other words, faculty members who spend the time and energy to implement, assess, and publish the results of a social media intervention may find that publication won't be weighed as heavily as another sort of publication would in the promotion and tenure process.

How then can we engage students, given the limited structures and resources afforded to us through our current educational system? As was explained in chapter 2, social media can be used in ways that help improve student involvement, and this type of intervention is a very efficient method of increasing engagement. Put another way, the time and resources spent in engaging students through the use of social media in the classroom yields far more powerful effects than time and resources spent in other types of educational interventions (Junco, Heiberger & Alonso-Garcia, in preparation; Junco, Heiberger & Loken, 2011). At a time when students spend more time in paid employment, less time on campus, and less time studying, we need more engaging learning spaces to help them be more academically integrated (Babcock & Marks, 2010; Kuh, 2009). The engagement benefits of social media translate into the classroom, with student online participation leading to improved quality and quantity of student class discussions (Bosch, 2009; Junco, Heiberger & Loken, 2011; Schroeder & Greenbowe, 2009). These benefits translate to broader educational gains. For instance, a Twitter intervention increased second-year persistence rates by 18 percent for students taking a first-year seminar. This increase was much larger than the 5 percent average difference found by Fidler (1991) for the persistence effects of first-year seminars (of note was the fact that Fidler (1991) did not find consistent benefits across all years of first-year seminars, a finding echoed by Keup's (2005–2006) study of nearly 20,000 first-year students).

Some educators who are interested in using social media in their courses hesitate because of fears that students will perceive such uses as an intrusion into "their space." During a two-year period, I conducted multiple studies integrating Twitter into courses and examining how Facebook might be used in similar ways. One interesting point emerged: when given the choice of technology to use as part of a course, students overwhelmingly chose Facebook (see also Hollyhead, Edwards & Holt, 2012; Hurt, Moss, Bradley, Larson & Lovelace, 2012). As part of one of these studies, we conducted extensive follow-up interviews with students. When we asked students about their preferences for the LMS, Twitter, or Ning (the technology used by students in a control condition), students overwhelmingly preferred Facebook. A couple of examples illustrate what many of them said:

> *"I think [using Facebook] would've been easier and a little more comfortable for people because I think pretty much everyone in my class had a Facebook and nobody had either one of these things."*
> *"I think that [Facebook] is a lot easier for people to use and since people generally get on there every day they are going to see the stuff and invites a lot quicker than others."*

Many of these students told us that they independently used Facebook to organize study groups, to ask questions of fellow classmates, and to catch up on missed work. So why did students prefer to use Facebook in their courses? Students in our sample gave us a variant of the same answer: all of their friends and classmates are on Facebook, and it's easy to use. In other words, Facebook has the user base to make academic conversations useful. In addition, since students are "always" on Facebook, it's easy to see when new comments are made to a post from a class (Junco, 2012a). This is in contrast to learning management systems (LMSs), which are unengaging and which students use only because of course requirements.

Other researchers have found similar results. Hurt and colleagues (2012) examined student outcomes from and preferences for Facebook use by assigning students to either use Facebook or the learning management system (LMS) in two courses. The researchers found that the Facebook group reported better educational outcomes than the LMS group. The researchers also found that 43 percent of the LMS users said they would have contributed more if they had used Facebook, while only 12 percent of Facebook users said they would have participated more with a switch to the LMS (Hurt, Moss, Bradley, Larson & Lovelace, 2012). Hurt and colleagues (2012) also found that students preferred Facebook because of its ease of use and their frequent use of the platform. Given this research as well as my work in this area, Facebook may be an effective and more engaging alternative to LMSs and course management systems.

Facebook

The Pearson survey found that faculty concern about privacy was a top barrier to implementation of social media, although only 15 percent of students in another study reported that they would feel their privacy was invaded by educational uses of Facebook (Roblyer, McDaniel, Webb, Herman & Witty, 2010). Furthermore,

187

students were more likely than faculty to agree that using Facebook for educational purposes would be convenient and less likely to agree that Facebook is "personal/social—not for education" (Roblyer, McDaniel, Webb, Herman & Witty, 2010). Roblyer and colleagues (2010) found that 23 percent of the 75 percent of faculty who had Facebook accounts were much more concerned about *their own* privacy being invaded if they used Facebook for educational purposes. Reluctant educators might already have the skills necessary to implement Facebook in their courses and might be helped by learning ways to use Facebook that would not allow students to invade their privacy. Interestingly enough, Mazer, Murphy, and Simonds (2007) found that teacher self-disclosure on Facebook was related to perceived student motivation, affective learning, and a more positive classroom climate, suggesting that faculty concerns about privacy are getting in the way of beneficial educational processes.

Students are more interested in using Facebook than any other social platform in their courses; however, academic uses must be appropriately framed (Hurt, Moss, Bradley, Larson & Lovelace, 2012; Junco, 2012a). If an educator says to students, "We're going to use Facebook in this course," students will be much less willing to do so than they would have if the educator had said, "We're going to use a Facebook group in this course to continue class discussions, to share course announcements, to post links to relevant news stories, and to document our work." An established and research-supported practice is to create a private group on Facebook and to have the instructor invite the students from the course. For instance, Hurt and colleagues (2012) described how instructors in their study created a private group and posted prompts to initiate discussion at least once a week. Using a private group would not allow students to have access to an educator's Facebook account and would alleviate the privacy concerns discovered in Seaman and Tinti-Kane's (2013) and Roblyer and colleagues' (2010) studies. In Hurt and colleagues' (2012) study, participation on Facebook was worth 8 percent of the students' final course grade, and instructors emphasized the importance of online discussion. Instructors shared a grading rubric with students that "outlined four main criteria: frequency of posts, connection to class material, conscientiousness, and critical thinking" (p. 6).

Facebook's affordances as an engaging tool far outweigh the affordances of the CMS and LMS discussion boards. Hollyhead and colleagues (2012) found that students preferred to create their own Facebook groups when no official course-related ones were available instead of using the LMS. Schroeder and Greenbowe (2009) found that while only 41 percent of a chemistry class joined the course Facebook group, there were 400 percent more posts on Facebook than on the course management system. Furthermore, these researchers reported that postings on the Facebook group "raised more complex topics and generated more detailed replies" than postings on the CMS (Schroeder & Greenbowe, 2009). Again, these increases in student engagement because of Facebook use echo the defining purpose of Facebook as a platform for engagement (Morrin, 2007). In the academic context, the affordances of Facebook, such as its emphasis on sharing, connecting, participation, and active engagement, align with the effective educational practices of active and collaborative learning—essential factors for student engagement (Chickering & Gamson, 1987; Kuh, 2009). Specifically, students' sharing of content such as links to news stories, communicating and collaborating with each other on course assignments, and engaging in class discussions in a Facebook group are exemplars of active and collaborative learning.

Using Facebook as a replacement for a CMS/LMS discussion board can help to improve student engagement and collaboration and lead to more in-depth discussions both online and offline (Hurt, Moss, Bradley, Larson & Lovelace, 2012; Junco, 2012c; Schroeder & Greenbowe, 2009). Indeed, using Facebook in this way can help students interact with educators, communicate more boldly, and improve in-class discussions (Bosch, 2009; Hurt, Moss, Bradley, Larson & Lovelace, 2012). Demystifying the professoriat is crucial in promoting student-to-student interactions and student-to-faculty interactions, both essential for student engagement, social and academic integration, and success (Bosch, 2009; Chickering & Gamson, 1987; Finn & Rock, 1997; Kuh, 2009; Kuh, Cruce, Shoup, Kinzie & Gonyea, 2008; Skinner, Kindermann & Furrer, 2009). Furthermore, demystifying the professoriat is exceedingly important in helping first-generation, low-income, and minority college students' academic integration (Pascarella & Terenzini, 2005). Through interactions on Facebook, students can learn that educators are approachable and can learn to seek help when they need it.

As suggested by my work (Junco, Elavsky & Heiberger, 2012) and the work of Hurt and colleagues (2012), it is vital that educators integrate Facebook into the course in educationally relevant ways (for instance, as a mode of discussing course content), that Facebook use be required, and that educators engage with students in the course group as much as possible. Forkosh-Baruch and Hershkovitz (2011) analyzed how higher education institutions were using social media and recommended that educators be encouraged to be involved on social media to enhance the social connections that make these sites academically useful. Hurt and colleagues (2012) found that students in one of the courses the researchers studied reported better outcomes, which the researchers believed resulted from the course instructor being much more engaged on Facebook. The researchers suggested that because the students perceived the instructor as more engaged, they were motivated to be more engaged themselves (Hurt, Moss, Bradley, Larson & Lovelace, 2012).

Twitter

To date, no controlled studies have evaluated the use of Facebook in order to improve student outcomes; however, the same does not hold for Twitter. We discovered that using Twitter in educationally relevant ways informed by Chickering and Gamson's (1987) seven principles for good practice in undergraduate education led to an increase in student engagement and overall semester GPA (Junco, Heiberger & Loken, 2011). This intervention had long-lasting effects, with students who were in the Twitter group being significantly more likely to be enrolled in their second year than those in the control group (Junco, Heiberger & Alonso-Garcia, in preparation). In a related study, we discovered elements for successful Twitter integration into a course (Junco, Elavsky & Heiberger, 2012). While some educators have used Twitter as a back channel to allow students to interact during course lectures, the most effective use of the platform is to engage students in ongoing academic and social dialogue. Just as with Facebook, the goal is to improve student relationships with each other and contact with professors and to enhance course discussions. As Bosch (2009), Schroeder and Greenbowe (2009), and Hurt and colleagues (2012) found with Facebook, we found that Twitter use led to more in-depth discussions that transferred to discussions in the classroom (Junco, Heiberger & Loken, 2011). Specifically, we found that students became more comfortable sharing their viewpoints in the online space, which led to increased social and academic integration, which in turn perhaps mediated additional outcomes such as self-esteem, satisfaction with university life, and performance proficiency—an example of how the online

191

disinhibition effect (described in chapter 3) helps students share more openly in offline academic settings when sharing online.

While Twitter can be a powerful tool for interaction, it does not have the same affordances as Facebook for classroom environments. Specifically, Twitter does not allow conversations to be easily viewed in their entirety (that is, threaded conversations). Additionally, viewing shared video, images, and other such content on Twitter often requires an additional step to access the content depending on the device or application used to access Twitter. Facebook also allows for the creation of closed groups, whereas on Twitter, all students' profiles must be set to private in order for there to be a semblance of privacy. Twitter affords students the ability to interact with more professional and scholarly sources than Facebook. For instance, students can follow scholars in their field and not only access the resources shared by these scholars but also ask questions about their work (Veletsianos, 2012). One semester, I had students write a blog post about the *Cluetrain Manifesto*, a book about online engagement for business. One of the students wrote a particularly interesting blog post that I tweeted to one of the authors of the book and that he then retweeted to his many followers. As with other uses of social media, educators who are going to ask students to use Twitter in this way are encouraged to understand and teach students the community norms for communication on the platform.

While lecture back channels have been popular on Twitter, they are not recommended for the classroom because of the potential for these unmoderated conversations to devolve into unproductive and even uncivil communication (boyd, 2009). Furthermore, our research shows that using Twitter as a course back channel does not impact student engagement or learning outcomes (Junco, Elavsky & Heiberger, 2012). Indeed, the most effective strategy is to use Twitter to continue class discussions and to interact with students in the ways they are accustomed to online.

As Hurt and colleagues (2012) and our work suggest (Junco, Elavsky & Heiberger, 2012), students will be more engaged with more engagement from the educator. Students are encouraged to respond to each other, retweet tweets from their peers and content relevant to the course, and share links. Two common practices involve either creating a Twitter account for the course or using the educator's personal Twitter account. The benefits of using the educator's personal Twitter account include being able to model appropriate online behaviors during the times the instructor is not posting to the course hashtag. Using a course account allows for the educator to keep his or her personal account separate and focused on content not related to the course.

Information Literacy and Evaluation

Students, like many in our society, rely on the Internet and social media for a great deal of their information needs; however, research has shown that information evaluation is difficult for students (Harris, 2008). Today, almost anyone with the requisite skills to access the Internet has the ability to create a website, web page, or blog to communicate information. Because the Internet is not peer reviewed, this ability leads to both wonderful opportunities for learning and growth, as well as the possibility of deception (whether intentional or not). Furthermore, social media allow users to disseminate information by methods such as posting and resharing status updates, tweets, and posts. Unfortunately, the speed by which information can spread online may lead to rapid dissemination of erroneous information. This reality led Matt Stempeck and his team at the MIT Media Lab to develop Lazy-Truth, a Gmail inbox extension that automatically provides users with correct information from FactCheck.org and PolitiFact when they receive e-mails containing myths, urban legends, and security threats (LazyTruth, 2013).

LazyTruth can't work for every situation; the need to teach *information literacy* in higher education has never been greater. The American Library Association's Presidential Committee on Information Literacy stated that for a person to be information literate, the person must be able "to recognize when information is needed and have the ability to locate, evaluate, and use effectively the needed information" (American Library Association, 1989). Gasser, Cortesi, Malik, and Lee (2012) expand the definition of information literacy to a framework for information quality that encompasses the process, contexts, and outputs of youth interaction with information.

The following are phases in youth's interactions with information (Gasser, Cortesi, Malik & Lee, 2012):

1. *Determining information needs:* There are three contexts that determine youth's information needs: personal, social, and academic. The need for information, and therefore the motivations associated with the information, varies according to context. For instance, students will engage with information much differently when they are searching for health-related information for themselves than when they are searching for research for a course.

2. *Searching for information:* Youth use search engines at high rates (Bilal & Ellis, 2011; Rowlands et al., 2008); however, they struggle to convert what they are searching for into appropriate keywords, struggle with search strategies, and have difficulties understanding the logic of results (Beheshti, Bilal, Druin & Large, 2010; Dhillon, 2007; Druin et al., 2009). For instance, youth rarely go beyond the first page of search results and often select one of the first results

(Druin et al., 2009). Research by Duarte Torres and Weber (2011) supports results from my own interviews with first-year seminar students showing that students can't distinguish between sponsored results and regular search results.

3. *Evaluating information:* The main criteria that youth use to evaluate search results are topicality, cues, heuristics, and visual and interactive elements (Gasser, Cortesi, Malik & Lee, 2012). As youth develop, their criteria for evaluating search begin to align with adult criteria (Livingstone, Haddon, Görzig & Ólafsson, 2011).

4. *Creating new information:* Content creation is broadly defined as creating anything from videos, images, and artwork to posts on social media. The act of creating online is related to student creativity and by extension related to the academic context. As student affairs professionals, we must prepare our students to engage in society more broadly, and online participation is an important facet of such participation.

A number of educational strategies focus on enhancing students' information literacy competencies in general and search and evaluation skills in particular (Gasser, Cortesi, Malik & Lee, 2012); however, higher education has been focused on teaching evaluation skills using a checklist approach, with a rigid set of evaluation criteria not transferable across contexts (Gasser, Cortesi, Malik & Lee, 2012; Meola, 2004). The most appropriate way to teach digital evaluation skills is to teach students how to think critically, not how to review a checklist that evaluates all content from an adult normative perspective. In fact, web search

195

evaluation exercises can be used to focus on helping students think critically about the content they discover—to be comfortable with nuance and not just a binary answer to the question "Is this information credible?"

Harris (2008) described her use of the *cognitive flexibility model* to induce cognitive dissonance with students and engage students in critical thinking about online content. She gave an example of teaching students the nuances of evaluation by using a website that meets many of the criteria for credibility using a checklist approach. The website, the Institute for Historical Review (http://www.ihr.org) is run by a Holocaust denial organization. Harris (2008) reported that the website "bears traditional credibility cues that are designed to trigger the authority heuristic," such as links to articles in the *Boston Globe* and *New York Times* as well as books from Harvard University Press; however, quotes are used as evidence of a powerful global Jewish conspiracy (p. 169). Harris (2008) also reported that students learned to "be alert to the additional cues that should trigger other conflicting credibility assessment heuristics" and that they could "track down the origins of selected quotes and compare the contexts in which they are used" (p. 169).

In teaching evaluation skills, it helps to consider how meaningful particular information is. For instance, students will be more motivated to conduct a thorough investigation when they conduct searches in the academic context and less motivated in certain aspects of the social context. Take for example a student who sees a friend post this status update:

> *It is official it was even on the news. Facebook will start charging due to the new profile changes. If you copy this on your wall your icon will turn blue and Facebook will be free for you. please*

pass this message on if not your account will be deleted if you don't pay (Snopes.com, 2013).

A student who reads and then shares that status update as the message suggests she might not be paying much attention to the update, as the student might be in a variety of psychological states. Perhaps the student is tired and not very interested in critically evaluating such information, or perhaps the student trusts the authority of the person posting the message. In making an assessment of cost versus reward before posting such a message, there is little psychological cost to posting such a status update and being wrong (not accounting for the obvious hit to the student's own credibility with her social media audience), whereas the reward of posting the message would be to be helpful to friends. Decisions to share information online are multifaceted; in a society where we must evaluate large volumes of information daily, these factors interact to determine evaluation decisions. Therefore, students might be more likely to investigate a claim if the information is meaningful to them, if the perceived cost of posting is lower than the reward, and if they are in a mental state where they have the cognitive resources available to make such evaluations.

Student evaluation decisions will be influenced by multiple factors and contexts. Therefore, it is critical to teach skills that are transferable across contexts. It is also helpful to realize that our students have been searching, evaluating, and creating information online for almost their entire lives. Understanding the personal, social, and academic contexts in which they have engaged in these searches helps us reduce our inclination to engage in the adult normative perspective when teaching students evaluation skills. Transitioning from the adult normative perspective and a reliance on the checklist approach helps us move toward a broader information evaluation model. In this way, we can teach students competencies that help them be more active and engaged citizens beyond college. For strong evaluation and critical thinking skills will transfer not just across the contexts of digital information evaluation, but to interpersonal and civic interactions as well.

CONCLUSION

Social media, when used in appropriate ways, can stimulate learning and lend an exciting balance to formal learning settings. Research shows not only that students prefer using social media over traditional course and learning management systems, but that certain uses of social media are related to more positive student outcomes (Ellison, Steinfield & Lampe, 2007; 2011; Ellison, Vitak, Gray, & Lampe, 2014; Heiberger & Harper, 2008; Hurt, Moss, Bradley, Larson & Lovelace, 2012; Junco, 2012b; 2012c; Junco, Heiberger & Loken, 2011; Schroeder & Greenbowe, 2009; Yu, Tian, Vogel & Kwok, 2010; Yang & Brown, 2013). Social media provide opportunities for teaching students and modeling habits of critical evaluation, allowing student affairs professionals to engage students using technological tools that match students' communication preferences, meet them where they are, and boast affordances superior to institutionally provided educational technologies. These sites have great potential to improve students' formal learning experience and also their informal learning related to social and academic integration, a strong predictor of student success. Student affairs professionals can leverage these sites to obtain desired outcomes of a college education. Specifically, student affairs professionals can help support formal and informal learning by understanding students' interactions with social media, leading students to grow further by helping translate formal learning to real-world outcomes.

Practical Tips

1. If you are going to use social media for formal learning, it is important to do the following:
   a. Explore whether social media are appropriate tools for your learning goals.
   b. Determine the desired learning outcomes of social media use.
   c. Ensure that the affordances of the social media tool coincide with your learning outcomes.
   d. Use theory to develop uses of social media in educationally relevant ways.
   e. Review effective uses of social media for formal learning based on the research.
   f. Engage with students on the platform.
   g. Engage in social media activities that lead to more positive learning outcomes.
   h. Model appropriate behavior when communicating online and explicitly identify these behaviors during class.
   i. Evaluate the outcomes of integrating social media into your course.
2. Understand the personal, social, and academic contexts and student motivations for searching in order to help students think critically about information they find online.

REFERENCES

American Library Association. (1989). *Presidential Committee on Information Literacy. Final Report.* Chicago: American Library Association.

Babcock, P., & Marks, M. (2010). Leisure College, USA: The Decline in Student Study Time. *American Enterprise Institute for Public Policy Research Education Outlook, 7.*

Beheshti, J., Bilal, D., Druin, A., & Large, A. (2010). Testing children's information retrieval systems: Challenges in a new era. *Proceedings of the American Society for Information Science and Technology, 47*(1), 1–4.

Bilal, D., & Ellis, R. (2011). Evaluating leading web search engines on children's queries. *Proceedings of the Human-Computer Interaction International Conference, Lecture Notes in Computer Science, 6764,* 549–558. Retrieved February 2, 2014, from http://www.springerlink.com/content/p45r64lvk1085708/.

Bosch, T. E. (2009). Using online social networking for teaching and learning: Facebook use at the University of Cape Town. *Communicatio: South African Journal for Communication Theory and Research, 35*(2), 185–200.

boyd, d. (2009). Spectacle at Web2.0 Expo…from my perspective. *Apophenia* (blog). Retrieved July 20, 2013, from http://www.zephoria.org/thoughts/archives/2009/11/24/spectacle_at_we.html.

Chickering, A. W., & Gamson, Z. F. (1987). Seven principles for good practice in undergraduate education. *AAHE Bulletin,* 3–7.

Dabbagh, N., & Kitsantas, A. (2011). Personal Learning Environments, social media, and self-regulated learning: A natural formula for connecting formal and informal learning. *The Internet and Higher Education, 15*(1), 3–8.

Dhillon, M. K. (2007). Online information seeking and higher education students. In M. K. Chelton & C. Cool (eds.), *Youth Information-Seeking Behavior II: Context, Theories, Models, and Issues* (pp. 165–205). Lanham, MD: Scarecrow Press.

Druin, A., Foss, E., Hatley, L., Golub, E., Guha, M. L., Fails, J., & Hutchinson, H. (2009). How children search the Internet with keyword interfaces. *Proceedings of the 8th International Conference on Interaction Design and Children* (pp. 89–96). Como, Italy: ACM.

Duarte Torres, S., & Weber, I. (2011, October). What and how children search on the web. *Proceedings of the 20th ACM International Conference on Information and Knowledge Management* (pp. 393–402). Glasgow, UK: ACM.

Ellison, N. B., Steinfield, C., & Lampe, C. (2007). The benefits of Facebook "friends": Social capital and college students' use of online social network sites. *Journal of Computer-Mediated Communication, 12*(4), 1143–1168.

Ellison, N. B., Steinfield, C., & Lampe, C. (2011). Connection strategies: Social capital implications of Facebook-enabled communication practices. *New Media & Society, 13*(6), 873–892.

Ellison, N. B., Vitak, J., Gray, R., & Lampe, C. (2014). Cultivating social resources on social network sites: Facebook relationship maintenance behaviors and their role in social capital processes. *Journal of Computer-Mediated Communication*, DOI: 10.1111/jcc4.12078.

Fidler, P. P. (1991). Relationship of freshman orientation seminars to sophomore return rates. *Journal of the Freshman Year Experience, 3*(1), 7–39.

Finn, J. D., & Rock, D. A. (1997). Academic success among students at risk for school failure. *Journal of Applied Psychology, 82*(2), 221–234.

Forkosh-Baruch, A., & Hershkovitz, A. (2011). A case study of Israeli higher-education institutes sharing scholarly information with the community via social networks. *The Internet and Higher Education, 15*(1), 58–68.

Gasser, U., Cortesi, S. C., Malik, M., & Lee, A. (2012). *Youth and Digital Media: From Credibility to Information Quality*. SSRN Electronic Journal. Retrieved February 2, 2014, from http://papers.ssrn.com/sol3/papers.cfm?abstract_id=2005272.

Hargittai, E. (2010). Digital na(t)ives? Variation in Internet skills and uses among members of the "Net Generation." *Sociological Inquiry, 80*(1), 92–113.

Harris, F. J. (2008). Challenges to teaching credibility assessment in contemporary schooling. In M. J. Metzger & A. J. Flanagin (eds.), *Digital*

Media, Youth, and Credibility. The John D. and Catherine T. MacArthur Foundation Series on Digital Media and Learning (pp. 155–179). Cambridge, MA: MIT Press.

Heiberger, G., & Harper, R. (2008). Have you Facebooked Astin lately? Using technology to increase student involvement. In R. Junco & D. M. Timm (eds.), *Using Emerging Technologies to Enhance Student Engagement.* New Directions for Student Services, Issue 124, pp. 19–35. San Francisco: Jossey-Bass.

Hollyhead, A., Edwards, D. J., & Holt, G. D. (2012). The use of virtual learning environment (VLE) and social network site (SNS) hosted forums in higher education: A preliminary examination. *Industry and Higher Education, 26*(5), 369–379.

Hurt, N. E., Moss, G. S., Bradley, C. L., Larson, L. R., & Lovelace, M. D. (2012). The "Facebook" effect: College students' perceptions of online discussions in the age of social networking. *International Journal for the Scholarship of Teaching and Learning.* Retrieved February 2, 2014, from http://digitalcommons.georgiasouthern.edu/ij-sotl/vol6/iss2/10/.

Junco, R. (2012a, January 17). College students prefer to use Facebook in their courses. *Social Media in Higher Education* (blog). Retrieved July 14, 2013, from http://blog.reyjunco.com/college-students-prefer-to-use-facebook-in-their-courses.

Junco, R. (2012b). Too much face and not enough books: The relationship between multiple indices of Facebook use and academic performance. *Computers in Human Behavior, 28*(1), 187–198.

Junco, R. (2012c). The relationship between frequency of Facebook use, participation in Facebook activities, and student engagement. *Computers & Education, 58*(1), 162–171.

Junco, R., & Chickering, A. W. (2010, September/October). Civil discourse in the age of social media. *About Campus, 15*(4), 12–18.

Junco, R., Elavsky, C. M., & Heiberger, G. (2012). Putting Twitter to the test: Assessing outcomes for student collaboration, engagement, and success. *British Journal of Educational Technology, 44*(2), 273–287.

Junco, R., Heiberger, G., & Alonso-Garcia, N. (in preparation). *Tweeting to stay: Fostering academic and social integration through Twitter.*

Junco, R., Heiberger, G., & Loken, E. (2011). The effect of Twitter on college student engagement and grades. *Journal of Computer Assisted Learning, 27*(2), 119–132.

Keup, J. (2005–2006). The impact of curricular interventions on intended second year re-enrollment. *Journal of College Student Retention, 7,* 61–89.

Kuh, G. D. (2009). What student affairs professionals need to know about student engagement. *Journal of College Student Development, 50*(6), 683–706.

Kuh, G. D., Cruce, T. M., Shoup, R., Kinzie, J., & Gonyea, R. M. (2008). Unmasking the effects of student engagement on first-year college grades and persistence. *The Journal of Higher Education, 79*(5), 540–563.

LazyTruth. (2013). *About.* Retrieved February 2, 2014, from http://www.lazytruth.com/?page_id=41.

Livingstone, S., Haddon, L., Görzig, A., & Ólafsson, K. (2011). *Risks and Safety on the Internet: The Perspective of European children.* Full findings and policy implications from the EU Kids Online survey of 9–16 year olds and their parents in 25 countries. London, UK: The London School of Economics and Political Science. Retrieved April 16, 2014, from http://www.lse.ac.uk/media%40lse/research/EUKidsOnline/EU%20Kids%20II%20(2009-11)/EUKidsOnline IIReports/D4FullFindings.pdf.

Mazer, J. P., Murphy, R. E., & Simonds, C. J. (2007). I'll see you on "Facebook": The effects of computer-mediated teacher self-disclosure on student motivation, affective learning, and classroom climate. *Communication Education, 56*(1), 1–17.

Meola, M. (2004). Chucking the checklist: A contextual approach to teaching undergraduates web-site evaluation. *portal: Libraries and the Academy, 4*(3), 331–344.

Moran, M., Seaman, J., & Tinti-Kane, H. (2011). *Teaching, Learning, and Sharing: How Today' s Higher Education Faculty Use Social Media.* Pearson Annual Survey of Social Media Use by Higher Education

Faculty. Retrieved July 6, 2013, from http://www.babson.edu/Academics/Documents/babson-survey-research-group/teaching-learning-and-sharing.pdf.

Morrin, D. (2007, August 29). A shift to engagement. *Facebook Developers* (blog). Retrieved February 2, 2014, from: https://developers.facebook.com/blog/post/30.

Osberg, D., & Biesta, G. (2008). The emergent curriculum: Navigating a complex course between unguided learning and planned enculturation. *Journal of Curriculum Studies, 40*(3), 313–328.

Pascarella, E., & Terenzini, P. (2005). *How College Affects Students: A Third Decade of Research.* San Francisco: Jossey-Bass.

Roblyer, M. D., McDaniel, M., Webb, M., Herman, J., & Witty, J. V. (2010, June). Findings on Facebook in higher education: A comparison of college faculty and student uses and perceptions of social networking sites. *The Internet and Higher Education, 13*(3), 134–140.

Rowlands, I., Nicholas, D., Williams, P., Huntington, P., Fieldhouse, M., Gunter, B., Withey, R., et al. (2008). The Google generation: The information behaviour of the researcher of the future. *Aslib Proceedings, 60*(4), 290–310.

Schroeder, J., & Greenbowe, T. J. (2009). The chemistry of Facebook: Using social networking to create an online community for the organic chemistry laboratory. *Innovate: Journal of Online Education, 5*(4). Retrieved April 16, 2014, from http://gator.uhd.edu/~williams/AT/ChemOfFB.htm.

Seaman, J., & Tinti-Kane, H. (2013). *Social Media for Teaching and Learning.* Pearson Annual Survey of Social Media Use by Higher Education Faculty. Retrieved February 2, 2014, from http://www.pearsonlearningsolutions.com/higher-education/social-media-survey.php.

Skinner, E. A., Kindermann, T. A., & Furrer, C. J. (2009). A motivational perspective on engagement and disaffection: Conceptualization and assessment of children's behavioral and emotional participation in academic activities in the classroom. *Educational and Psychological Measurement, 69*(3), 493–525.

Snopes.com (2013). Facebook charges. Retrieved July 7, 2013, from http://snopes.com/computer/facebook/fbcharge.asp.

Veletsianos, G. (2012). Higher education scholars' participation and practices on Twitter. *Journal of Computer Assisted Learning, 28*(4), 336–349.

Yang, C., & Brown, B. B. (2013). Motives for using Facebook, patterns of Facebook activities, and late adolescents' social adjustment to college. *Journal of Youth and Adolescence, 42*(3), 403–416.

Yu, A. Y., Tian, S. W., Vogel, D., & Kwok, R. C.-W. (2010). Can learning be virtually boosted? An investigation of online social networking impacts. *Computers & Education, 55*, 1495–1503.

CHAPTER 6

Planning, Implementing, and Assessing Social Media Interventions

Social media interventions are actions or processes taken to improve an identified educational issue—for instance, using Twitter to improve student engagement in a course. Social media interventions are, just like any other intervention, an attempt by student affairs professionals to implement something (like a program or a process) that will lead to desired positive student outcomes. All too often student affairs professionals implement programs without evaluating their effectiveness, and the same is true when they use social media to convey messages and engage with their students. To date, little has been done to assess how official institutional social media use impacts student engagement, well-being, social and academic integration, and academic success. For instance, while campus activities professionals have used social media to market their programs, no evaluations have been reported showing whether this kind of marketing leads to increased participation in events (Doan, 2010).

Typically the assessment process is described separately from the intervention.[1] For the purposes of this chapter, however, social media implementation and assessment will be discussed together (Schuh & Upcraft, 2000; Upcraft & Schuh, 1996). There are parallels inherent in these processes, as background work necessary to develop a successful social media intervention will yield important information for the assessment process. For instance, conducting a literature review focusing on how social media use can influence student engagement can yield ideas for effective implementations of these technologies but also ideas about how student engagement can be measured. The assessment and intervention processes should be guided by theory. A strong theoretical basis for an intervention will make it easier both to guide the implementation of the intervention and to assess the outcomes of that intervention. If you believe that time on academic tasks increases student engagement, then you might believe that using Twitter to discuss course content would lead to student engagement; a literature review in this area shows ways that Twitter can be used effectively for student engagement and which evaluation instruments can be used to measure engagement (Junco, Elavsky & Heiberger, 2012; Junco, Heiberger & Loken, 2011).

Program evaluation does not have to be a Herculean task. In fact, when the evaluation of programs is built into the planning process, the evaluation itself becomes a small effort compared with the planning and implementation phases. Although student affairs professionals did not explicitly sign up to do assessment and evaluation, they are an implicit and necessary part of the job. Asking student leaders to debrief a program is assessment. Guiding resident assistants through the process of building sociograms about the students on their floors is evaluation. The work is already being done; it's just not often called assessment. Student affairs professionals need to apply the same standards to understand the outcome of their efforts in the same way that they implore students to do so.

Higher education has faced many challenges in the early 2000s. Up through that time, it was an all-but-certain truism that higher education institutions were not affected by downturns in the nation's economy. In fact, downturns in the national economy have often led to increased enrollments in higher education, usually by people who lost their jobs and were looking to retrain for new careers (Carnevale, Jayasundera & Cheah, 2012). Additionally, higher education has, until recently, been viewed as one of the only ways that people can engage in upward socioeconomic mobility. Regrettably, this is no longer the case. Furthermore, college costs have outpaced inflation since the early 1980s (United States Bureau of Labor Statistics, 2010). With the increased cost in attendance—even at publicly funded institutions—has come an increased scrutiny of what institutions are doing to add value to students' lives and a resultant increase in accountability. In other words, politicians and society in general want to know that we are delivering on our promise to educate and prepare students for the future. Student affairs should heed this clarion call.

The rise of for-profit institutions has compounded the call for accountability. New models of course delivery such as the MOOC (massive open online course) have grown exponentially in popularity. Online-only programs and universities have seen sharp increases in enrollment. Sadly, many of these online service delivery models assume that *content delivery* is the special sauce of higher education—or, put another way, that providing students with content knowledge is the necessary and sufficient requirement for desired student outcomes. Most educators can assure you that this assumption is far from the truth. Student learning is measured, not only in quiz scores, but in psychosocial development, interpersonal skills, critical thinking, peer-to-peer learning, and learning to be a lifelong learner. Student affairs professionals may know that these aspects of student learning are important, but we have done little to show how our work impacts students in these important ways. Social media allow for some very unobtrusive methods of data collection, which, coupled with basic outcomes assessments, can make for powerful evidence of how what we do makes an impact on student outcomes. With social media, we have tangible evidence of how many students participate in the intervention, the level at which they participate, and whether they continue to participate.

An assessment does not have to be grandiose to be helpful, but it does need to be well planned. If you are spending time in developing a social media intervention, spend a little extra time and effort planning its assessment. This chapter will first review the dynamics of resistance to social media interventions. The following sections provide an outline of the social media planning and assessment process, the results of which can not only help convince a supervisor of the intervention's importance but also serve as evidence for accountability and gather support for further interventions, resources, and collaborations.

SOCIAL MEDIA SKEPTICS AND CRUSADERS

The current state of the field is such that many student affairs professionals are skeptical of the value of social media. Pearson's social media survey results can help us understand the dynamics of this resistance. In the Pearson survey, older faculty were less likely to use social media, and one of the most-cited barriers to implementation of social media interventions was lack of institutional support (Seaman & Tinti-Kane, 2013). The *social media skeptics* are often upper-level professionals who have not "grown up with" social media in their lives and who often have a direct role in providing "institutional support." On the other hand, *social media crusaders* are typically professionals who are newer to the field and who have had much more experience with social media as part of their developmental life experiences. Of course, like any dichotomy, this is a simplification of the roles and attitudes found in the field, as there is a broad spectrum of attitudes, with many professionals falling between the two extremes; however, this dichotomy also allows us to view the dynamics of the state of the profession and to make recommendations about bridging these gaps.

The dichotomy between social media skeptics and crusaders helps us understand the paradigms under which we are currently working. In his seminal work, *The Structure of Scientific Revolutions*, Thomas Kuhn (1962) outlined how advances in scientific thought resulted not from a progressive development of evidence but from more sudden *paradigm shifts*. His idea of scientific revolutions can be specifically applied to the state of social media uptake in education. Kuhn's (1962) idea of a *paradigm* can be thought of as a model of scientific thought that is based on one or more scientific achievements. Paradigms are scientific achievements that share two characteristics: they have great impact because of their unprecedented ability to draw away a group of adherents from competing schools of thought, and they are adequately open-ended so that this new group of practitioners can have ample problems to solve (Kuhn, 1962).

The following are Kuhn's (1962) three phases of scientific revolutions:

1. *Pre-paradigm:* In this phase, there are scientists conducting work; however, there are no accepted schools of thought (or theories). Typically there are a number of theories that are often incompatible at this stage.
2. *Normal science:* This phase begins when a paradigm develops during the first phase and draws a critical mass of adherents. Research during this phase is based on achievements and research activities that scientists agree form a base for their practice.
3. *Revolutionary science:* During the course of normal science, new discoveries are made that don't fit within the dominant paradigm. Some of these discoveries are disproved; however, others "stick" and start to attract a growing body of adherents. As the evidence and the proportion of adherents grow for the new paradigm, there is a revolution resulting in a paradigm shift.

While Kuhn (1962) was primarily concerned with scientific thought, methods of conducting experiments, and apparatus, his most prominent contributions were to the understanding of the cultural and social aspects of the scientific process. The concept that accepted schools of thought (cultures) shift because of prodding from those with new ideas lends itself well to thinking about many social phenomena, including tensions in student affairs about using social media to promote informal learning. Of course, there is not as much scientific data driving the paradigms in student affairs as in a field like chemistry or biology. The field of student affairs then is at the *normal science* phase: it has established theories, some of which have been supported by a small amount of research evidence. The field of student affairs also has a delineated school of thought—a way of *being* student affairs professionals, if you will. Some of the theories student affairs professionals adhere to include that a more engaged student is a better student, that it is important to both challenge and support our students, that psychological and physical well-being are essential, that academic success is closely tied to what students do when they are not in class, and that students should spend an appropriate amount of time studying for their courses.

Enter the dichotomy between social media skeptics and crusaders. Social media skeptics are operating under the dominant paradigm in student affairs, which does not involve employing technology to affect student learning outcomes, perhaps because of the focus on face-to-face interactions. In fact, those within the dominant paradigm might categorize social media use as a time-wasting activity that detracts from students' focus on academics and the social aspects of university life. While an adherence to these popular myths is understandable, especially for those who have not grown up with social media (and other information and communication technologies), there is research showing that social media use is in fact related to increased face-to-face interactions, the building of stronger friendships, and social and academic integration (see Ellison, Steinfield & Lampe, 2007; 2011; Ellison, Vitak, Gray & Lampe, 2014; Junco, 2012a; Junco, Heiberger & Alonso-García, in preparation; Junco, Heiberger & Loken, 2011; Manago, Taylor & Greenfield, 2012; Selwyn, 2009; Valenzuela, Park & Kee, 2009; Ward, 2010; Yang & Brown, 2013; Yu, Tian, Vogel & Kwok, 2010). In fact, research has yet to be published showing a link between social media use and fewer offline interactions (and if you happen to come across such a study, please make sure to send it to me).

Social media crusaders, in contrast, are working under a newer and distinct paradigm. The desire to use social media as part of their repertoire of communication tools might very well be linked to other traits they share as educators. Crook (2008) described the "Web 2.0 mentality," which is a worldview driving the uptake of social media tools. Those with a Web 2.0 mentality might share personality styles and interests that correlate with or are perhaps the third, fourth, or fifth variables which explain the social media crusader's interest in using these technologies to engage students. The Web 2.0 mentality may be reflective of a broader cultural movement that emphasizes "participation, informality and irreverence" (Crook, 2008, p. 56). Social media crusaders then might be reflecting a paradigm that is focused on changing not only how students are engaged in higher education but how members of our society are engaging with each other.

Unfortunately, social media crusaders are often so enthusiastic about using social media with their students that they are incapable of seeing these sites from a more balanced perspective. What I often hear from new or mid-level student affairs professionals is, "My institution just doesn't get [fill in the social media site]!" This perspective has led not just to frustration on their part but to an "us versus them" mentality with respect to colleagues who are not as well versed in social media. Furthermore, the crusaders' great enthusiasm has actually worked against examining how student affairs professionals can use social media to benefit students, for if one "already knows that something works," there is no reason to evaluate its impact. Of course, this idea is far from the truth. Student affairs practice needs data, outcome studies, and information about how work with students makes an impact in their lives.

If you can't find data in the literature to support your intervention, then you must collect outcomes data yourself. This task can be extremely rewarding; however, it can be met with much resistance from the very people who are excited about using social media. Indeed, the Pearson survey found that more than half of faculty said that inability to measure effectiveness was a major barrier to implementation of social media in their courses (Seaman & Tinti-Kane, 2013). Luckily, there is some existing evidence to show that using social media in clearly defined ways is related to the learning and developmental outcomes of interest to student affairs professionals. Social media use has been found to be related to self-esteem (Gonzales & Hancock, 2011; Mehdizadeh, 2010; Tazghini & Siedlecki, 2013), shyness (Orr et al., 2009), Big Five personality traits such as Extraversion and Neuroticism (Bachrach, Kosinski, Graepel, Kohli & Stillwell, 2012; Gosling, Augustine, Vazire, Holtzman & Gaddis, 2011; Moore & McElroy, 2012; Ong, Ang, Ho, Lim & Goh, 2011; Ross et al., 2009; Seidman, 2012), political participation (Kim & Khang, 2014; Vitak et al., 2011), life satisfaction, social trust, civic engagement, and political participation (Valenzuela, Park & Kee, 2009), development of identity and peer relationships (Pempek, Yermolayeva & Calvert, 2009), relationship building and maintenance (Ellison, Steinfield & Lampe, 2007; 2011; Ellison, Vitak, Gray & Lampe, 2014; Manago, Taylor & Greenfield, 2012; Valenzuela, Park & Kee, 2009; Yang & Brown, 2013), perceptions of social support (DeAndrea, Ellison, LaRose, Steinfield & Fiore, 2011; Manago, Taylor & Greenfield, 2012), student engagement (Heiberger & Harper, 2008; HERI, 2007; Junco, 2012a; Junco, Elavsky & Heiberger, 2012; Junco, Heiberger & Loken, 2011), and social and academic integration (Selwyn, 2009; Yu, Tian, Vogel & Kwok, 2010). Student affairs professionals can use these research findings to lend support to their use of social media in similar ways.

THE PLANNING PROCESS

Preparation

Previous research, learning, or developmental theories should guide the development of an intervention. Reason and Kimball (2012) described the importance of the interaction between

215

formal and informal theories in student affairs practice and proposed a model integrating these with input from the institutional environment. However, student affairs practitioners are often consciously unaware of the formal theories that guide their practice (Bresciani, Gardner & Hickmott, 2010), when they are in fact putting these formal theories into practice. This is different from saying that new student affairs professionals rely mostly or solely on informal theories (Reason & Kimball, 2012). Rather, new professionals remember and maintain schemas of formal theory and integrate them into their informal theories and their practice. However, because informal theories are more proximate, they are the ones most commonly held in conscious awareness.

Therefore, when student affairs professionals come up with an idea for a social media intervention, it is likely that they have connected the intervention with formal theory, but they may have done so unconsciously. In the many conversations I've had with new professionals about their desire to use social media with their students, they have been able to articulate a formal theory-to-practice connection when prompted. It is imperative that practitioners connect theory to their proposed interventions; luckily, this step should not be difficult given their ability to articulate the connection between theory and practice. For example, a professional may be interested in involving students in residence hall activities because it seems like a good idea for students to be socially active. Upon additional reflection, the professional might make the connection that student involvement is shown to be related to a myriad of psychosocial and learning outcomes, not least of which is social integration—which is related directly to student persistence (Astin, 1984; Kuh, 2009; Pascarella & Terenzini, 2005; Tinto, 1993).

Here are some questions to answer when preparing to implement a social media intervention.

Why are you using social media? Refer back to the theory guiding the development of the intervention and ask whether social media provide the best tools to reach your objectives. All too often, the "cool factor" of social media gets in the way. Elsewhere I've written about the long-standing misconception that "throwing technology at an educational problem will automatically produce better learning outcomes" (Junco, 2012b). Nothing is farther from the truth: as you may recall from the research presented in chapter 2, how social media are used is perhaps the crucial factor in predicting outcomes, because social media are simply tools. In fact, an intervention not enabled by technology may be the best intervention to attain your desired outcomes.

Why are you assessing the use of social media? It is important to evaluate social media interventions for the sake of our students (so we can adjust these interventions and our approach to them for maximum benefit) and for the sake of our profession (so that we can learn about what works and what doesn't); however, other circumstances may also drive assessment efforts. You may be asked to support your division's mission to prove accountability or to justify the need for additional staffing or reallocation of your time.

What are your desired learning or developmental outcomes? There is a difference between goals and outcomes: goals are general, while outcomes are measurable and specific. Student affairs practitioners generally think in terms of goals for their students—for example, for students to develop mature interpersonal relationships or a strong sense of identity—and have difficulty articulating learning and developmental outcomes. The operationalization of outcomes will be discussed later in the section on assessment.

Once you have identified desired outcomes and have evaluated whether social media are the best modality for an intervention that you are planning, the next step is investigating similar work that has been conducted. Have researchers examined the relationship between social media use and your desired outcomes? If so, what proportion of the variance can be attributed to how social media were used? How can you leverage social media to reach those goals? If no research has been conducted on related social media sites or outcomes, have student affairs professionals at other institutions conducted similar interventions using different modalities? If so, what were their successes and challenges? How can you use what you learned from peer institutions to inform your intervention? How can you translate another institution's similar work to meet your specific needs? Interestingly enough, you can use social media to engage your personal learning network (PLN, described in more detail in chapter 7) to find out whether colleagues have conducted similar interventions. If there is no research evidence and there are no examples of similar interventions, then it is especially important to have strong ties between your intervention and a guiding theory. When we first examined how educationally relevant uses of Twitter would influence student outcomes, there was no previous research to suggest how we might use social media to support student learning, so we used Chickering and Gamson's (1987) seven principles for good practice in undergraduate education to guide the development of our intervention.

A crucial step in the preparation process is to consider which students you will leave out by focusing on a social media intervention. As reviewed in chapter 1, there are differences in the ways that minority students and those from lower socioeconomic levels use technologies generally and social media in particular. These digital inequalities affect use of the sites and could substantially limit the benefits received from the intervention. Indeed, my research suggests that students at a digital disadvantage might not even engage in the intervention in the first place (Junco, 2013). As such, it is important to plan how to reach disenfranchised and disconnected students with the intervention, an issue discussed in the section on training later in this chapter. It is also important to think about how digital inequalities will affect the assessment and to plan analyses appropriately. For instance, student gender, race, ethnicity, and socioeconomic status can be used as control variables when analyzing the results.

Enlisting Buy-In

Student affairs professionals who are excited about implementing social media interventions often have to convince a supervisor about the value of the tools. We know from the Pearson social media survey that older faculty are less likely to engage in personal, professional, and classroom uses of social media than their younger counterparts (Seaman & Tinti-Kane, 2013). We can extrapolate this dynamic to student affairs, of course with the caveat that the dynamic may not always hold true—on a few occasions, I've witnessed very skeptical professionals who have also grown up in the age of social media. For these reasons, it's valuable to enlist the support of a wide range of individuals in your social media intervention. Seek out other social media crusaders on campus, whether they work in student affairs or not, and make an effort to solicit input from social media skeptics.

While it is important to collaborate with those who will help you implement these new ideas, it's just as important to recognize how you will frame the intervention with those who might not share your enthusiasm. Put another way, it is important to temper your excitement in order to educate your colleagues on the value of social media. Take their side, understand the roots of their skepticism, and empathize with their concerns so that you may

219

best present evidence to garner support. If you solicit input from skeptics, making them a part of the process, they are more likely to be supportive of your intervention and interested in the results. Additionally, skeptics may lend a different perspective in interpreting your findings that may help strengthen future interventions. In addition to broad-based support, it is especially vital to ensure that you have the support of everyone who is directly involved in the intervention.

The *Web 2.0 mentality* is a possible confounding factor that explains the positive outcomes of social media use: a student affairs professional who is interested in integrating emerging technologies into their programs may have other personality characteristics and interests that correlate with positive student outcomes (Crook, 2008). These educators might be more willing to experiment with engaging educational methods. They might also be more willing to take "educational risks" and to learn from and adjust to the results. It is wholly possible that the personality characteristics of those carrying out the intervention are the major influencing factor on the outcome of interest. Student affairs professionals with a Web 2.0 mentality, then, are more likely to implement new technology interventions, and positive outcomes may not be due to the use of the technology but to a conscious or unconscious belief about working with students that leads intervention participants to behave a certain way. Because of the confounding possibilities, if your goals are to evaluate how your intervention can be used across programs, departments, or institutions, then it is essential to include educators who might not have a Web 2.0 mentality to help implement your intervention.

Collaboration across departments and divisions is helpful not only in building and implementing a social media intervention but also for assessing its effectiveness. While any single student affairs division may have few professionals interested in social media, there are likely professionals in various departments

220

on campus interested in different facets of social technologies. Faculty in sociology, computer science, communications, marketing, education, and psychology may all have interests in collaborating on social media projects, and they may have projects of their own that would apply to student affairs work. Additionally, professionals in other departments can help with implementation of the social media assessment. Individuals in statistics, institutional research, information technology, admissions, or counseling may be able to help with evaluation techniques. Unfortunately, student affairs professionals sometimes have difficulty collaborating with academic affairs professionals and often blame this difficulty on the resistance or attitudes of academic departments. In order to foster strong collaborations, student affairs professionals must meet other departments and faculty where they are, just like we do with students. Focusing on *win-win-win* propositions helps in enlisting collaboration—when approaching people in other departments, it's good to have articulated an idea of how collaborating with you can help them. For example, a junior faculty member in education might be interested in studying the effects of social media on student learning, and you can offer to help with a publication using your data. Conversely, someone in institutional research might be interested in including data about social media use in their next report, and you might collect that data as part of your intervention.

Training

Training for both staff and student employees should follow a similar model. Some social media interventions are simple, and one person can handle the management of the social media accounts or activities; other interventions are more complex or address the needs of more students and need to be handled by multiple people. The intervention also needs to follow and comply

221

with an institution's social media policy. As with nondigital programming, staff need training to implement the intervention. Training involves recruiting individuals who have a basic level of technological knowledge and interest in the intervention, delineating the intervention's learning outcomes, and outlining how social media will be used to attain those outcomes. When planning training, assume that staff are at the most basic level of knowledge with social media.

Educators and noneducators alike make the mistake of assuming that all college students are equally skilled in the use of technology. Research on digital inequalities illuminates the distinction between *access* and *use*: access to technology does not guarantee a high level of skill. Students from lower socioeconomic levels or from minority racial or ethnic backgrounds are at a disadvantage in how they use technology and how these uses are related to academic and developmental outcomes (boyd, 2007; Hargittai, 2010; Hargittai & Litt, 2011; Junco, 2013). These inequalities begin at an early age and are propagated throughout students' academic careers (Brown, Higgins & Hartley, 2001; Milone & Salpeter, 1996; Pisapia, 1994; Warschauer, Knobel, & Stone, 2004; Warschauer & Matuchniak, 2010). Unfortunately, little is done in the university setting to help address these inequalities as students transition into the workforce. Therefore, we need to be careful not to propagate these inequalities in our interventions.

One strategy that serves a dual purpose is to teach students and staff about the social media used in the intervention. Some attendees may be bored by the training because of their high level of technological skill, but it is preferable to bore some than to exclude traditionally digitally disenfranchised students and staff members. In addition, standardizing how social media will be used (including language used, tone of messages sent, and specific information shared) as part of the intervention leads to consistency for the student experience.

The following are two main goals for training efforts (Cabellon, 2013).

1. *Help staff shift how they view social media from a social-personal to a social-educational perspective.* If your staff already have experience using social media, most of this experience will be in the social-personal context, with communications not intended to have educational value but instead focused on personal interactions with friends and family. Training can help staff consider how uses of social technologies can aid in student growth, development, and learning and how such communications are qualitatively different from the ways that staff have already been using these sites and services.

2. *Establish what your organization's "voice" will be*—that is, your organization's communication style. It is important for organizations to be consistent with their online voice, especially given the difficulties inherent in understanding tone in online spaces (Epley & Kruger, 2005; Kruger, Epley, Parker & Ng, 2005). Will the tone be professional or humorous; will the organization use language congruent with that of students? Check to see whether your institution already has overarching guidelines for institutional voice. Cabellon (2013) suggests that staff be trained to be congruent with the organization's voice in the same way that you might train them to answer the phones or to give campus tours.

Cabellon (2013) discusses content to include in social media staff training:

1. *Online self-presentation* (which he refers to as *digital identity*) training involves educating staff about how they've already used social media in the social-personal context and helping them shift to the social-educational context. Participants are encouraged to evaluate how others may make judgments about them based on what they find about them online. One strategy is asking participants to Google themselves and to discuss how they may be judged by others based on what they've found.

2. *Social media lexical instruction* helps staff learn about the idiosyncrasies of the terms used for each site. As explained in chapter 1, a message to all followers on Twitter is called a "tweet," while on Facebook it is referred to as a "post." Discussing the language used for each site also segues nicely into discussing the cultural norms of use for each site and how users are expected to interact in those communities. Additionally, Cabellon (2013) recommends explicit teaching of privacy settings and controls, a topic also covered in chapter 1.

3. *Scenario solving* includes showing staff how to actively engage on the sites being used in the intervention and then having them participate by engaging on the sites themselves. For instance, Cabellon (2013) recommends asking participants to post content on the organization's Facebook page or sending a tweet to the organization's Twitter account. Such participation engages active learning and allows for refinement of the transition to the social-educational context and adoption of the organization's voice.

Training should include relevant stakeholders. At some institutions, for instance, the central communications office oversees all official university communications on social media. Even if your marketing and communications staff do not have oversight for your social media programming, it's helpful to have them collaborate in developing training content and participate in training delivery.

Assessment

The preparation section earlier in this chapter reviewed the importance of identifying the learning or developmental outcomes of interest. Outcomes should be measurable and meaningful in relation to the student experience. These outcomes can be measured with qualitative methods, quantitative methods, or a combination of both (often called *mixed methods*). Qualitative methods are those that involve collecting descriptive information about people, events, situations, and interactions (Upcraft & Schuh, 1996). Qualitative data collection techniques include interviews, focus groups, observations of behavior, and document analysis (for instance, reviewing student portfolios). In contrast, quantitative methods use numbers to measure outcomes of interest. Quantitative data collection techniques include surveys, tests, and other instruments that quantify responses. The key difference is in the types of data collected—quantitative techniques yield numerical data while qualitative techniques yield data that are either written or spoken language. Quantitative techniques are useful in describing how *most* students use and are affected by the social media intervention, while qualitative data are useful for describing individual experiences. Quantitative methods usually allow for data that are more generalizable to the population than qualitative data. Additionally, qualitative methodologies can serve as crucial starting point when examining newer phenomena like social media. In these cases, qualitative inquiry can lead to a better understanding of what quantitative data need to be collected in future studies.

Learning or developmental outcomes need to be operationalized in order to be measurable. *Operationalization* is the translation of outcomes into discrete and measurable variables. Often, operationalized outcomes approximate but do not fully encompass a construct of interest. Consider the construct of student engagement as an outcome. It is not possible to measure "physical and psychological energy," so we use other variables, often called *proxy variables*, to approximate and triangulate the construct (Astin, 1984). With a complex construct such as student engagement, it's often a good idea to use multiple proxy variables. Figure 6.1 illustrates some of the variables that can be used to operationalize student engagement. In this example, engagement can be approximated by using scores on a nineteen-item engagement

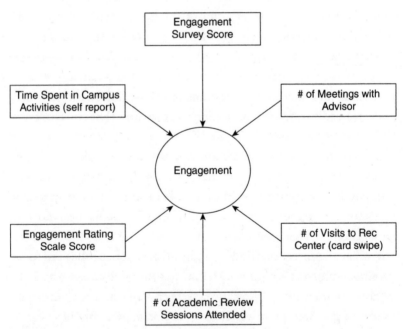

Figure 6.1. Representation of proxy variables to measure student engagement.

survey (Junco, Heiberger & Loken, 2011), by asking students to report how much time they spend in campus activities, by observing and rating student classroom engagement, by counting the number of times a student meets with their advisor, by the number of times they swipe their ID card to enter the student recreation center, or by the number of academic review sessions they attend for their Introduction to Psychology class. You'll notice that both the metrics and how they are collected differ—some variables are measured through self-report, while others are measured without student input.

Social media and the increased use of educational technologies on college campuses present an opportunity to collect user-generated data for assessments efficiently. *Learning analytics* is the collection and analysis of student-generated data in order to predict outcomes and adapt educational techniques. Learning analytics are examined in greater detail in chapter 8; while the field of learning analytics typically deals with predicting student outcomes, the methods of data collection used in the field are applicable to the assessment process. Indeed, student affairs professionals are already using student-generated data to track resource utilization, and it won't be long before these methods are used to identify proxies for student learning and developmental outcomes. As suggested in the previous paragraph, the number of visits to the campus recreation center can be evaluated through student card swipes when they check in. These card swipes might serve as a proxy measure of student involvement and student engagement.

It is critical to select an evaluation technique that is reflective of and congruent with the outcomes of interest. If you are interested in obtaining quantitative data and are planning to use a survey or a measure of a construct, then it is important to pick an appropriate measure. Conduct a literature review to evaluate existing measures and the evidence for their *construct validity*—that

227

is, their actual ability to measure the phenomenon they purport to measure. A thorough exploration of appropriate methods to show evidence for instrument reliability and validity is beyond the scope of this chapter; however, there are a few important points to keep in mind:

1. *Reliability* refers to data showing evidence that an instrument measures consistently. If you step on a scale, step off it, and step back on and get the same reading of twenty pounds each time, we would say the scale showed evidence of reliability.

2. *Validity* refers to evidence that an instrument is measuring what it is supposed to measure. Such evidence is obtained by collecting both data on the instrument and also data on a measure (or measures) independent from the instrument, and comparing the two. For example, data to support a nineteen-item engagement instrument's validity can include correlating scores on the instrument with observational measures of engagement or with self-report of time spent in campus activities. In the scale example in the preceding paragraph, you have evidence from other measures that you weigh a lot more than twenty pounds; therefore, there is little evidence of validity for the scale.

3. Instruments themselves do not harbor the quality of being reliable or valid. In other words, we cannot say "the nineteen-item engagement scale is a reliable and valid measure of student engagement." Instead, we can say that data have been collected that support the reliability and validity of the instrument.

There are different ways to measure reliability and validity. For instance, we can give students an IQ test and then give it to them again ten weeks later to see whether the scores are consistent—this is called *test-retest reliability*. *Internal consistency* is a form of reliability that examines the extent to which item responses are consistent with each other. Evidence for validity can be collected through evaluating *construct validity*, which is made up of concurrent validity and discriminant validity. *Concurrent validity* is the extent to which two measures of the same construct that theoretically should be related are indeed related. *Discriminant validity* is the opposite—the extent to which two measures of different constructs that theoretically should be unrelated are indeed unrelated.[2]

As discussed earlier, an assessment does not have to be intricate in order to be helpful. If you are interested in moving beyond merely describing how students participated in an intervention to being able to infer whether the intervention caused changes in a particular outcome, the assessment must be designed appropriately—in other words, such an assessment becomes a research project that needs to be planned based on the methodological principles and institutional requirements of a research study. For a thorough treatment of such research designs, the interested reader is referred to Kazdin's *Research Design in Clinical Psychology* (Kazdin, 2002). In most cases, to make strong causal inferences about an intervention requires using a *pre-test/post-test control group design*, which is also called a *classic controlled experimental design*.

These are the requirements of a pre-test/post-test control group design:

1. *Random assignment of participants from the same population into an experimental and a control group.* Adding a control group allows one to measure how much a student changes on the variable of interest without the intervention. Participants must all be members of the same population (for example,

229

all students at your institution) and be randomly assigned into either the control or experimental group; that is, each participant in the sample should have an equal chance of being assigned to either group.

2. *Administering a pre-test to participants in both groups.* In this case, the pre-test will evaluate the learning or developmental outcomes of interest. A pre-test also helps one evaluate whether the control and experimental groups were different on the variable of interest at the onset of the study (if they were, the researcher should suspect that random assignment was not successful and plan accordingly).

3. *Ensuring that both groups experience the same conditions except that the experimental group will experience the intervention.* This is perhaps the most difficult part of conducting a pre-test/post-test control group design because there is little we can do to influence the real-world experiences of the control group. However, there are variables that we can control—for example, ensuring that the control group is not part of the experimental intervention's Facebook group. Research involving social media sites should be planned accordingly: What is it that students in the experimental group will do on the site or sites that will be different from the control group? Will simple exposure to the site affect your construct of interest? Identify the variables that you can control, and plan the intervention in ways that will help minimize spillover of the intervention to the control group.

4. *Administering the post-test to participants in both groups.* At the end of the intervention, both groups are given the post-test, which is the same instrument as the pre-test.

5. *Assessing the amount of change in the construct(s) of interest from the pre-test to the post-test for participants in each group.* The

easiest method of evaluating change in a design that involves a single pre-test and a single post-test is by calculating a difference score—subtracting the pre-test score on the measure or measures of interest from the post-test score. Then, *inferential statistics* are conducted to see whether there are differences between the two groups. Furthermore, control variables (unchangeable variables that may influence the results such as racial or ethnic background) are identified and included as part of the analyses.

Karl Popper (1963) described the idea of *falsifiability*, which in this context refers to research that is designed so that hypotheses can be proved false. Although no number of positive outcomes can confirm a hypothesis, a single negative outcome is logically conclusive. For example, there is no way to verify the assertion that "all swans are white," yet it is easy to falsify the assertion with the observation of a single black swan. In the context of assessment, this idea means that evaluations should be planned so that they can refute your hypothesis. An excited student affairs professional who is interested in showing that an innovative social media intervention helps students reach identified learning or developmental outcomes might think that the possibility of obtaining a "negative result" means that all of the work the professional put into the intervention and the assessment was for naught. Nevertheless, having a negative result is very important as it leads the student affairs professional to critically consider and learn what didn't work. Negative results may come about because the way that social media were used was inappropriate for the intended outcomes or a student affairs professional was not engaged in a way that supported student development (Junco, Elavsky & Heiberger, 2012). It is necessary to determine

231

what did or didn't happen and to continue learning and developing from the process.

Implementation

The implementation phase begins once you have defined your learning outcomes, trained your staff, and decided upon an appropriate assessment strategy. The following are important steps in the social media intervention implementation process:

1. *Define your target population.* Will you focus your intervention on a certain group of students? Perhaps you are interested in engaging students in a particular residence hall or students who are academically at risk based on their previous semester's grades.

2. *Select the platform or platforms you will use.* Will you focus on just using a Facebook page or will you also include Twitter in your engagement strategy? Which platforms have affordances that are congruent with your learning outcomes? For instance, if you want to host threaded conversations related to career development, Twitter might not be the best choice, and you may want to use a blog or a Facebook page instead.

3. *Plan content and engagement.* What will the process of engagement on social media look like? Will you encourage students to interact with specific individuals in your area? What topics will you cover with your posts and interactions with students? Consider the types of content: Will you post pictures, memes, links to news stories, relevant university information? Along with the process, topics, and types of content, you should determine posting frequency—although frequency may vary from intervention to intervention, it is important to maintain consistency. For instance, if you regularly post two links to news stories every day, you will not

want to go a few days without posting a news story. Some social media managers use an editorial calendar to schedule when content will be shared and to make sure that all intended topics are covered.

4. *Who will engage?* It is important to indicate who will have the responsibility of engaging with students on the social media site or sites. If there is more than one person responsible for doing so, frequent meetings will help ensure that the institution's voice is being maintained and that the content is being shared according to your plan.

5. *Administer pre-tests.* If they are part of your assessment strategy, send out pre-tests. Begin a database to track the participants in the intervention and, if you will collect server-level data, have the collection method and database ready.

6. *Engage with students.* Remember that a key reason for using social media is their ability to effectively engage students. Therefore, it is important that staff tasked with running the social media outlets actively participate in conversations with students. Social media are less about the program or the institution and more about the students—bring them into the conversation by asking them to submit content, reply to posts, and so on.

7. *Provide accurate information.* It is essential to build credibility with your target population of students. One way to do so is to make sure that you are providing accurate information. The staff member directing the social media platform should have easy access to other staff who can help with answers the staff member might not know. Don't sacrifice the speed of social media communications at the cost of accuracy—it's OK to tell a student that you will research the question and send them an answer when you find out.

8. *Engage in social media listening.* Social media listening is achieved through actively searching social media sites (using

233

keyword searches) to see what students are talking about. Chapter 4 provides a number of examples of departments that engaged in social media listening to reach out and support students in need.

9. *Administer post-tests.* Again, if it is part of your assessment strategy, administer evaluation instruments when the intervention has concluded.

10. *Continuity after intervention.* Will you provide continuity once your intervention has concluded? In our research on social media, some students will continue using the sites and project accounts even after the intervention has concluded. Further engagement with these students will continue to provide benefit; however, it is important to decide whether you will continue to engage with students or not and to let them know.

ANALYSES, INTERPRETATION, AND REPORTING

Analyses

Once data collection is complete, analyses must be conducted to describe, summarize, or draw conclusions. If quantitative methods were used, *descriptive statistics* are used to describe the data. These include measures of central tendency (like mean, median, and mode) and measures of dispersion or spread (like range, quartiles, variance, and standard deviation). *Inferential statistics* can also be employed to draw conclusions from quantitative data. Inferential techniques include comparing differences between group means (with, for example, analyses of variance (ANOVA) and t-tests) and measuring the relationship between two or more variables (using, for example, correlation and regression). Qualitative results are summarized and presented as overarching themes, by using selected quotes (called exemplars) and by reporting evaluations of observations or document reviews. If the assessment team did not already include someone versed in interpretation and reporting of statistical or qualitative data, it's important to enlist the assistance of a person available to do statistics or research consulting. Often, there is an institutional research person or a student affairs research person who can provide guidance. Data analyses, especially for quantitative data, must address many nuances to obtain usable data. Therefore, it's imperative either to have someone on the assessment team with a great deal of data analysis experience or to consult with such an expert before proceeding to the interpretation stage.

Descriptive statistics are used in describing data like the demographic characteristics of survey respondents. In contrast, inferential statistics are used when evaluating whether an intervention affected the engagement survey scores of the students who received the intervention as compared with those who didn't. Inferential statistics provide information on whether differences between groups are statistically significant, yet they don't provide information about the real-world significance of the findings. In our original Twitter study, the control group's and the experimental group's overall semester GPAs were compared after the semester and intervention were complete (Junco, Heiberger & Loken, 2011). The control group had a mean semester GPA of 2.28, while the experimental group had a mean semester GPA of 2.79. The group of students who used Twitter as part of a course had a statistically significant higher GPA than the students who didn't— but was this difference meaningful in the real world? Indeed, the mean increase of 0.51 in GPA had real-world significance—in fact, such an increase would make a difference in whether a student continued in a major (in this case pre-health professionals). Framed another way, if we could help all students improve their overall semester GPA by half a point just by having them use Twitter in educationally relevant ways in one course, we would jump at the chance! This example illustrates the importance of

235

considering the real-world impact of your results: Do they matter in practical ways to students or to the institution?

Interpretation and Reporting

Data analyses provide useful information that summarizes findings and, depending on the assessment methodology, may even provide information from which you can make inferences about the effectiveness of an intervention. Selecting and creating appropriate reporting methods is essential for communicating what you have found. University administrators (and most other faculty and staff) have little time to toil through lengthy assessment reports to find the most important highlights. However, a lengthy report might be exactly what is needed when submitting evaluation results as part of the university's yearly strategic planning assessment. Therefore, it is helpful to know the needs and communication style of your intended audience.

Infographics

Information graphics or *infographics* are visual representations that are intended to communicate complex data easily and clearly. There are two reasons that infographics are important to consider as a method for reporting assessment results. First, infographics are not just popular online but are also being increasingly used to communicate evaluation findings in educational institutions. Second, infographics are an easy way to communicate complex data and can be easily and quickly understood by individuals who are focused on many other things (and may have increased cognitive load and little additional processing capacity).

For a time, the way infographics were being used in the media was dreadful; popular online news sources spread infographics that misrepresented research data (including some of my own work). Unfortunately, because readers were interested in the infographic but not interested enough in the supporting research to evaluate the original source, erroneous information was propagated widely. Of course, this speaks to a broader issue of information literacy (discussed in detail in chapter 5); however, there is no way to influence the existing habits of millions of Internet goers. I decided to contribute to countering this trend by (1) deconstructing a few of the infographics in posts on my blog (see Junco, 2011), and (2) understanding that writing a rebuttal to an infographic that spread all over the Internet is of little utility in improving the information literacy of the masses, I issued a call for a graphic designer to collaborate with me on infographics to communicate the results of a research study—both its findings and limitations. Figure 6.2 shows one of these infographics. The online response was overwhelming: the blog post hosting the infographic received more visitors than any other of my previous blog posts. Additionally, the infographic was used on many other blogs and news sites and raised awareness of the research paper on which it was based—in fact, it is one of my more frequently cited papers.

REFINEMENT

This chapter has focused on using assessment data for supporting divisional and institutional goals, convincing supervisors of the value of implementing social media interventions, and general accountability. While these other functions are important motivators for assessing social media interventions, assessing the intervention for its own sake is perhaps the most basic function of assessment. In other words, *how do we know that what we are doing works?* And if it doesn't work, *how can we adjust it so that it does?* Assessment data play a crucial role in answering these questions. As suggested earlier in the chapter, finding out that your intervention does not affect your intended outcomes is important because you then have information about what to adjust in future

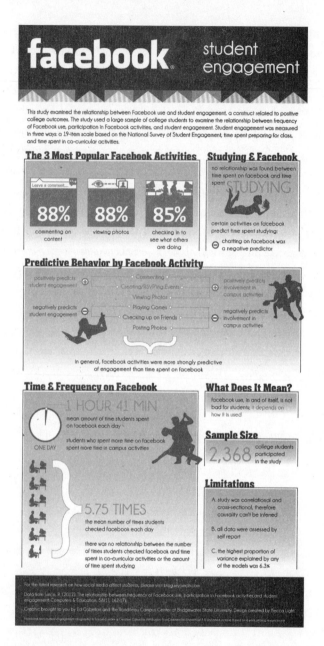

Figure 6.2. Facebook and student engagement infographic based on my journal article on the same topic (Junco, 2012a).

implementations of the intervention. In one of our studies, we discovered that certain uses of Twitter in the classroom were not related to the outcomes of engagement or academic performance (Junco, Elavsky & Heiberger, 2012). Of course, the instructor of the course was disappointed; however, he gained valuable information about how to use Twitter in future courses. Furthermore, we gained valuable information about what works and what doesn't and were able to communicate this information to other educators.

Once assessment data are collected, interpreted, and shared and ideas for refinement are identified, the process can begin anew. Continuous iterations of the intervention and assessment process lead to greater efficiencies and more detailed information about what works. Perhaps you have learned that your intervention works only with certain students or only during a specific point in the semester, or you've learned whom to include in future collaborations. Furthermore, you may have learned that your assessment instruments and methods perhaps did not capture what you were interested in examining; refinement would include identifying additional or replacement methods of evaluating your desired outcomes.

CONCLUSION

Even though extrapolations can be made from some research to support the use of social media interventions, little has been done to assess how practical applications of these interventions impact student engagement, well-being, social and academic integration, and academic success. Increased calls for accountability and skepticism about the value of social media in students' lives support the need to assess how what we do with our students both off and on social media has an impact on their learning and developmental outcomes. Assessments don't have to be as intricate as

239

a full-fledged research study involving a pre-test/post-test control group design in order to be helpful. Focus groups, satisfaction surveys, and descriptions of differences in social media use can help guide further and effective institutional uses of social media. The future of social media is full of possibilities for innovative assessment techniques. For instance, the ability to collect student-generated data will drive important assessment efforts and will be explored in chapter 8 on the future of social media.

Practical Tips

1. Consider your desired learning outcomes and decide whether social media are the appropriate tool for your intervention.
2. Ensure that you are not engaging in reproducing digital inequalities by using methods or tools that put disenfranchised students at further disadvantages.
3. Enlist buy-in from your colleagues, supervisors, and individuals from other departments.
4. Train your staff in using social media as part of the intervention process.
5. Choose appropriate evaluation tools (such as relevant surveys) and methods (quantitative versus qualitative) to evaluate your desired learning outcomes.
6. Report your results using formats congruent with the needs and communication styles of your intended audience.
7. Use data collected to refine your social media intervention for future semesters.

REFERENCES

Astin, A.W. (1984). Student involvement: A developmental theory for higher education. *Journal of College Student Personnel, 25,* 297–308.

Bachrach, Y., Kosinski, M., Graepel, T., Kohli, P., & Stillwell, D. (2012). Personality and patterns of Facebook usage. *Proceedings of the 3rd Annual ACM Web Science Conference,* 24–32.

boyd, d. (2007). Why youth (heart) social network sites: The role of networked publics in teenage social life. *MacArthur Foundation Series on Digital Learning: Youth, Identity, and Digital Media* (ed. David Buckingham). Cambridge, MA: MIT Press.

Bresciani, M. J., Gardner, M. M., & Hickmott, J. (2010). *Demonstrating Student Success: A Practical Guide to Outcomes-Based Assessment of Learning and Development in Student Affairs.* Sterling, VA: Stylus.

Brown, M. R., Higgins, K., & Hartley, K.. (2001). Teachers and technology equity. *Teaching Exceptional Children, 33*(4), 32–39.

Cabellon, E. (2013). Staff training for managing social media communication. *On the Go with Ed Cabellon* (blog). Retrieved January 31, 2014, from http://edcabellon.com/tech/smstafftraining/.

Campbell, D. T., & Fiske, D. W. (1959). Convergent and discriminant validation by the multitrait-multimethod matrix. *Psychological Bulletin, 56*(2), 81–105.

Carnevale, A. P., Jayasundera, T., & Cheah, B. (2012). *The College Advantage: Weathering the Economic Storm.* Georgetown Public Policy Institute: Center on Education and the Workforce Report. Retrieved September 14, 2013, from http://www9.georgetown.edu/grad/gppi/hpi/cew/pdfs/CollegeAdvantage.ExecutiveSummary.081412.pdf.

Chickering, A. W., & Gamson, Z. F. (1987). Seven principles for good practice in undergraduate education. *AAHE Bulletin,* 3–7.

Crook, C. (2008). *Web 2.0 Technologies for Learning: The Current Landscape: Opportunities, Challenges and Tensions.* British Educational Communications and Technology Agency (BECTA) Report: Web 2.0 Technologies for Learning at Key Stages 3 and 4. Retrieved February 3, 2014, from http://dera.ioe.ac.uk/1474/1/becta_2008_web2_currentlandscape_litrev.pdf.

DeAndrea, D. C., Ellison, N. B., LaRose, R., Steinfield, C., & Fiore, A. (2011). Serious social media: On the use of social media for improving students' adjustment to college. *The Internet and Higher Education, 15*(1), 15–23.

Doan, J. (2010, October). Be a fan: Building social media into campus programming. *Campus Activities Programming,* 20–21. Retrieved February 2, 2014, from https://www.naca.org/SiteCollection Documents/Doan_article.pdf.

Ellison, N. B., Steinfield, C., & Lampe, C. (2007). The benefits of Facebook "friends": Social capital and college students' use of online social network sites. *Journal of Computer-Mediated Communication, 12*(4), 1143–1168.

Ellison, N. B., Steinfield, C., & Lampe, C. (2011). Connection strategies: Social capital implications of Facebook-enabled communication practices. *New Media & Society, 13*(6), 873–892.

Ellison, N. B., Vitak, J., Gray, R., & Lampe, C. (2014). Cultivating social resources on social network sites: Facebook relationship maintenance behaviors and their role in social capital processes. *Journal of Computer-Mediated Communication.* DOI: 10.1111/jcc4.12078.

Epley, N., & Kruger, J. (2005). When what you type isn't what they read: The perseverance of stereotypes and expectancies over e-mail. *Journal of Experimental Social Psychology, 41,* 414–422.

Gonzales, A. L., & Hancock, J. T. (2011). Mirror, mirror on my Facebook wall: Effects of exposure to Facebook on self-esteem. *Cyberpsychology, Behavior and Social Networking, 14*(1–2), 79–83.

Gosling, S. D., Augustine, A. A., Vazire, S., Holtzman, N., & Gaddis, S. (2011). Manifestations of personality in online social networks: Self-reported Facebook-related behaviors and observable profile information. *Cyberpsychology, Behavior and Social Networking, 14*(9), 483–488.

Hargittai, E. (2010). Digital na(t)ives? Variation in Internet skills and uses among members of the "Net Generation." *Sociological Inquiry, 80*(1), 92–113.

Hargittai, E., & Litt, E. (2011). The tweet smell of celebrity success: Explaining variation in Twitter adoption among a diverse group of young adults. *New Media & Society, 13*(5), 824–842.

242

Heiberger, G., & Harper, R. (2008). Have you Facebooked Astin lately? Using technology to increase student involvement. In R. Junco & D. M. Timm (eds.), *Using Emerging Technologies to Enhance Student Engagement*. New Directions for Student Services, Issue 124, pp. 19–35. San Francisco: Jossey-Bass.

Higher Education Research Institute (HERI). (2007). College freshmen and online social networking sites. Retrieved February 2, 2014, from http://www.heri.ucla.edu/PDFs/pubs/briefs/brief-091107 -SocialNetworking.pdf.

Junco, R. (2011, May 3). Thoughts on the "Is Social Media Ruining Students?" infographic. *Social Media in Higher Education* (blog). Retrieved February 2, 2014, from http://blog.reyjunco.com/thoughts-on -the-is-social-media-ruining-students-infographic.

Junco, R. (2012a). The relationship between frequency of Facebook use, participation in Facebook activities, and student engagement. *Computers & Education, 58*(1), 162–171.

Junco, R. (2012b). Giving students iPads does not lead to better learning outcomes. *NBC Latino*. Retrieved February 2, 2014, from http:// nbclatino.tumblr.com/post/23546757626/opinion-giving -students-ipads-does-not-lead-to-better.

Junco, R. (2013). Inequalities in Facebook use. *Computers in Human Behavior, 29*(6), 2328–2336.

Junco, R., Elavsky, C. M., & Heiberger, G. (2012). Putting Twitter to the test: Assessing outcomes for student collaboration, engagement, and success. *British Journal of Educational Technology, 44*(2), 273–287.

Junco, R., Heiberger, G., & Alonso-Garcia, N. (in preparation). Tweeting to stay: Fostering academic and social integration through Twitter.

Junco, R., Heiberger, G., & Loken, E. (2011). The effect of Twitter on college student engagement and grades. *Journal of Computer Assisted Learning, 27*(2), 119–132.

Kazdin, A. E. (2002). *Research Design in Clinical Psychology*. Upper Saddle River, NJ: Pearson.

Kim, Y., & Khang, H. (2014). Revisiting civic voluntarism predictors of college students' political participation in the context of social media. *Computers in Human Behavior, 36*, 114–121.

Kruger, J., Epley, N., Parker, J., & Ng, Z. (2005). Egocentrism over e-mail: Can we communicate as well as we think? *Journal of Personality and Social Psychology, 89*(6), 925–936.

Kuh, G. D. (2009). What student affairs professionals need to know about student engagement. *Journal of College Student Development, 50*(6), 683–706.

Kuhn, T. S. (1962). *The Structure of Scientific Revolutions.* Chicago: University of Chicago Press.

Manago, A. M., Taylor, T., & Greenfield, P. M. (2012). Me and my 400 friends: The anatomy of college students' Facebook networks, their communication patterns, and well-being. *Developmental Psychology, 48*(2), 369–380

Mehdizadeh, S. (2010). Self-presentation 2.0: Narcissism and self-esteem on Facebook. *Cyberpsychology, Behavior and Social Networking, 13*(4), 357–364.

Milone, M. N., & Salpeter, J. (1996). Technology and equity issues. *Technology and Learning, 16*(4), 38–47.

Moore, K., & McElroy, J. C. (2012). The influence of personality on Facebook usage, wall postings, and regret. *Computers in Human Behavior, 28*(1), 267–274

Ong, E., Ang, R., Ho, J., Lim, J., & Goh, D. (2011). Narcissism, extraversion, and adolescents' self-presentation on Facebook. *Personality and Individual Differences, 50*, 180–185.

Orr, E. S., Sisic, M., Ross, C., Simmering, M. G., Arseneault, J. M., & Orr, R. R. (2009). The influence of shyness on the use of Facebook in an undergraduate sample. *Cyberpsychology & Behavior, 12*(3), 337–340.

Pascarella, E. T., & Terenzini, P. T. (2005). *How College Affects Students: A Third Decade of Research.* San Francisco: Jossey-Bass.

Pempek, T. A., Yermolayeva, Y. A., & Calvert, S. L. (2009). College students' social networking experiences on Facebook. *Journal of Applied Developmental Psychology, 30*(3), 227–238.

Pisapia, J. (1994). *Technology: The Equity Issue.* Richmond, VA: Metropolitan Educational Research Consortium.

Popper, K. (1963). *Conjectures and Refutations: The Growth of Scientific Knowledge.* London: Routledge.

Reason, R. D., & Kimball, E. W. (2012). A new theory-to-practice model for student affairs: Integrating scholarship, context, and reflection. *Journal of Student Affairs Research and Practice, 49*(4), 359–376.

Ross, C., Orr, E. S., Sisic, M., Arseneault, J. M., Simmering, M. G., & Orr, R. R. (2009). Personality and motivations associated with Facebook use. *Computers in Human Behavior, 25*(2), 578–586.

Schuh, J. H., & Upcraft. M. L. (2000). *Assessment Practice in Student Affairs: An Applications Manual.* San Francisco: Jossey-Bass.

Seaman, J., & Tinti-Kane, H. (2013). *Social Media for Teaching and Learning.* Pearson Annual Survey of Social Media Use by Higher Education Faculty. Retrieved February 2, 2014, from http://www .pearsonlearningsolutions.com/higher-education/social-media -survey.php.

Seidman, G. (2012). Self-presentation and belonging on Facebook: How personality influences social media use and motivations. *Personality and Individual Differences, 54*(3), 402–407.

Selwyn, N. (2009). Faceworking: Exploring students' education-related use of Facebook. *Learning, Media and Technology, 34*(2), 157–174.

Tazghini, S., & Siedlecki, K. L. (2013). A mixed method approach to examining Facebook use and its relationship to self-esteem. *Computers in Human Behavior (29)*3, 827–832.

Tinto, V. (1993). *Leaving College: Rethinking the Causes and Cures of Student Attrition* (2nd ed.). Chicago: University of Chicago Press.

United States Bureau of Labor Statistics. (2010). *Back to College.* United States Department of Labor. Retrieved January 31, 2014, from http://www.bls.gov/spotlight/2010/college/.

Upcraft, M. L., & Schuh, J. H. (1996). *Assessment in Student Affairs: A Guide for Practitioners.* San Francisco: Jossey-Bass.

Valenzuela, S., Park, N., & Kee, K. F. (2009). Is there social capital in a social network site? Facebook use and college students' life satisfaction, trust, and participation. *Journal of Computer-Mediated Communication, 14*(4), 875–901.

Vitak, J., Zube, P., Smock, A., Carr, C. T., Ellison, N., & Lampe, C. (2011). It's complicated: Facebook users' political participation in the

245

2008 election. *Cyberpsychology, Behavior and Social Networking, 14*(3), 107–114.

Ward, T. H. (2010). *Social network site use and student retention at a four-year private university.* Ph.D. diss., The Claremont Graduate University.

Warschauer, M., Knobel, M., & Stone, L. (2004). Technology and equity in schooling: Deconstructing the digital divide. *Educational Policy, 18*(4), 562–588.

Warschauer, M., & Matuchniak, T. (2010). New technology and digital worlds: Analyzing evidence of equity in access, use, and outcomes. *Review of Research in Education, 34*(1), 179–255.

Yang, C., & Brown, B. B. (2013). Motives for using Facebook, patterns of Facebook activities, and late adolescents' social adjustment to college. *Journal of Youth and Adolescence, 42*(3), 403–416.

Yu, A. Y., Tian, S. W., Vogel, D., & Kwok, R. C.-W. (2010). Can learning be virtually boosted? An investigation of online social networking impacts. *Computers & Education, 55*, 1495–1503.

NOTES

1. A particular exception is the Logic Model described by the Kellogg Foundation: http://www.wkkf.org/knowledge-center/resources/2006/02/wk-kellogg-foundation-logic-model-development-guide.aspx.

2. Campbell and Fiske (1959) introduced the concept of creating a *Multitrait-Multimethod Matrix* (MTMM) in order to comprehensively evaluate *construct validity.* The MTMM calls for evaluating several constructs (so that *concurrent* and *discriminant validity* can be examined) by each of several methods (for instance, using a survey, through direct observation, and by measuring performance). The MTMM is a superior method for evaluating the validity of an instrument; unfortunately, a literature search for instruments used in student affairs assessments that have been evaluated through an MTMM method yielded no results.

CHAPTER 7

Using Social Media for Professional Development

Professional development comprises educational activities performed outside of the typical duties and regular schedule of work; by participating in professional development activities, student affairs professionals can engage in continuous and lifelong learning. Professional development allows for the opportunity to learn about new research, theories, and methods that help improve the work we do with our students. It also allows for the building and maintenance of a professional social network that helps support healthy work attitudes and practices. Emotionally intense work, such as the kind performed in human service fields like student affairs, is related to burnout (Burke, Noblet & Cooper, 2013). Burnout in turn can result in increased psychological and health problems, decreased performance, increased turnover, and substance abuse (Alarcon, 2011; Swider & Zimmerman, 2010). However, the social networking, professional support, and knowledge building received through professional development opportunities may help alleviate the psychological stressors that lead to burnout in student affairs (Bährer-Kohler, 2013).

A personal learning network (PLN) is an informal learning network that supports practitioners and can be thought of as a cultivated community of interest in a professional area. Using social media to build PLNs is popular among K–12 educators (Warlick, 2009); however, only relatively recently have professionals in higher education begun to adopt the concept. In the past, PLNs were created by attending conferences and workshops or by connecting with nearby educators. Indeed, student affairs professionals have experience with these types of offline PLNs from being involved in national and regional organizations and attending conferences. In graduate school, most student affairs professionals are encouraged to network when they attend the larger national conferences because these networks open up possibilities for new professional opportunities, collaborations, information about new research and resources, and professional and personal support. Additionally, online graduate programs in many education fields have intentionally created online PLNs for their student cohorts— encouraging them and often requiring them to communicate and collaborate, both to explicitly learn about course content and also to implicitly learn PLN building and maintenance.

Previously, sharing information, resources, and support was more difficult for student affairs professionals who lacked adequate professional development funds. Lack of these funds often correlates with diminished institutional or divisional resources

248

and in fact signals a need for increased professional development, as institutions that have to "tighten their belts" when it comes to professional development funds also have fewer resources for hiring personnel. Fewer personnel resources mean that staff have to handle larger caseloads of students, residents, and advisees, in addition to perhaps many other responsibilities; these overworked staff are the ones who would benefit most from additional professional development. Luckily, social media can facilitate something akin to an ongoing professional conference for development. When student affairs professionals build PLNs, they are connecting with a group of peers who may be facing similar challenges and who may be at similar places in their career development. Student affairs professionals use social media for professional purposes in much the same way as students use social media to build and maintain social capital; building and maintaining a network of professional peers (a PLN) allows professionals to reap the benefits accrued from these relationships. A student affairs professional with a large advising caseload might seek and receive support from her PLN in order to have a healthier work-life balance. Another educator might ask his PLN for information about effective learning outcome evaluation instruments.

Twitter has been a very popular tool used by professionals in higher education to build and maintain PLNs (Veletsianos, 2012). Twitter allows educators to build communities of practice—something that becomes increasingly important when educators' interests or chosen functional areas are specialized or unusual. For instance, it might be easy to find another residence hall director on campus, but it might not be easy to find another student affairs professional whose specialty interest area is supporting students who are lesbian and from a minority racial background. Research has been conducted to examine how social media are used to engage with a PLN. For instance, Veletsianos (2012) examined the Twitter practices of popular higher education scholars.

249

The following are categories of Twitter activities engaged in by higher education scholars with more than 2,000 followers (Veletsianos, 2012):

- *Information, resource, and media sharing:* This was the primary Twitter activity of higher education scholars, accounting for 39 percent of all tweets. Scholars tweeted about research and other items related to their professional activities as well as sharing personal information. Sometimes scholars tweeted about content being shared at a conference they were attending.
- *Expanding learning opportunities beyond the confines of the classroom:* Scholars in the sample used Twitter to make classroom activities and content available to others but also to connect their students with outside individuals and resources.
- *Requesting assistance and offering suggestions:* Individuals used Twitter to build and maintain their own PLNs by asking their networks for information to intentionally improve their own knowledge and practice. They also engaged their PLNs by offering assistance to others.
- *Living social public lives:* Scholars shared information about their day-to-day activities, likes, dislikes, personal lives, and profession, providing important social commentary.
- *Digital identity and impression management:* As discussed later in this chapter in the section on self-presentation, scholars used Twitter to build or promote their professional online image.
- *Connecting and networking:* The scholars networked with others but also served as connectors between individuals (for instance, connecting their students with others in the field).
- *Presence across multiple online social networks:* Because they were also active on other social networking websites, scholars tweeted about content they shared on those sites.

Scholars' "networked participation is a complex and multi-faceted human activity where personal and professional identities blend, and where participatory digital practices meet individual reflections, fragmented updates, and social interaction" (Veletsianos, 2012, p. 345). In other words, scholars' Twitter activity not only provides good suggestions for how student affairs professionals might use Twitter themselves but also hints at what kinds of information they will obtain when engaging their PLNs. One way to build a PLN is to follow professionals and scholars who share information related to the professional area in which you are interested. For instance, if you are interested in using social media for marketing programs and campus services, you might follow other Twitter users who work in social media marketing and who share information and resources about their work. Another method of building a PLN is by engaging established communities of practice whose tweets are aggregated using a hashtag.

In a crowdsourced paper, we described "#sachat," a Twitter hashtag and PLN for student affairs professionals (Junco et al., 2010). A word, phrase, or code preceded by the "#" symbol on Twitter is called a *hashtag* and is a clickable keyword. When a user clicks on the hashtag on the Twitter website, and on most Twitter clients, she or he receives the results of a search for all tweets containing that tag; users can also do a search for a hashtag in the Twitter search box or using a Twitter mobile or desktop application. The #sachat hashtag represents a community of student affairs professionals interested in connecting, sharing their experiences, and engaging in personal and professional development. Indeed, numerous subcommunities and hashtags have branched off from the original group, including #safit for student affairs professionals interested in motivating themselves and others to keep up with their fitness goals, #satech for student affairs professionals interested in technology, #sagrad for graduate students in

251

student affairs, and #sadoc for doctoral students in student affairs. One of the more interesting offshoots of #sachat has been the #sagrow community—begun by Ed Cabellon because of an interaction he had on Twitter in which he wondered whether he could connect new professionals with mentors. Shortly thereafter, Ed created the #sagrow community by matching seasoned student affairs professionals mentors with new professionals.

When #sachat began, almost all of the participants were also interested in using social media and technology in student affairs; although many are still interested in doing so, technology adoption across the profession has expanded, and so the community has become more inclusive of all student affairs professionals, regardless of professional interest. The #sachat community engages in regular live "chats." Before each #sachat session, an online poll is conducted to choose a topic. Each week during #sachat, a volunteer moderator helps participants stay on topic by asking pointed questions and encouraging critical thinking. These sessions serve as large-scale discussions in which participants can share their thoughts, their experiences at their institution, and good practices. An examination of the transcripts of these chats shows that participants learn from each other, ask questions, and share resources to further the development of those in the community. Moreover, these conversations often continue after the designated chat times, either on Twitter or through other media. Outside of #sachat chat times, community members continue to use the hashtag to engage their PLNs by posting links and resources, questions, and seeking support.

Hashtags are also used to aggregate tweets related to offline professional conferences—often referred to as "participating in the conference back channel" (see figure 7.1). A back channel is a running conversation that happens "behind the scenes" of an event such as a conference and that allows participants to engage with one another, often with session presenters, and with their

Figure 7.1. Examples of tweets using the #ACPA13 conference hashtag during the opening speaker's session.

broader PLNs. Of importance for professional development, individuals who are unable to attend the conference are often able to follow along with the back channel and learn about what is being discussed. This has become easier to do with more people live-tweeting from conference sessions and sharing pictures of slides, links to sites that contain their notes, and sometimes even audio or video of the session. Sometimes, presenters acknowledge this form of participation by creating a sub-hashtag for their session and by posting presentation materials online before a talk so that those participating in the back channel can more easily follow along. This process can become symbiotic, with presenters able to promote their work and those following along from other locations able to engage in professional development without ever leaving their home or office.

When you attend professional conferences, it is helpful for you to share what you are learning with your PLN. This process creates a positive feedback loop, with you sharing helpful content with your community and then members of your PLN viewing you as someone who shares useful information. Share with your PLN by live-tweeting conference sessions and posting relevant materials for those not able to attend such as pictures of slides, handouts, and videos of particularly interesting segments. You can also post relevant quotes from conference sessions and share both references that are discussed and also references *not* being discussed but appropriate to the session content. Live-tweeting has become something of an art at professional conferences—advanced tweeters combine their ability to take shorthand notes along with their speed in sharing on Twitter to form uninterrupted streams of session content. Even if one or more such tweeters are in your session, participate by sharing your own experiences—important content is worth repeating, especially for well-attended and well-tweeted conferences. In addition, interact with other conference participants on the back channel—retweet their content and engage in discussions of session content or conference happenings.

One facet of the norms and mores of the culture of early Twitter users was an emphasis on egalitarianism. Early interactions on Twitter involved users from different statuses interacting as equals—for instance, a programmer might easily interact with a technology company CEO. This early emphasis on egalitarianism has continued and has spread to how Twitter is used in the field of education. Veletsianos's (2012) work identifies how scholars interact with their followers on Twitter. His examples show how junior scholars, educators, and the public at large can connect with senior scholars in ways never before possible—but it's not just about the actual connection, it's about how Twitter interactions help flatten the hierarchies that exist in higher education. Aside from short interactions on campus or at a conference, where else can a graduate student have ongoing conversations with a senior student affairs officer? These types of interactions on Twitter open up the possibilities for new types of learning—as TJ Logan writes, "imagine getting a pre-press paper by Junco and Chickering through Twitter just by asking the right questions in the right circles" (personal communication, 2013).

Communities of practice with horizontal structures (in which everyone in the community is treated as an equal) are more productive and produce higher-quality work, with increased creativity a by-product of working in an environment that welcomes diverse ideas. This dynamic has its parallels in the online disinhibition effect, for if junior professionals feel more comfortable taking interpersonal risks online, they are more likely to reach out and build relationships with senior professionals and reap the career rewards of doing so. Such interactions on Twitter afford junior professionals the ability to build social capital in career relationships in ways that they never could have done before; however, this ability also places a great deal more responsibility

255

on new professionals. They must be keenly aware of how they are interacting online. They must understand not just the norms of the social technology on which they are interacting, but also the norms of interactions by their fellow professionals on that technology, as well as the norms of the profession at large. It is especially valuable for professionals to understand these norms and to actively consider how they will shape and display their online image.

SELF-PRESENTATION

Just as students need to think about how they present themselves online, student affairs professionals have to do the same. Unfortunately, graduate preparation programs are not educating student affairs professionals about online self-presentation. In the midst of technological progress, student affairs graduate preparation programs have held on to a rigid set of core curricula and have not added courses and experiences to help graduate students use social media to support student learning and for their own professional growth. The problem perhaps stems from the fact that faculty members, who produce the majority of the scholarship in student affairs, have little interest in conducting research on how social media affect students. Therefore, almost all student affairs graduate students are left to learn about how to use these technologies on their own and have little to no formal guidance on using social media to build and enhance their professional self-presentation.

Online professional self-presentation is colloquially referred to as "promoting your brand"—a term that has businesslike connotations and is often interpreted negatively. Although the parallels between professional self-presentation and marketing are clear (you are "selling a product"), it is more appropriate to conceptualize this idea by using the psychological concept of self-presentation introduced in chapter 3. Many student affairs professionals use the term *digital identity development* to refer to online professional self-presentation; however, it is important to tease apart the differences between using social media as part of the exploration and development of identity and using social media to present oneself in a certain way. Labeling the latter *digital identity development* confounds a developmental process with a professional communication strategy. Furthermore, labeling online professional self-presentation *digital identity development* may keep the field of student affairs from more critically and deeply examining how the emerging adult identity development process is affected by online interactions.

Online professional self-presentation is the building of an ideal image through content that is publicly shared in online spaces. In this sense, professional self-presentation involves presentation dynamics very similar to those that apply to a job interview—we must be aware of how we are communicating and coming across, we must be mindful of promoting our strengths and acknowledging our weakness without seeming narcissistic or incompetent, and we must interact with others in a professional, cordial, and civil manner. In a sense, we are cultivating an online reputation that is tied to our personal and professional reputations. Our followers, friends, and lurkers will make value judgments about our offline persona based on what we share online and will also make value judgments about what they find out about us through a Google search. Just as we teach graduate students to wear a suit for their interviews, it is also necessary to teach them how to be aware and take control of their professional online image—especially in an age when many employers Google potential employees and make hiring decisions based on what they find on their social media profiles (CareerBuilder.com, 2012). Professional online self-presentation, then, is akin to wearing a digital suit for a never-ending job interview.

The absence of an online presence is not acceptable—if you don't take control of sites high in the search results for your name, someone else will. A colleague once said that she didn't take any academic seriously who didn't have control over the content of the first few results in a Google search of their name. There are plenty of easy-to-use sites and services that allow student affairs professionals to have highly ranked Google search results related to their name. Having control over these results allows a person to present and promote themselves in the ways that are important to that person. In this way, our online professional self-presentation is tied to our identity development: perhaps we want to be seen as a competent midlevel manager with an appropriate level of experience, or perhaps a new professional wants to be recognized for their groundbreaking work in their institution's LGBT center. For example, many new student affairs professionals post their top five StrengthsQuest talent themes on their Twitter profiles. How you define yourself online will be very closely tied to how others will define you, either as their first impression of you or on an ongoing basis in lieu of any other interactions.

There are two general categories of sites and services that student affairs professionals can use to promote their professional online image.

1. *Static websites:* Sites in this category host content that is not updated regularly; these include biography pages on your institution's website, profile pages on services like about.me, and personal websites.
2. *Dynamic websites:* These are typically social media sites and services that are usually updated more frequently than static websites, including Facebook, Twitter, LinkedIn, blogs, Academia.edu, and so on.

While not essential to have both types of sites, it is certainly helpful to have a static page that serves as the digital equivalent of a CV or resume and a dynamic site that promotes current projects and philosophies.

The student affairs blogging community continues to grow and develop as an important facet of student affairs professionals' PLNs. Bloggers write about and share their experiences and thoughts, develop their philosophies as professionals, and also solicit feedback on their writing through blog comments, tweets, and Facebook posts. Blogs such as *On the Go* by Ed Cabellon, Liz Gross's blog, and *This Side of Theory* by Stacy Oliver have provided personal and career advice to student affairs professionals, while the *Women in Student Affairs (WISA)* blog has provided opportunities for women in the profession to share content with a wider audience. Indeed, the WISA blog has greater readership than perhaps any blog that can be developed by a new or emerging professional and becomes a great place to showcase one's work and to begin to develop a professional online presence.

Successful online self-presentation, however, can help student affairs professionals reap astounding professional benefits. Participating on Twitter has helped me spread word of my research and realize an untold number of benefits, including connecting with new collaborators, receiving feedback on research results, enhancing media and public awareness of my work, and learning about career opportunities. Blogging about your work creates a type of digital portfolio, as blogs can be searchable and permanent. A blog that reflects your practice can become a way for future employers to evaluate your growth as a professional and serves the secondary purpose of highlighting your technology skills—for if you can communicate about yourself effectively in online digital spaces, you can do the same for a new division. Once, I blogged about the difficulties I was having in my job search and received wonderful feedback that helped me successfully land an ideal job soon thereafter. However, this wouldn't have happened without having a preexisting online presence showing the progression of my work.

Professional self-presentation is more difficult in the online space because we are always "on," unlike in the offline world. Because of the online disinhibition effect (also reviewed in chapter 3), we are more likely to say something online than we are in face-to-face interactions, and it's difficult if not impossible for a reader to interpret tone in online communications (Kruger, Epley, Parker & Ng, 2005). Therefore, it is much more difficult to cultivate a positive online image than it is to do the same in the offline world. While the offline world affords us the ability to see how our reactions affect others (at the very least through nonverbal communication), the online world has no such cues. Additionally, in offline interactions, we can explain our faux pas, which are much harder for a social media audience to forgive. The public nature of most social media also makes it so that we often don't know who is reading (and reacting) to our posts. There are many stories about people losing their jobs for things they posted on social media; however, possible problems can be more than merely binary—for example, if you share negative feelings about a department initiative or other such content that upsets your colleagues and makes your work more difficult.

The *90-9-1 principle* (also referred to as the *1 percent principle*) refers to the understanding that 90 percent of people in any online space will only *lurk*—that is, view content without participating—while 9 percent will edit, remix, or share content, and only 1 percent will create new content. It is helpful to keep this principle in mind in the context of professional self-presentation because it is never apparent whom you are reaching. In fact, someone might follow your posts over a long period of time and develop an opinion of you, without you ever knowing. Understanding the *90-9-1 principle* allows us the opportunity to consider that our online presence influences people in substantial ways and to

260

adjust our online presence accordingly. But don't fret too much about who might be reading your posts and how they might view your online image. Instead, focus on sharing good content—because the upside of having lurkers follow your online presence is that you have plenty of opportunities to be seen as an effective and innovative student affairs professional. Having a good idea of what is helpful and well received by others allows one to build a mental framework to help guide what and how you share on social media.

WHAT SHOULD BE SHARED?

Social media like Facebook were originally developed for users to share personal identities and content. However, the lines become blurred for some when using social media professionally. To alleviate this tension, some educators have separate personal and professional social media accounts. However, segmenting one's online image in that way is not helpful for professional self-presentation. The adage of not "mixing work and play" doesn't really hold for these sites. Chapter 5 describes how educators must demystify the professoriat in order to help students with their academic integration—especially students from disenfranchised backgrounds. The same is true for student affairs professionals; however, student affairs professionals, by virtue of the nature of their career, already have less social distance between themselves and their students. So why increase this social distance online? One possibility is the fear of slipping up on social media and suffering negative job consequences as a result. Certainly, that is an issue to consider; however, it is also helpful to consider how the personal-professional dichotomy plays out in the offline world.

In any offline professional environment, employees always have personal relationships. For instance, coworkers invite each other to dinner or to have a drink after work. Some division heads invite their supervisees and direct reports to their home for get-togethers. Furthermore, personal relationships extend and blend into work time—colleagues who are friends talk about what they did with their families over the weekend. Social media are analogous to such interactions; just as you wouldn't arrive at your dean's house drunk, you wouldn't embarrass your department publicly on social media. In this sense, there is not much difference between the offline and online world; therefore, student affairs professionals are encouraged to interact on social media using their real identities in order to build an online professional presence. It is not as important that we have a sanitized online professional image as it is to have an image that is professional yet congruent with our personal identities. In other words, the person you are in your position as a student affairs professional should shine through on social media in the same way as the person you are shines through in interactions with colleagues and students.

There is evidence to show that sharing professional information online leads to desirable professional outcomes. Eysenbach (2011) found that there was a significant correlation between the number of tweets mentioning an academic article within the first seven days after publication and citations to that article. Furthermore, Eysenbach (2011) found that "highly tweeted articles were 11 times more likely to be highly cited than less-tweeted articles." In other words, promoting a research paper on Twitter leads to more citations for the paper, presumably because more people find out about and read the article. Melissa Terras, from the London School of Economics and Political Science, wondered whether making all of her papers publicly available and blogging and tweeting about them would influence the impact of her work (Terras, 2012). She discovered that there were huge spikes in download counts for her papers after she blogged and tweeted about them—and that her download counts were substantially higher than those of her colleagues (who, Terras reported, were also doing great work). Terras (2012) found that the papers she blogged and tweeted about were eleven times more likely to be downloaded; she concluded, "If you want people to find and read your research, build up a digital presence in your discipline, and use it to promote your work when you have something interesting to share. It's pretty darn obvious, really."

Even though Eysenbach's (2011) and Terras's (2012) findings focused on academic publishing, they are directly applicable to student affairs. Imagine how this process might work for student affairs professionals: You are excited about a major initiative you've directed on your campus, which has shown a positive impact. Then, you blog about this initiative and tweet about it using the #sachat hashtag to reach a broad community of student affairs professionals. The next thing you know, deans, SSAOs, and other professionals are asking you to comment about implementing the same initiative at their college or university. Not only have you contributed your work in a positive way to the community, but you have also added value to your online professional image. Continuing to share your work and other resources that might be helpful to the broader community of student affairs professionals helps to establish your image as a capable student affairs expert in others' eyes.

Information literacy skills are important for student affairs professionals, not just to possess themselves, but also to model in online social spaces. Don't retweet, share, or post things that you haven't read and critically evaluated. You wouldn't cite a journal article that you haven't read in your academic writing, so why would you share something online that you haven't read? Doing so shows a lack of information evaluation skills at best and at worst could suggest you agree with a viewpoint that does not comport with your own beliefs and may even be seen as distasteful by others. Pay particular attention to and take additional precautions with provocative headlines. Take it upon yourself to model behavior that shows strong information evaluation skills, not just to your students, but also to others in your PLN. Indeed, when you critically evaluate an article and find inferential gaps, share that information on social media. Doing so helps position your online professional image as a person who will evaluate all information with the academic rigor expected of all professionals in higher education.

One method of learning what an appropriate online professional image looks like is to review the social media presence of other professionals. In other words, become a lurker and learn about the culture of online professionalism in higher education and student affairs before becoming an active member of the community. Ed Cabellon often reflects about online professional presentation on his blog, *On the Go with Ed Cabellon*. In one post, Cabellon (2013) reflected on some ideas for using social media to constructively build an online professional image.

The following are ideas for social media activities to build an online professional image (Cabellon, 2013):

- "Check in" to events, buildings, service areas, and so on by adding a location to your Facebook posts, checking in on Facebook places, or by checking in on FourSquare and posting the check-in to Twitter. Doing so shows not only your participation in events but also your presence on campus.
- Tag colleagues in pictures, videos, or location check-ins on Facebook, or @reply colleagues on Twitter, along with sending them a positive message. This helps build engagement with your posts and communicates interest in a collegial relationship with fellow professionals.
- When you share anything you'd classify as professional on Facebook, make sure that the post is shared publicly. If you

are posting professional content on Twitter, ensure that your tweets are set to be public. As discussed earlier, doing so shows others what you are doing and helps them perceive you as a competent professional.

· Share helpful articles that you are reading on Twitter. Showing members of the online community what you found helpful adds to others' PLNs but also shows where your interests lie.

· Connect with students on Facebook by friending them, interacting with student group pages, and tagging them in content (such as pictures from events). Doing so extends your student affairs work into online social spaces and can support students' academic and social integration.

· Connect with students and other members of your institutional and local community on Twitter by doing keyword searches for your institution's name and location. Then, interact by replying to questions and providing helpful suggestions. Doing so models a commitment to the institution that will likely be modeled by students, further increasing their academic integration.

· Share useful tweets with colleagues who aren't on Twitter via e-mail. Not only does such sharing extend the resources of your PLN, it might serve to help build your PLN by attracting more colleagues to the site.

Cabellon (2013) emphasizes the need to share your accomplishments, "especially those that involved your staff, students, and other divisional staff members. Whether it's a new program or service; publication; or honor bestowed upon [us], no one tells the Student Affairs story better than us." Cabellon (2013) suggests that social media can be used in this way to add qualitative data to show our impact—and as discussed in the previous section,

265

showing our impact publicly makes a positive impact on our division as well as on our professional online image.

CONCLUSION

Social media can be used as efficient and effective tools for student affairs professionals to support their professional development. Indeed, evidence shows that sharing professional work on social media leads to positive career outcomes. Social technologies can be used to build and maintain a personal learning network that allows a professional to build social capital; these communities of practice can support career development and also help professionals convey their accomplishments to a broader audience. Twitter is often used to build PLNs by aggregating communities of practice around hashtags. In student affairs, the #sachat hashtag hosts a weekly live chat as well as an ongoing open forum for professionals to interact with others across institutions. This forum is especially helpful for student affairs professionals in divisions with limited resources; in fact, the building of social capital through Twitter can help decrease job stress.

Student affairs professionals need to be well versed in promoting their online professional image, as it is no longer acceptable to have no online presence. Social media can be used to develop and project this professional image and to showcase a professional's skills. Using social media effectively can help student affairs professionals showcase their communication, information literacy, collaboration, technology, and functional area skills. Communication skills can be highlighted when a professional's online interactions show that the person can communicate effectively not just within their division but also across institutions. Information literacy can be demonstrated by evaluating shared content critically and by sharing only content that has been screened for quality. Professionals can show their collaboration skills by highlighting how they work with those in their PLN and their technology skills by showcasing creative ways they are using technology—such as creating videos of their work or designing a blog theme. Finally, student affairs professionals can use social media to help broadcast their professional skills to interested parties. Using social media for professional development will help the field of student affairs grow in ways previously unimagined and ultimately will help us serve our students more effectively.

Practical Tips

1. Develop a personal learning network to help support your professional development.
2. Follow conference hashtags to supplement your professional development.
3. Cultivate your online professional image through blog posts and participation in professional social media communities.
4. Find the right balance between sharing personal and professional information on social media.
5. Use social media to communicate your professional accomplishments.

REFERENCES

Alarcon, G. M. (2011). A meta-analysis of burnout with job demands, resources, and attitudes. *Journal of Vocational Behavior*, 79(2), 549–562.

Bährer-Kohler, S. (2013). *Burnout for Experts: Prevention in the Context of Living and Working*. New York: Springer.

Burke, R. J., Noblet, A. J., & Cooper, C. L. (2013). *Human Resource Management in the Public Sector*. New Horizons in Management Series. Northampton, MA: Edward Elgar.

Cabellon, E. (2013). Your student affairs selfie. Retrieved January 31, 2014, from http://edcabellon.com/leadership/saselfie/.

CareerBuilder.com. (2012). Thirty-seven percent of companies use social networks to research potential job candidates, according to new CareerBuilder Survey. Retrieved February 2, 2014, from http://www.careerbuilder.com/share/aboutus/pressreleasesdetail.aspx?id=pr691&sd=4%2F18%2F2012&ed=4%2F18%2F2099.

Eysenbach, G. (2011). Can tweets predict citations? Metrics of social impact based on Twitter and correlation with traditional metrics of scientific impact. *Journal of Medical Internet Research, 13*(4).

Junco, R., Dahms, A. R., Bower, M. L., Craddock, S., Davila, D. S., Hamilton, M., & Kane, C. (2010). Media review: #sachat on Twitter. *Journal of Student Affairs Research and Practice, 47*(2), 7.

Kruger, J., Epley, N., Parker, J., & Ng, Z. (2005). Egocentrism over e-mail: Can we communicate as well as we think? *Journal of Personality and Social Psychology, 89*(6), 925–936.

Swider, B. W., & Zimmerman, R. D. (2010). Born to burnout: A meta-analytic path model of personality, job burnout, and work outcomes. *Journal of Vocational Behavior, 76*(3), 487–506.

Terras, M. (2012). The verdict: Is blogging or tweeting about research papers worth it? *The Impact Blog*. Retrieved February 2, 2014, from http://blogs.lse.ac.uk/impactofsocialsciences/2012/04/19/blog-tweeting-papers-worth-it/.

Veletsianos, G. (2012). Higher education scholars' participation and practices on Twitter. *Journal of Computer Assisted Learning, 28*(4), 336–349.

Warlick, D. (2009). Grow your personal learning network: New technologies can keep you connected and help you manage information overload. *Learning & Leading with Technology, 36*(6), 12–16.

268

CHAPTER 8

The Future of Social Media in Student Affairs

Up to this point, we've been discussing the *present*—social media sites and services students are currently using. We often think that technological innovation is tied to societal progress; however, we also tend to think that most emerging technologies will be short-lived. One thing is certain: technological progress moves ahead at a lightning speed, while societal and psychological adaptation to these technologies lags behind. We've seen this with other technologies that create great societal tensions about their use, like the typewriter, telephone, and television. *Moore's Law* is the proposition that the number of transistors on integrated circuits will double about every eighteen months. Moore (1965) described this trend, and it has proved surprisingly accurate over the years (see figure 8.1). You might be wondering how Moore's Law, about

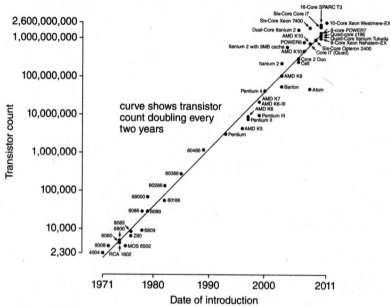

Figure 8.1. Graph illustrating Moore's Law: a plot of the actual number of transistors in computer central processing units over time. Note that there has been exponential growth, with transistor counts doubling every two years.

transistors, applies to social media. We can extrapolate from Moore's Law to forecast the proliferation of new social technologies and new methods for interacting with them. Social technologies will likely continue to evolve and develop in ways that we might not be able to imagine, with a resultant lag in societal understanding and adaptation.

Years before Facebook was invented and when Mark Zuckerberg was still in high school, Wellman (2001) described how the Internet was helping people extend their offline social networks. He wrote, "It is becoming clear that the Internet is not destroying

270

community but is resonating with and extending the types of networked community that have already become prevalent in the developed Western world" (Wellman, 2001, p. 2032). Although I've focused on the applications we now call *social media*, it is clear that the Internet was used for social connections well before we had these containers for our social interactions (such as Facebook, Twitter, Instagram, and LinkedIn). We've been social online long before the advent of our current set of social media, and we'll be social long after Facebook and Twitter have been forgotten. But what comes next?

Perhaps not exactly paraphrasing Oscar Wilde, "social media imitate life, and life imitates social media." In other words, new technologies are developed all the time that help people be more social, more productive, and so on. However, only a few catch on to reach the popularity of Facebook and Twitter. Perhaps the primary reason some social media are adopted and some fall to the wayside is that certain sites and services fill a social or societal need at the time they are developed. Sometimes, as is the case with the sites popular today, it was unclear there was a need until after the sites were developed and adopted. Clearly, college students wanted a technologically mediated way to learn about and interact with their on-campus peers, and Facebook gave them that. Widespread adoption after Facebook was opened up to all users showed a societal need for increased connection. Indeed, as Western society has become more affluent, individuals move around more and have less opportunity to establish strong offline bonds (Oishi, 2010). Social media sites and services like Facebook allow people to maintain and strengthen already existing connections even after moving away geographically.

Carl Sagan's seemingly bleak reflections on our *technological adolescence* are pertinent when thinking about the social tensions inherent in technological growth: because of our technological progress, Sagan thought we might destroy ourselves before reaching greater states of human, technological, and industrial development. We may be so captivated by technological progress that we would develop an alluring technology that, when used, would destroy life. In the movie version of his book *Contact*, Sagan expanded this idea to address the tension between technological progress and social isolation. The main character, Ellie, is selected as the only human to travel in a machine and to meet an alien. When she meets the alien, who has taken the form of her deceased father, he reflects on the human condition: "You feel so lost, so cut off, so alone. Only you're not. See, in all our searching the only thing we've found that makes the emptiness bearable is each other." Humans have a need to connect, and the progress of industrialization has forced onto us increased social distance; however, with social technologies, we are able to take a piece of that very industry that made us disconnected and use it to connect and "make the emptiness bearable." Think about this need for connection in the context of a new student moving away from home and onto campus for the first time. He or she has a strong need to affiliate, to connect with peers, to feel validated, and ultimately to feel loved (Maslow, 1943). Social media help us seek these connections in new ways.

While social media allow us to connect in ways we were unable to in the past, social tensions do arise as society progresses along the social media adoption curve. Other chapters have covered the adult normative perspective: the viewpoint that interprets youth behavior in terms of adult norms. Traditional media outlets really benefit by promoting the negatives of youth social media use, and these messages are adopted by adults and often by youth themselves. Additionally, these messages are integrated into K–12 education; while policies are starting to change, almost all K–12 school districts ban the use of social media. Traditional media outlets typically select stories about social media because they are provocative and garner viewership or readership; unfor-

272

tunately, almost exclusively the most popularized stories are about negative impacts of social media use. Further, reporters are not scientists so (1) they don't seek evidence that contradicts their theories and (2) they rarely judge the scientific methods of a story, especially one focused on research about social media. Clearly, some negative outcomes are associated with social media use, but the positive outcomes must be considered as well. Social tension arises because we as a society "write off" social media or, worse, see social media as eroding the fabric of our society and ruining our youth. Part of this tension, no doubt, stems from a lack of understanding from those who didn't grow up with social media.

It's a lot easier to stick with a preconceived notion than to try to collect evidence to negate that notion. If we rigidly believe that social media are "bad," then we are also saying that youth are engaging in harmful behavior daily, even though these technologies are integrated fully into the fabric of their normal social lives and psychological development. Student affairs professionals do not get to have the luxury of following along with the status quo—they must engage in personal and professional soul-searching to best help support and challenge students. To be clear, there are situations and reasons requiring us to be mindful of the dangers of social media use and to communicate that information to students. However, these communications will be much better received and more effective when we engage with students from their perspective, not ours. As suggested in earlier chapters, there's no better way to "lose" a student than to take a prescriptive approach. The goal is not for students to think, "This person knows nothing about what I do online and yet they are telling me what I do is wrong," but instead to think, "This person understands what I do online and is helping me see some of the ways that I can use social media to my benefit."

New technologies are developed and adopted at such a rapid rate that they allow us little time to "catch up" psychologically and socially. Mobile phones have changed the way we communicate in obvious and not-so-obvious ways. Commenting on her own observations as well as data from Neilsen about mobile phone use, Paul (2011) exclaimed, "nobody calls me anymore." Paul (2011) was commenting on the social phenomenon of preferring text messaging to voice calls and pointed out that some people become annoyed when they receive an unplanned phone call. Another psychological and societal tension involving mobile phones is texting and driving. Texting while driving is hazardous (Drews, Yazdani, Godfrey, Cooper & Strayer, 2009) and doubles the chances of a crash or near-crash (Fitch et al., 2013). Nevertheless, drivers still text. Part of the reason is that our judgments about the safety of texting and driving are just developing; this issue was not a concern before the advent of mobile phones that made texting easier through the use of a keyboard, cell phone plans that allowed unlimited texting, and a societal shift away from making phone calls to texting. In this sense, and as Sagan warned, individually and as a society we have to catch up with technology before our behaviors associated with that technology quite literally kill us; in other words, we have to survive our technological adolescence. More people are becoming aware of the dangers of text messaging, and as of this writing forty-one states have passed laws making it illegal to text while driving (though legislation is not necessarily the best way to handle this issue, at least these states recognize the problem).

Student affairs professionals must work to understand how students are using emerging technologies, both discovering what is normative and beneficial and also learning about how these technologies can (and do) harm students. The goal is to help students minimize the negative impacts of technology while promoting the positive. Understanding the social and psychological tensions inherent in the adoption of technology in general will help you predict how students will react to new technologies with similar affordances. For instance, it is no surprise that youth use Snapchat to send silly, embarrassing, or provocative pictures, given that Snapchat has affordances similar to those of Instagram and texting (the ability to send a picture directly to a friend's phone) as well as 4chan (the "temporary" and ephemeral nature of the pictures (Bernstein et al., 2011; Madden et al., 2013)). Another social tension that Snapchat may fuel in the future is an increase or a shift to communicating via images instead of text messages, given the rapid growth in technologies that enable such sharing.

The founder of Snapchat, Evan Spiegel, said, "The minute you tell someone that images on your server disappear, everyone jumps to sexting" (Gallagher, 2012). Even though he's trying to minimize this issue, it does seem that Snapchat affords users more comfort with sexting. Snapchat, then, is a good example of the tensions between how youth use and understand a technology and how adults interpret their behaviors. American society has interesting double standards about sexuality. We have a puritanical taboo against talking about sexuality very directly, even though we support rather explicit portrayals of sexuality in movies, television, and advertising. We sexualize and exploit children in advertising, turning girls into part-objects that bear little resemblance to what women actually look like, yet we have a great problem thinking and talking about emerging adult sexuality. As a result, sexting is automatically seen as something negative. What if adolescents *are* sexting? What if, and I posit that this is actually the case, sexting is a healthy and normative outlet of young adult sexuality?

Sexting doesn't indicate a significant change in teen sexual behavior or risk taking. Instead, sexting just makes teen sexual behaviors more visible to adults. Research has shown a correlation between sexting and being sexually active; however, there is no relationship between sexting and riskier sexual behaviors like unprotected sex (Rice et al., 2012). Additionally, longitudinal data show that the proportion of US adolescents who are sexually active has declined in recent years (Finer & Philbin, 2013; Klein, 2005). Other research has also suggested that sexting is a normal facet of young adult sexual activity (Lenhart, 2009) used by older teens as yet another way to explore and develop their identities (Katzman, 2010). Sexting is especially important for young adults who are exploring an LGBT identity (Rice et al., 2012). Of course, the danger inherent in sending nude pictures of oneself is that those pictures will be sent to other parties or even posted on the Internet for the public to see. Having pictures shared publicly becomes yet another tension in the relationship among society, technology, and different modes and cultures of use because of societal norms about nudity and sexuality as well as what my colleague Eric Gordon and I call the "asshole problem."

The "asshole" problem: Sexting is a normative part of emerging adult (and even emerged adult) sexual expression. However, some unscrupulous actors (who are appropriately termed *assholes*) will release these images publicly and break the trust of the sender. Such behaviors are perhaps related to the asshole's inability to process discontent about the subject of the picture in a healthy way. The person whose image is shared is at an added risk because US society has a problem not only with young adult sexuality specifically but with nudity in general. Indeed, we have criminalized nudity in public spaces like beaches, an idea anathema to a majority of European Union citizens. So when an image is released that has been shared in confidence, it is not evaluated as a mistake of youth but instead is seen as that person's sexual deviancy.

Ideally, it would be understood in our culture that young adults, teens, and college students can actually engage in normal and normative expressions of sexuality. The tension that arises when sexting images are released publicly is between youth who use sexting as a natural form of self-expression and sexual identity exploration and individuals who have not spent their formative years using technology in the same ways. As examined in chapter 1, this dilemma speaks to the issue of digital inequalities expressed when those with privilege, like an admissions officer or a potential boss, pass judgment on a younger person because of cultural differences in behavior. Luckily, this doesn't happen often, with one study finding that only 2 percent of sexters had their photo shared with someone they didn't want to see it (Cox Communications, 2009). While it is unlikely that a future employer or admissions officer could see a photo shared in confidence, it is more likely that peers will share and shame the sexter for the image. But it's not the peers' fault. Adolescents who would shame someone for having taken a nude photograph are just reacting in the same way that we do as a society—engaging in double standards about sexuality.

Sexting has parallels in other cultural taboos. For example, in American culture we rarely discuss the fact that as adults we are sexually active, yet many adults have children. This discussion is necessarily provocative when viewed through the adult normative lens, which serves to emphasize the point that just because youth are engaging in a behavior doesn't mean it is incorrect or "wrong," and just because an individual thinks something is "right" doesn't mean it's right for everybody. In fact, research by the Pew Internet and American Life Project shows that adults aged twenty-five to thirty-four are more likely to sext than any other age group (Lenhart & Duggan, 2014). Perhaps as we mature as a society, some of these tensions will dissipate, though they may well be replaced by new tensions between emerging technologies

277

and social forces. These are some dynamics to be aware of as future technologies develop that allow for sharing of more intimate details of our lives. Indeed, in late 2013, Google released its Glass product, which is a device that is worn like eyeglasses and which offers much of the functionality of a mobile phone— including the capability to take pictures and videos. One can see the opportunity for youth to use Glass to document even more private details of their lives and easily share them publicly.

Expect that the future will bring new social media technologies that will help us move closer together and battle the social distance inherent in our fast-paced and mobile worlds. What exactly these technologies will look like is beyond the prognosticating abilities of this author; however, I have great hope that these technologies will be positive outlets for students and others to explore their identities, share, connect, create, and build communities and networks to support their psychosocial and physical development. Furthermore, and of importance to student affairs professionals, how students use these technologies will predict their benefits (and risks). Using new technologies for connection and communication will likely continue to predict positive outcomes, while using new technologies for disconnection and isolation will lead to negative outcomes. The processes are important to understand as student affairs professionals keep up with new technological trends—and the most straightforward way to do this is to talk to the students themselves.

Don't believe the hype when you hear about a new technology "ruining our youth," because perhaps that new technology is helping youth connect and engage in ways never before possible (Ridenhour, Shocklee, Sadler & Drayton, 1988). Take it upon yourself, as an educator who specializes in the culture of students, to explore with them how they are using the technology, what it means to them, and its affordances. Learn about the technology yourself: What are the benefits and pitfalls? Sign up for an account—if there is such a thing as an account—and explore the technology yourself. Oliver Sacks (1995) titled one of his books *An Anthropologist on Mars*—a phrase used by Temple Grandin, who was diagnosed with autism, to describe her inability to understand the nuances of human emotion. To compensate, she would attempt to discern cognitively how people would behave in certain situations. In other words, she was an observer of human interactions and emotions, cognitively learning from them as much as she could to balance out her inability to understand them emotionally.

Student affairs professionals are urged to be "anthropologists on Mars" when it comes to current and future technology use. Be curious and view students' digital worlds through their eyes; then, tie their experiences to your knowledge of student development to help students in their growth. Make sure, however, that by doing so you are not driving a wedge between yourself and your students. One of my biggest professional regrets is that some readers interpreted the information in our *Connecting to the Net. Generation* book to mean that our students are so different from us that we can never truly understand them (Junco & Mastrodicasa, 2007). This interpretation is perhaps exactly opposite to the book's intention and a most unfitting viewpoint for someone working in the field of student affairs. As educators, we must strive to build interpersonal connections with our students that will help engage them, add to their social and academic integration, and challenge and support them through their college years (and perhaps beyond). Thinking that our students are very different from us because they do things differently is the same as stereotyping, say, all Latino or all lesbian students. So, as you move forward and consider new technologies that emerge and, more important, how students use those technologies, it helps to take a curious stance, more like an anthropologist than a student affairs professional. The more you can learn about student normative behavior, the better you will be at connecting with students and making a positive difference in their lives.

In terms of personal adoption of new technologies, if you are a social media crusader, try your best to be a social media skeptic, and vice versa. As you have no doubt gathered from reading this book, the gray area of social media enthusiasm—where you understand that there are benefits and pitfalls and that these depend on how the technologies are used—is a good place from which to examine and figure out what is best for our students. Removing ourselves from the poles of the crusader-skeptic dichotomy allows us to be more critical about the methods we are using to engage students in educationally relevant interventions. By reducing our ego investment in a particular outcome based on our preexisting viewpoint, we become more open to evaluating the effectiveness of our interventions. Put another way, being open to being wrong about the benefits (and the pitfalls) of social media allows us to have a clearer view of what is actually happening in the lives of our students. This outlook will propel us to address new technologies with vigor and to be on the leading edge of supporting students.

LEARNING AND TRACE ANALYTICS

While a number of currently emerging technologies might be of potential benefit to student development and learning, none seems more promising and more suitable to an evidence-based approach than learning analytics. *Learning analytics* is the use of student-produced data to predict outcomes and tailor education and is often thought of as a practical application of big data in education. An example of the use of big data outside of education is the way a website like Amazon.com knows the kinds of things that you like based on your shopping and web browsing habits. Another example is the way Google tracks your browsing habits in order to provide ads uniquely tailored to you on the web pages you visit: Google crunches data using "secret sauce" algorithms to predict what you want to buy and what you will buy, based not just on your own behavior, but also on the behavior of other like-minded users. Although these examples may be seen as under-handed marketing practices, the same methods can be used to benefit students in educational settings.

Up to this point, student affairs professionals have had to rely on limited sources of data to predict student success and to identify students with whom they might need to intervene. For instance, how can we tell whether a student is struggling academi-cally? Typically we have relied on students' overall, semester, or (when available) midterm grade point averages. Sometimes, when we work closely with students, they might share their course exam and paper grades with us. These data, however, are of limited use in helping students succeed—for if a student comes to us for help once they've already failed a few exams or, worse, an entire semes-ter, it is much more difficult to help the student get back on track. Advisors often suggest that first-semester students drop a course instead of receiving a poor grade because of the potential blow to their overall GPA, which affects continued enrollment in a major or at the institution. Surveys, learning outcomes assessments, and student demographic information have been other sources tradi-tionally used to try to identify students in need of help—again, with limited predictive ability.

Imagine that you could have data, collected unobtrusively, showing which students might need additional support in real time. Learning analytics can be used to provide important data about student success without having to rely on traditional, weak measures. The process of learning analytics is focused on collect-ing large amounts of data in order to identify patterns that will help tailor education more precisely for each student. This process has its roots in the big data revolution—the use of massive amounts

281

of data along with great computing power to find patterns and make predictions. These processes have been applied to making predictions about personal traits, behaviors, and shopping habits. In a study exemplifying the predictive ability of simple data, Kosinski, Stillwell, and Graepel (2013) found that Facebook "likes" predicted, with a high degree of accuracy, traits such as age, gender, sexual orientation, race, religious preference, and political affiliation. Facebook likes also predicted with a good degree of accuracy relationship status, substance use, whether a user's parents stayed together or separated before the user reached the age of 21, and the personality traits of Openness, Extraversion, and intelligence (Kosinski, Stillwell & Graepel, 2013). To put it simply, online behavior that doesn't seem to be related to complex information such as a person's sexual orientation or the fact he or she is an extrovert actually yields a great deal of predictive power for such outcomes.

The following five steps of analysis characterize the learning analytics process (Campbell & Oblinger, 2007):

1. *Capture:* Data are collected or captured through various methods, such as a course or learning management system, enrollment databases, or the student information system.
2. *Report:* Once data have been captured, aggregated, and stored in a location such as a database, those with access can run basic descriptive reports.
3. *Predict:* Ultimately, the goal of learning analytics is to build predictive models using statistical techniques like linear and logistic regression.
4. *Act:* Predictive models help administrators and student affairs professionals take actionable steps, whether to

provide students with information or to develop and implement an intervention.

5. *Refine:* The final step is to use information from the process to improve further iterations of the system.

In practice and up to this point, the majority of learning analytics projects collect data from learning and course management systems. Purdue University's Signals analytic project exemplifies how colleges and universities are using learning analytics today. The Signals project mines data from the student information system (SIS), course management system (CMS), and grade book to flag at-risk students by posting a traffic signal indicator on the CMS homepage (Arnold & Pistilli, 2012). Signals uses the following four components to predict a student's risk status: percentage or points earned in the course, the student's interactions on the Blackboard CMS compared with their peers, their academic background (high school GPA, SAT scores), and student characteristics. Based on the results of this predictive model, the traffic signal indicator may be changed, an e-mail message or text message sent, or a referral made to an academic advisor or for a face-to-face meeting with a course instructor (Arnold & Pistilli, 2012). Typically, activity data collected through learning analytics tools include information about engagement with the learning community, uploading content, quiz scores, and number of logins (Dawson, McWilliam & Tan, 2008; Macfadyen & Dawson, 2012). However, *engagement* is typically narrowly defined as posts on discussion forums, chat sessions, and CMS message access (Dawson, McWilliam & Tan, 2008).

Research shows a relationship between CMS activity and course outcomes. In a study at a single university, Macfadyen and Dawson (2012) found that the number of discussion messages posted, the number of discussion messages read, and the number of discussion replies posted were all significantly related to final course grades. A similar study by Smith, Lange, and Huston (2012) found that log-in frequency, site engagement, weighted log-in frequency, weighted site engagement, and points submitted were all correlated with successful course outcome (that is, whether students earned a final letter grade of C or higher). The problem with these analyses is that course grade is partly dependent on CMS activity, and therefore correlations between CMS activity and course grades reflect students' completion of actual assignments. Put another way, correlating CMS activity with final course grade is similar to correlating required assignments to final course grade—there will always be a strong relationship between the two, for if students don't complete the assignments, they don't pass the course. Although this distinction seems simple, it serves to illustrate that the results of current implementations of predictive analytics are weaker than reported. If these projects were to parse out the variance associated with required online activity, their predictive power would likely suffer. Furthermore, while some learning analytics systems like Purdue Signals include data from sources extraneous to the CMS, most do not.

Unfortunately, typical projects fall short of the promise of learning analytics because they use limited types and amounts of data (such as number of posts and discussion views). In addition, the predictive statistics uncovered are often exaggerated because of an existing relationship between assignment completion and course outcomes. What is needed in the field of learning analytics is an expansion of the systems to collect and use data that bolster predictive models and that allow for more fine-tuned interventions. With any predictive model, increasing the number and quality of the predictors should, to a point, produce more accurate results. As we have seen from research outside of education, such as that of Kosinski and colleagues (2013), seemingly meaningless data can be used to make strong predictions about people and their behaviors.

Trace analytics is the term I have coined to refer to using seemingly irrelevant user-generated data to predict learning outcomes. These data are usually disregarded or not even thought about by the end user. Some examples of data that can be used for trace analytics include time spent on various computer activities, geolocation data, check-ins, proportion of social and recreational uses of technology versus academic uses, and incidental activities on websites (such as Facebook likes or Twitter retweets). You might wonder how these activities could possibly predict academic outcomes. The concept behind such "spooky analytics" is almost purely psychometric and requires a discussion of the difference between observed and true scores. In psychometrics, classical test theory presumes that each person has a *true score* on any given construct (such as intelligence), which is the score that would be obtained if there were no errors in measurement of that construct. However, we can never correctly know a person's true score and must approximate it by understanding that the true score is a combination of the *observed score* on a test along with *error*.

We can extend this idea to constructs. A major problem of correlational research is the "third, fourth, fifth, etc. variable problem"—that is, that a presumed causal relationship between two variables might actually be caused by an unmeasured third, fourth, or fifth variable (or some combination of variables). As explained in chapter 1, the negative correlation discovered between Facebook use and grades may be caused by a student's self-regulation or lack thereof (Junco, 2012; Kirschner & Karpinski, 2010). In such a case, self-regulation would mediate the relationship between Facebook use and grades as well as be related to both. A student who has less motivation to engage in

285

academic pursuits may be one who uses Facebook more and may have lower grades—not because the student uses Facebook more but because the student is not motivated to engage in academic-related activities. In such a case, the relationship between Facebook and grades is spurious. While my study (Junco, 2012) and the one by Kirschner and Karpinski (2010) did not measure self-regulation, student Facebook use might have been a proxy for this construct. Of course Facebook use does not fully equate to self-regulation; however, in this example, Facebook use might share enough variance with student self-regulation that it serves well as a proxy. Extrapolating this example out further and in combination with research showing that seemingly irrelevant data can predict significant outcomes, we can see how social media trace analytics might serve useful purposes in predicting student success.

The Association for Middle Level Education (AMLE) defines formative assessment as part of the educational process; when "incorporated into classroom practice, it provides the information needed to adjust teaching and learning while they are happening" (Garrison & Ehringhaus, 2007, p. 1). Furthermore, "formative assessment helps teachers determine next steps during the learning process as the instruction approaches the summative assessment of student learning" (Garrison & Ehringhaus, 2007, p. 2). Adding trace analytics to existing learning analytics methods can enhance their ability to serve as formative assessments in order to identify student struggles and intervene as necessary. Therefore, one way to greatly increase the predictive ability of existing learning analytics systems would be to add to the predictive models the time students spent using search engines, on Facebook, and using word processing applications. Adding additional data would not only increase the models' predictive ability but also help provide data at more regular intervals that can be used to "check in" on how students are doing. Put another way, faculty and administrators could know which students may be at risk before they complete their very first course assignment.

Research has found a number of noncognitive variables that are related to student success, such as time spent studying and appropriate use of study skills (Ackerman, 1987; Annis, 1985; Ryan, 1984; Steinberg, Fegley & Dornbusch, 1993), Study Management and Academic Results Tests (SMART) scores (Kleijn, Ploeg & Topman, 1994), cognitive strategy (Naumann, 1999), self concept/efficacy (Obrentz, 2012; Tobey, 1997), Test of Reaction and Adaptation to College (TRAC) scores (Falardeau, Larose & Roy, 1989), and student motivation as measured by the Kaufman-Agars Motivation-orientation Scale (KAMS) and personality characteristics such as the Big Five personality factor Conscientiousness (Kaufman, Agars & Lopez-Wagner, 2008; Komarraju, Karau & Schmeck, 2009; Komarraju, Karau, Schmeck & Avdic, 2011). Trace analytics can serve as a way to measure, via proxy, these noncognitive variables critical to student success.

Self-regulation has emerged as a noncognitive variable that is strongly related to student success (Duckworth & Carlson, 2013). Duckworth and Carlson (2013) define *self-regulation* as "the voluntary control of attentional, emotional, and behavioral impulses in the service of personally valued goals and standards" (p. 209). Some researchers have suggested that self-regulation is almost identical to the Big Five personality factor of Conscientiousness (Caspi & Shiner, 2010; Moffitt et al., 2011). The links between Conscientiousness and academic outcomes are well established (Kaufman, Agars & Lopez-Wagner, 2008; Komarraju, Karau & Schmeck, 2009; Komarraju, Karau, Schmeck & Avdic, 2011). While not currently possible, research is under way to identify *trace data* that can be easily collected and can serve as proxies for these noncognitive variables. The goal is to provide faculty members and interested administrators the ability to conduct real-time monitoring and assessment of student progress well before the student submits any formal learning assessment in a course.

Geolocation data might be an effective source of trace analytics. De Montjoye, Hidalgo, Verleysen, and Blondel (2013) studied a dataset of about 1.5 million mobile phone users. As with any mobile phone, each time a user initiates or receives a call or a text message, the location of the connecting antenna is recorded in the mobile operator's log. De Montjoye and colleagues (2013) used the geospatial trace data collected by such use and found that they could uniquely identify 95 percent of individuals using just four of these geospatial points. In other words, data gathered automatically and without the knowledge of mobile phone users can reveal private information about an individual. Anyone with access to such data can uniquely identify you and then reidentify you at any time without any additional information.

While the De Montjoye and colleagues (2013) study has serious privacy implications, especially for those who use location-based social networks like FourSquare, the study's findings suggest that such information might be used to support student learning. Adding geolocation data to predictive analytics can help us build even stronger predictive models of student success. Perhaps it's the case that students who visit the library more do better on their chemistry exams but not on their psychology exams, and that students who do better on their psychology exams happen to visit the psychology building more. Aggregating these geolocation data with other trace analytics like digital textbook usage data could serve to bolster the identification of students who are at risk of performing poorly in their psychology and chemistry courses even before they take an exam. Alerting faculty, advisors, and student support professionals of potentially at-risk students as early as possible can help educators engage in conversations with these students to address their needs, which could have an impact on proximate course outcomes. Perhaps chemistry students may not need to be encouraged to visit the library more (although that's probably a good idea); instead, it may be that library usage is tied to another critical student success variable like self-regulation. So knowing that a student is using the library less might be an indicator that we have to help her or him with organizational skills, study strategies, or self-regulation.

How Might Trace Analytics Be Used in Practice?

In the past, we have identified "at-risk" students based on categories—lumping all students who are from low socioeconomic status backgrounds or all first-generation college students in one group. Categorical groupings based on background characteristics help focus our attention, yet they also include many more students than we need to focus on. Such groupings also exclude at-risk students who don't share these background characteristics. However, trace analytics allow us to move beyond these categorical groupings and identify specific students who are at risk based on their behaviors. This is a key distinction; anyone who has worked in higher education long enough has met students in the "at-risk" category who are more motivated, focused, and successful than the general population of students. Trace analytics would allow student affairs professionals an efficient and unobtrusive method of quantifying student characteristics such as engagement, a factor that has been difficult to measure until now. Imagine a residence hall director who has access to predictive results based on trace analytics. These results might show that one of the students in their hall will likely become disengaged within the next few weeks. Since we know that disengaged students are less likely

289

to persist, the residence hall director might choose to intervene more directly with the student in order to improve the student's engagement and, ultimately, persistence.

Trace analytics can effectively predict student learning outcomes. Some of my research has shown that even when controlling for prior academic achievement, user-generated digital textbook usage data can predict student course grades. Furthermore, digital textbook usage data are as strong a predictor of academic outcomes as prior academic achievement (and sometimes an even stronger predictor). This evidence means that we can use a real-time indicator of academic outcomes based on behaviors linked to positive educational outcomes. In other words, a student's reading behavior in any given week of the semester can help inform us about how well that student will do in the class, allowing us to intervene to help the student make fine-tuned adjustments in how he or she is working in a course. A student background characteristic like prior academic achievement will allow us to categorize students only once, into the "at-risk" or "not at-risk" category, whereas digital textbook use data allows us to categorize students at any time during a course—which allows us to be much more effective, because the way that students engage with the course may change at any time during the semester.

Of course, privacy issues need to be addressed when using trace data. Significantly, trace data have roots in commercial applications of big data; therefore, only third parties have the expertise, infrastructure, and processing ability to collect and process these data. That fact means that novel applications of user-generated data in educational contexts will no doubt be handled by vendors not related to the colleges or universities that are using their services. It is crucial, then, that educational institutions delineate privacy ground rules with these companies to protect student data.

The following are some privacy issues that educational institutions must address with technology vendors:

- How will data be collected and transmitted? User data should be decoupled from identifying information at its source. For instance, if textbook analytics data are being collected, then an ID number should be assigned to each student. Data should be encrypted when sent to the vendor handling the analytics.
- How will data be protected when handled by the vendor? What kinds of storage and encryption techniques will be used? Who will have access to the data and under what circumstances? Policies and procedures need to be in place so that the vendors comply with Family Educational Rights and Privacy Act (FERPA) requirements.
- How will the vendor use the data collected beyond their analytics reporting? Will data be used for product improvement? Research and development?
- What happens to student data when the contract with the vendor ends?

While learning analytics is a relatively new field, the potential of trace analytics has not yet begun to be realized. As more interesting applications of these technologies emerge, privacy issues related to them must be addressed. In my work on the textbook analytics project as well as in a larger trace analytics research study, students have reported being comfortable with the data collected and the purposes for which data are used. Transparency is essential in communication with students about trace analytics data collection—indeed, students become more comfortable with such new programs when they know how their information is being used, particularly when they know their data are being used to support their academic success. Since the field of educational trace analytics is in its infancy, it will be crucial to keep tabs on the privacy implications of collecting, analyzing, and reporting such data.

WHAT MIGHT THE CLASSROOM OF THE FUTURE LOOK LIKE?

Looking toward the future, readers of this book are likely to be most interested in technologies that help further engage students in active learning. Currently, there is a movement supporting the *flipped classroom*, where content is delivered outside class (through various technologies) and the actual work (conducted through active learning) happens inside the classroom. Lectures are minimized or removed altogether from flipped classrooms, and they become more engaging academic spaces. Perhaps not all courses or subjects are appropriate for a fully flipped classroom, but the movement will no doubt have an impact on all educational processes. Extrapolating from this movement, we can imagine that the classroom of the future will be an engaging social space, where vigorous conversation and debate are encouraged while technologies are employed to help students collaborate, communicate, and build a sense of classroom community.

The near-term future should bring more social dynamics to the classroom. Chapter 5 outlined how research findings can be used to implement educationally relevant uses of social media in formal learning settings. With more research and more faculty implementing these technologies in relevant ways, there will be a shift in student expectations. Within the next five years or so, it is likely that an increased percentage of faculty will use social media like Facebook as a replacement for LMS threaded discussions and that more will use Twitter to extend classroom discussions and help students build community, as well as integrating these and other technologies in novel ways related to positive academic and social outcomes.

Student affairs practitioners will likely also integrate social media even more in their practice in the near future. The fact that you are reading this book is perhaps a good indicator of the interest in the field for such work. There are already novel and relevant ways to use social media with students in the cocurriculum (see chapter 4), and student affairs professionals will no doubt think of other very creative interventions. The near future will likely also bring more rigorous examination of social media interventions and dissemination of that information so that others may learn from the outcomes. Student affairs professionals are in a unique position to use geolocation to engage students. The location-based gaming platform SCVNGR was used by student affairs professionals to build digital scavenger hunts as part of student orientation activities and to improve academic and social integration. SCVNGR allowed student affairs professionals to build challenges that included "checking in" and completing tasks at campus locations. While SCVNGR is no more, similar platforms are available (like Edventure Builder) or are under development. These kinds of platforms can be adapted to *gamify* engagement in academic and cocurricular activities.

A number of popular new technologies so far have been purposefully omitted from this chapter as well as this book. Two of the most notable are massive open online courses (MOOCs) and badges. MOOCs are large-scale web-based courses open to anyone who wants to take them. MOOCs are popular in higher education partly because a number of well-regarded institutions (like Harvard, MIT, and Berkeley) have been strong proponents. Badges are digital objects intended to be alternative forms of credentialing for skills and achievements. Badges can represent either in-class academic achievement or out-of-class skills. Early in their development, badges were conceptualized as serving as credentials for completing MOOCs and other online open courses. I haven't spent much time discussing MOOCs and badges because I am not yet convinced of their viability as effective platforms. MOOCs are exactly the same as traditional online-only courses and can be thought of as a digitization of a correspondence course. In other words, MOOCs are not engaging platforms, and I'm interested in technologies that allow us to increase student engagement, not the opposite. My concerns about badges are somewhat different. The concept behind badges is solid; however, it's not yet clear whether educational institutions will use them in ways that promote their adoption. In other words, the microcredentialing movement is both interesting and potentially impactful for higher education, yet the badges container may not be the best choice. Time (and research) will tell whether badges can be a viable solution to document student skill sets for future employment and educational opportunities.

CONCLUSION

Perhaps surprisingly to some, the Internet was used for social interaction, connection, and social networking long before the current crop of social media sites and services appeared. This chapter has reviewed the societal forces and tensions that have led up to and resulted from the development of new technologies. Even though Sagan believed that we will either get through our technological adolescence or destroy ourselves, perhaps it's best to accept that human psychology and society will always lag behind technological progress. If we think of it as an evolutionary process, and to the chagrin of those who would tell you that "the human brain is being rewired because of the use of technology," it may take hundreds of thousands of years before our biological

294

(and in turn psychological and social) processes evolve to adapt fully to technological changes. By that time, there will likely be new technological standards to which to adapt. Viewed graphically, human adaptation to technological progress would most likely resemble an asymptote.

Student affairs professionals, then, are encouraged to keep societal and psychological forces in mind when evaluating future technologies for their ability to be used in ways that help or harm our students. Psychological and societal forces make certain technologies more likely to be created and adopted. Societal forces are also what make student affairs professionals generally more inclined to see what students do online as inappropriate, deviant, or wrong. Examining the future of social technologies involves continually balancing our adult normative views with the experience of our students. As we do so, we'll align with the ideas and philosophies behind the flipped classroom movement, which places more trust (and therefore responsibility) on students for their own learning, and we will usher in progressive and expansive new paradigms in student affairs philosophies.

As this book is being written, new research is being produced, and the social media platforms on which that research is based are changing. Technology is a reflection of who we are. As a society we develop and support social media because they add value to our lives. It stands to reason that we'll continue building new technologies for interpersonal connection and that some of these technologies will be widely adopted by society. In the current phase of social technological expansion, youth have been the driving force behind adoption. Perhaps that will change, or perhaps it's the willingness of youth to try new things and to be less rigid and set in their ways that drives adoption of emerging technologies. Either way, as new interaction and communication platforms are developed, youth will continue to use them throughout their psychosocial development to explore themselves and

295

their interpersonal relationships. As new technologies are created that make communication more efficient, they will also make engaging with and supporting student learning more efficient. It is up to us as student affairs professionals to learn about these tools and to leverage them to support our students.

The best way for you as a student affairs professional to keep up with social technology development and adoption is to talk with your students. Have them show you how they use social media and identify how these uses relate to the desired outcomes of a college education. As you learn, be skeptical but keep an open mind. Examine social media as a biologist would examine a single-celled organism under a microscope—with a sense of inquisitiveness and desire to learn. Temper your excitement about new technologies, and don't let it get in the way of appropriate evaluations—it is important to learn both about what works and what doesn't. Integrate assessment strategies when you put into practice social media programs and interventions. Then, share your results with your PLN and the broader student affairs community.

As evidenced by the book you have just finished reading, we know a lot about how using social media relates to student development and learning. However, we have much more to learn, especially about causal links between site usage and particular outcomes. A number of examples of how student affairs professionals are using social media were discussed in chapter 4. Even though these seem to be effective uses of social technologies, how do we know what actually works? How do we know that social media themselves have an impact on student growth? We need to conduct research to answer these questions and parse out the variance among the social technologies, how they are used, and the engagement style of the student affairs professionals using them.

You, as a student affairs professional, have great power to help our students change. With your help, a first-generation student can learn what it's like to be a college student, a disengaged student can be helped to be more engaged, a student who is homesick can feel welcomed in the university environment, and a student who is on the path to self-discovery can be supported along the way. While these tasks can be accomplished by those not in student affairs, we occupy a unique place in colleges and universities and in the lives of our students. Not only can we do these things, we are best suited to do them because of our training and the collective values of our profession. Student affairs professionals can help others in higher education see the benefits of using social media to support students and balance out the negative messages being propagated through society. Student affairs professionals can lead the way in showing others how social media can be leveraged to *meet students where they are* and to bring them along to where we want them to be.

Practical Tips

1. Consider ways that you can support psychological and societal transitions inherent in the adoption of new technologies.
2. Explore the affordances and impacts of emerging technologies along with your students.
3. Look for new ways of using available data to help support student developmental and learning outcomes.
4. Investigate ways that you can encourage students to use new technologies for informal learning.
5. Be skeptical of the promise of new technologies and collect data to evaluate their effectiveness whenever possible.

REFERENCES

Ackerman, P. L. (1987). Individual differences in skill learning: An integration of psychometric and information processing perspectives. *Psychological Bulletin, 102*(1), 3–27.

Annis, L. F. (1985). Student-generated paragraph summaries and the information-processing theory of prose learning. *Journal of Experimental Education, 54*(1), 4–10.

Arnold, K. E., & Pistilli, M. D. (2012). Course Signals at Purdue: Using learning analytics to increase student success. *Proceedings of the 2nd International Conference on Learning Analytics and Knowledge,* 267–270.

Bernstein, M., Monroy-Hernández, A., Harry, D., André, P., Panovich, K., & Vargas, G. (2011). 4chan and /b/: An analysis of anonymity and ephemerality in a large online community. *Proceedings of the Fifth International Association for the Advancement of Artificial Intelligence Conference on Weblogs and Social Media.* Retrieved April 18, 2014, from https://www.aaai.org/ocs/index.php/ICWSM/ICWSM11/paper/viewFile/2873/4398.

Campbell, J. P., & Oblinger, D. G. (2007). *Academic Analytics.* EDUCAUSE Report. Retrieved July 16, 2013, from http://net.educause.edu/ir/library/pdf/PUB6101.pdf.

Caspi, A., & Shiner, R. L. (2010). Temperament and personality. In M. Rutter, D. Bishop, D. Pine, S. Scott, J. Stevenson, E. Taylor, & A. Thapar (eds.), *Rutter's Child and Adolescent Psychiatry* (5th ed., pp. 182–199). London: Blackwell.

Cox Communications, in partnership with the National Center for Missing and Exploited Children, and John Walsh. (2009). *Teen Online & Wireless Safety Survey: Cyberbullying, Sexting, and Parental Controls.* Retrieved April 18, 2014, from http://ww2.cox.com/wcm/en/aboutus/datasheet/takecharge/2009-teen-survey.pdf.

Dawson, S., McWilliam, E., & Tan, J. P. (2008). Teaching smarter: How mining ICT data can inform and improve learning and teaching practice. In *Proceedings ascilite Melbourne* (pp. 221–230).

De Montjoye, Y. A., Hidalgo, C. A., Verleysen, M., & Blondel, V. D. (2013). Unique in the crowd: The privacy bounds of human mobility. *Nature Scientific Reports, 3,* 1–5.

298

Drews, F. A., Yazdani, H., Godfrey, C. N., Cooper, J. M., & Strayer, D. L. (2009). Text messaging during simulated driving. *Human Factors: The Journal of the Human Factors and Ergonomics Society, 51*(5), 762–770.

Duckworth, A. L., & Carlson, S. M. (2013). Self-regulation and school success. In B. W. Sokol, F. M. E. Grouzet, & U. Müller (eds.), *Self-Regulation and Autonomy: Social and Developmental Dimensions of Human Conduct* (pp. 208–230). New York: Cambridge University Press.

Falardeau, I., Larose, S., & Roy, R. (1989). *Test de Réactions et d'Adaptation au Collégial (TRAC)*. Sainte-Foy: Cégep de Sainte-Foy.

Finer, L. B., & Philbin, J. M. (2013). Sexual initiation, contraceptive use, and pregnancy among young adolescents. *Pediatrics, 131*(5), 886–891.

Fitch, G. A., Soccolich, S. A., Guo, F., McClafferty, J., Fang, Y., Olson, R. L., Perez, M. A., Hanowski, R. J., Hankey, J. M., & Dingus, T. A. (2013, April). *The Impact of Hand-Held and Hands-Free Cell Phone Use on Driving Performance and Safety-Critical Event Risk*. Report No. DOT HS 811 757. Washington, DC: National Highway Traffic Safety Administration.

Gallagher, B. (2012). No, Snapchat isn't about sexting, says co-founder Evan Spiegel. *TechCrunch*. Retrieved February 2, 2014, from http://techcrunch.com/2012/05/12/snapchat-not-sexting/.

Garrison, C., & Ehringhaus, M. (2007). Formative and summative assessments in the classroom. *Association for Middle Level Education Report*. Retrieved April 18, 2014, from http://www.amle.org/Browseby Topic/Assessment/AsDet/TabId/180/ArtMID/780/ArticleID/286/Formative-and-Summative-Assessments-in-the-Classroom .aspx.

Junco, R. (2012). Too much face and not enough books: The relationship between multiple indices of Facebook use and academic performance. *Computers in Human Behavior, 28*(1), 187–198.

Junco, R., Gross, L., & Mastrodicasa, J. (2012). *Game Dynamics in the Classroom: Badges to Improve Student Engagement and Learning in Large Lecture Courses*. Proposal submitted to the MacArthur Foundation Digital Media and Learning Competition. Retrieved August 31,

2013, from http://blog.reyjunco.com/wp-content/uploads/2012/02/JuncoBadgesProposal.pdf.

Junco, R., & Mastrodicasa, J. (2007). *Connecting to the Net.Generation: What Higher Education Professionals Need to Know about Today's Students.* Washington, DC: NASPA.

Katzman, D. K. (2010). Sexting: Keeping teens safe and responsible in a technologically savvy world. *Paediatrics and Child Health, 15*(1), 41–42.

Kaufman, J. C., Agars, M. D., & Lopez-Wagner, M. C. (2008). The role of personality and motivation in predicting early college academic success in non-traditional students at a Hispanic-serving institution. *Learning and Individual Differences, 18*(4), 492–496.

Kirschner, P. A., & Karpinski, A. C. (2010). Facebook and academic performance. *Computers in Human Behavior, 26,* 1237–1245.

Kleijn, W. C., Ploeg, H. M., & Topman, R. M. (1994). Cognition, study habits, test anxiety, and academic performance. *Psychological Reports, 75,* 1219–1226.

Klein, J. D. (2005). Adolescent pregnancy: Current trends and issues. *Pediatrics, 116*(1), 281–286.

Komarraju, M., Karau, S. J., & Schmeck, R. R. (2009). Role of the Big Five personality traits in predicting college students' academic motivation and achievement. *Learning and Individual Differences, 19*(1), 47–52.

Komarraju, M., Karau, S. J., Schmeck, R. R., & Avdic, A. (2011). The Big Five personality traits, learning styles, and academic achievement. *Personality and Individual Differences, 51*(4), 472–477.

Kosinski, M., Stillwell, D., & Graepel, T. (2013). Private traits and attributes are predictable from digital records of human behavior. *Proceedings of the National Academy of Sciences of the United States of America, 110*(15), 5802–5805.

Larose, S., & Roy, R. (1995). Test of Reactions and Adaptation in College (TRAC): A new measure of learning propensity for college students. *Journal of Educational Psychology, 87*(2), 293–306.

Lenhart, A. (2009). *Teens and Sexting.* Pew Internet and American Life Project Report. Retrieved February 3, 2014, from http://

300

pewinternet.org/~/media//Files/Reports/2009/PIP_Teens_and _Sexting.pdf.

Lenhart, A., & Duggan, M. (2014). *Couples, the Internet, and Social Media: How American Couples Use Digital Technology to Manage Life, Logistics, and Emotional Intimacy within Their Relationships.* Pew Internet and American Life Project Report. Retrieved April 18, 2014, from http://www.pewinternet.org/2014/02/11/couples-the-internet -and-social-media/.

Macfadyen, L. P., & Dawson, S. (2012). Numbers are not enough: Why e-learning analytics failed to inform an institutional strategic plan. *Educational Technology & Society, 15*(3), 149–163.

Madden, M., Lenhart, A., Cortesi, S., Gasser, U., Duggan, M., & Smith, A. (2013). *Teens, Social Media, and Privacy.* Pew Internet and American Life Project Report. Retrieved July 7, 2013, from http:// www.pewinternet.org/Reports/2013/Teens-Social-Media-And -Privacy.aspx.

Maslow, A. H. (1943). A theory of human motivation. *Psychological Review, 50*(4), 370–96.

Moffitt, T., Arseneault, L., Belsky, D., Dickson, N., Hancox, R., Harrington, H. L., & Caspi, A. (2011). A gradient of childhood self-control predicts health, wealth, and public safety. *Proceedings of the National Academy of Sciences, 108*(7), 2693–2698.

Moore, G. E. (1965). Cramming more components onto integrated circuits. *Electronics,* 114–117.

Naumann, W. C. (1999). Predicting first-semester grade point average using self-regulated learning variables. *Dissertation Abstracts International Section B: The Sciences and Engineering, 59*(8-B), 4503.

Obrentz, S. B. (2012). Predictors of science success: The impact of motivation and learning strategies on college chemistry performance. Diss., Georgia State University. Retrieved February 3, 2014, from http://scholarworks.gsu.edu/cgi/viewcontent.cgi?article=1078& context=epse_diss.

Oishi, S. (2010). The psychology of residential mobility: Implications for the self, social relationships, and well-being. *Perspectives on Psychological Science, 5*(1), 5–21.

Paul, P. (March 18, 2011). Don't call me, I won't call you. *The New York Times*. Retrieved September 30, 2013, from http://www.nytimes .com/2011/03/20/fashion/20Cultural.html.

Rice, E., Rhoades, H., Winetrobe, H., Sanchez, M., Montoya, J., Plant, A., & Kordic, T. (2012). Sexually explicit cell phone messaging associated with sexual risk among adolescents. *Pediatrics*, *130*(4), 667–673.

Ridenhour, C., Shocklee, H., Sadler, E., & Drayton, W. (1988). "Don't believe the hype," on *It Takes a Nation of Millions to Hold Us Back*, Columbia (audio recording).

Ryan, M. P. (1984). Monitoring text comprehension: Individual differences in epistemological standards. *Journal of Educational Psychology*, *76*, 248–258.

Sacks, O. (1995). *An Anthropologist on Mars: Seven Paradoxical Tales*. New York: Knopf.

Smith, V. C., Lange, A., & Huston, D. R. (2012). Predictive modeling to forecast student outcomes and drive effective interventions in online community college courses. *Journal of Asynchronous Learning Networks*, *16*(3), 51–61.

Steinberg, L., Fegley, S., & Dornbusch, S. M. (1993). Negative impact of part-time work on adolescent adjustment: Evidence from a longitudinal study. *Developmental Psychology*, *29*, 171–180.

Tobey, P. E. (1997). Cognitive and noncognitive factors as predictors of retention among academically at-risk college students: A structural equation modeling approach. *Dissertation Abstracts International*, *57*(7-A), 2907.

Wellman, B. (2001). Computer networks as social networks. *Science*, *293*, 2031–2034.

NAME INDEX

SUBJECT INDEX

Page references followed by *fig* indicate an illustrated figure; followed by *t* indicate a table.

Users: California's Do Not Track Kids Act allowing deletion of online content by youth, 16; digital inequalities among, 31–36; Facebook's history of disregarding privacy of, 11–12; high rates of privacy settings used by youth, 14; psychological aspects of privacy among, 14–15; as social media products to advertisers, 11. *See also* Students

Ushahidi, 22

V

Validity: concurrent, 229; construct, 227–228; description of, 228; different ways to measure, 228–229; discriminant, 229

Video sharing. *See* Image and video sharing

Vine: description and function of, 27; hashtags adopted by, 23

W

Web 2.0 mentality, 71–72, 220

Western Michigan University, 158–161

White students: African American youth use of Twitter over, 24, 33; Facebook use by, 33

Wikipedia, "Criticism of Facebook" page of, 12

Wilde, Oscar, 271

Willis, TJ, 153–155

Women in Student Affairs (WISA) blog, 259

"World's Most Influential Person" poll (*Time* magazine), 110

Y

Yahoo, 12

Your First College Year (YFCY) survey, 58

Youth: Jezebel's public shaming of racist tweets made by, 15–16; racial differences in Twitter use by, 24; "right to be forgotten" legislation proposed to protect, 16; sexting by, 275–278; smartphone ownership of, 29–30. *See also* Age differences; Students

YouTube, 11, 139–142

Z

Zuckerberg, Mark: Chris "moot" Poole's opposite view on anonymity from, 110–111; Facebook founded by, 19–20; on online identification as issue of integrity, 109

Want to connect?

Like us on Facebook
www.facebook.com/JBHigherEd

Subscribe to our newsletter
www.josseybass.com/go/higheredemail

Follow us on Twitter
www.twitter.com/JBHigherEd

Go to our Website
www.josseybass.com/highereducation

WILEY

If you enjoyed this book, you may also like these:

Supporting Online Students
by Anita Crawley
ISBN: 9781118076545

The Mobile Academy
by Clark N. Quinn
ISBN: 9781118072653

WILEY